AF184399

RECURSIVE DESCENT COMPILING

A. J. T. DAVIE, B.Sc.
and R. MORRISON, B.Sc., M.Sc., Ph.D.
Department of Computational Science
University of St. Andrews
Scotland

ELLIS HORWOOD LIMITED
Publishers · Chichester

Halsted Press: a division of
JOHN WILEY & SONS
New York · Brisbane · Chichester · Toronto

First Published 1981
Reprinted in 1982

ELLIS HORWOOD LIMITED
Market Cross House, Cooper Street, Chichester, West Sussex, PO19 1EB, England

The publisher's colophon is reproduced from James Gillison's drawing of the ancient Market Cross, Chichester.

Distributors:

Australia, New Zealand, South-east Asia:
Jacaranda-Wiley Ltd., Jacaranda Press,
JOHN WILEY & SONS INC.,
G.P.O. Box 859, Brisbane, Queensland 40001, Australia

Canada:
JOHN WILEY & SONS CANADA LIMITED
22 Worcester Road, Rexdale, Ontario, Canada.

Europe, Africa:
JOHN WILEY & SONS LIMITED
Baffins Lane, Chichester, West Sussex, England.

North and South America and the rest of the world:
Halsted Press: a division of
JOHN WILEY & SONS
605 Third Avenue, New York, N.Y. 10016, U.S.A.

©A. J. T. Davie and R. Morrison/Ellis Horwood Ltd.

British Library Cataloguing in Publication Data
Davie, A. J. T.
Recursive descent compiling –
(The Ellis Horwood series in computers and their applications)
1. Compiling (Electronic computers)
2. Electronic digital computers
I. Title II. Morrison, R.
001.64'25 QA76.6

Library of Congress Card No. 81–6778 AACR2

ISBN 0-85312-386-1 (Ellis Horwood Ltd. – Library Edn.)
ISBN 0-470-27270-8 (Halsted Press – Library Edn.)
ISBN 0-85312-539-2 (Ellis Horwood Ltd. – Student Edn.)
ISBN 0-470-27361-5 (Halsted Press – Paperback Edn.)

Typeset in Press Roman by Ellis Horwood Limited
Printed in England by R. J. Acford, Chichester

COPYRIGHT NOTICE –
All Rights Reserved. No part of this publication may be reproduced, stored in a retrieval system, or transmitted, in any form or by any means, electronic, mechanical, photocopying, recording or otherwise, without the permission of Ellis Horwood Limited, Market Cross House, Cooper Street, Chichester, West Sussex, England.

Table of Contents

Authors' Preface 9

1 Introduction

1.1 What are Compilers? 11
1.2 The Phases and Passes of a Compiler 12
1.3 Recursive Descent Compiling. 15
1.4 History of Recursive Descent and LL(1) 17
1.5 Informal Introduction to S--algol 18

2 Mathematical Preliminaries

2.1 Introduction. 23
2.2 Relations 24
2.3 Digraphs 25
2.4 Properties and Algebra of Relations 27
2.5 Closure of Relations. 28
2.6 Boolean Matrix Representation 29
2.7 Calculation of Closures. 30
2.8 Summary. 33

3 Grammatical Preliminaries

3.1 Grammars and Languages 34
3.2 Chomsky's Stratification. 36
3.3 Context Free Grammars 38
3.4 Sentence Generation and Recognition 40
3.5 Derivations. 41
3.6 Ambiguity and Syntax Trees 42
3.7 A General Top Down Method 45
3.8 Bottom Up Methods 49
3.9 Summary. 50

4 Testing and Manipulating Grammars
4.1 The Need for Deterministic Methods . . . 52
4.2 LL(1) Grammars . . . 52
4.3 FIRST and FOLLOW Relations . . . 55
4.4 Factorisation and Substitution . . . 59
4.5 Left Recursion and its Elimination . . . 61
4.6 Cheating . . . 63
4.7 Summary . . . 65

5 Compiler Construction
5.1 The Role of S-algol . . . 67
5.2 The One Pass Nature of Recursive Descent Compilers . . . 67
5.3 Stepwise Refinement . . . 69
5.4 The Structure of a Recursive Descent Compiler . . . 71
5.5 The Layers of the Compiler . . . 71
5.5.1 Syntax Analysis . . . 71
5.5.2 Lexical Analysis . . . 72
5.5.3 Context Free Error Diagnosis and Recovery . . . 72
5.5.4 Type Checking . . . 72
5.5.5 Environment and Scope Checking . . . 73
5.5.6 Context Sensitive Error Reporting . . . 73
5.5.7 Abstract Machine Definition . . . 73
5.5.8 Code Generation . . . 74
5.6 Summary . . . 75

6 Syntax Analysis
6.1 The First Layer . . . 76
6.2 The Lexical Analysis Abstractions . . . 76
6.3 BNF and Coding . . . 78
6.4 The Syntax Analyser . . . 80
6.5 Expressions and Block Expressions . . . 83
6.6 Summary . . . 87

7 Lexical Analysis
7.1 The Function of a Lexical Analyser . . . 88
7.2 Scanning . . . 88
7.3 S-algol Scanning . . . 90
7.4 Screening . . . 95
7.5 Lexical Errors . . . 97
7.6 Listing the Source Program . . . 98

7.7 Mustbe and Have 99
7.8 Summary 99

8 Syntax Error Diagnosis and Recovery
8.1 What can we do about Errors? 101
8.2 The Pascal Error Recovery Scheme 103
8.3 The S-algol Error Recovery Scheme 104
8.4 Error Reporting 107
8.5 Summary 107

9 Type Matching
9.1 Context Sensitive Analysis 109
9.2 Type Matching Rules 109
9.3 The Representation of the Data Types 111
9.4 Checking the Equality of two Types 113
9.5 Type Errors 114
9.6 The Type Checking Layer 116
9.7 Summary 124

10 Name and Scope Checking
10.1 The Need for a Symbol Table 125
10.2 Symbol Table Organisation 125
10.3 Modelling Scope 128
10.4 Declarations 129
10.5 Accessing the Binary Tree 130
10.6 Refinement of the Syntax Analyser 132
10.7 Summary 135

11 Abstract Machine Design
11.1 Compiler Output 136
11.2 The S-algol Abstract Machine 138
11.3 The Stack 138
11.4 The S-algol Stack 139
11.5 The Heap 141
11.6 Heap Organisation 142
11.7 The Abstract Machine Code 143
11.8 The Stack Instructions 144
11.9 The Heap Instructions 145
11.10 Flow of Control Instructions 146
11.11 Summary 147

12 Code Generation
12.1 Similated Evaluation of the S-algol Machine 149
12.2 Declarations and the Use of the Symbol Table 153
12.3 The Final Refinement of the Syntax Analyser 155
12.4 Summary 163

13 Bootstrapping and Portability
13.1 The Need to Port Languages 164
13.2 T-Diagrams 165
13.3 Cross Compilation 167
13.4 Bootstrapping by Pushing 167
13.5 Bootstrapping by Pulling 171
13.6 Summary 173

Appendices
AA S-algol Syntax 174
AB Type Matching Rules 177
AC Procedure number 178
AD The Abstract Machine Code 180
AE S-code Generated by the S-algol Compiler 187

Index 189

Authors' Preface

The computing community is well served with texts, good, bad and indifferent, on the subjects of compiling and compilers. One of the most popular methods of implementing a compiler is that of recursive descent and many compilers, including ones for the languages Algol 60, Pascal, Algol 68R and BCPL, have been written using this technique. It is therefore surprising that comparatively little has been written about it. This text sets out to bridge this unexpected gap.

The subject matter of the text has formed the basis of lecture courses at St.Andrews University for both undergraduates and graduates. Naturally the courses have developed, and will continue to do so, over the years. At present the material appears in, but does not form the whole body of, lectures on Graph Theory, Grammars and Automata and Compiling Techniques.

The text sets out to give an introductory look at compiling in general through the medium of one particular technique. It does not therefore claim to be a complete reference guide to all aspects of compiling. Several topics, for instance that of optimization, are only touched on briefly. The intention has been to set out the main problems encountered in any compiler, however simple, and show how to tackle each of these in the relatively straightforward way which recursive descent imposes.

Students who embark on any course on compilers will be expected to know something about programming languages. This text assumes that the readers have such knowledge, that they will be fairly proficient at programming computers and that they will know about the fundamentals of program and data structures and how to manipulate them. It does not assume knowledge of any *particular* programming language. However familiarity with a block or procedure structured language such as one of the Algols or Pascal would be an advantage. As far as elementary mathematics is concerned, only basic set theory and logic are assumed as prerequisites.

The book is divided roughly into three parts. The first, which consists of Chapter 1 by itself, is a general introduction. The second, comprising Chapters 2, 3 and 4, is mainly theoretical in nature. Chapter 2 introduces some essential mathematical notions chiefly that of closure. These are used in Chapters 3 and 4 which are about linguistic specification and testing whether languages are suitable for the recursive descent treatment. Some hints are also given about how to massage a linguistic specification into the correct form.

The third and major part of the book is about the practical realisation of a recursive descent compiler. This is done by specifying a syntax-recognising skeleton and adding flesh and muscle to it layer by layer. Chapter 5 gives an overview of this process and outlines the different layers. Chapter 6 describes the skeleton in detail and Chapter 7 the lexical analysis phase. Layers dealing with errors and types are added in Chapters 8 and 9 and ideas of scope and naming are discussed in Chapter 10. Chapters 11 and 12 deal with code generation, the former with what code is generated and the latter with how to generate it. The final chapter stands on its own. It is, strictly speaking, not specific to our particular kind of compiler; but we felt that the subjects of bootstrapping and portability were too important to be left out of any book about compilers.

We are indebted to many for helping with this book both directly and indirectly: To many of our Honours students for reading and proofreading early and later versions of various chapters and, by so doing, revising for their examinations: To our colleagues, especially Pete Bailey and Iain Adamson, for many useful comments, suggestions and criticisms: To our former colleague, Dave Turner, for his expertise and influence on our views about compilers: To our wives who have put up with it all and provided nourishment and encouragement. We must also show our gratitude to our children who, in spite of the fact that they have actively hindered this book's production, have amused and entertained us by way of diversion.

Tony Davie and Ron Morrison
St.Andrews
May 1981

CHAPTER 1

Introduction

1.1 WHAT ARE COMPILERS?

A **compiler** is a computer program which translates another program called the **source program** into yet a third called the **object program**. The source programs are written in the **source language** and each solves a particular problem for a user; the object program produced for it solves the same problem but is expressed in the **object language**. In general, the source language should be one in which users find it easy and natural to solve their problems, and the object language, whilst probably quite opaque in meaning to users, will be a natural one for some machine to execute. Thus we can view a compiler as a tool which transforms programs from the users' domain of problem solving into the machine's domain of problem execution, without varying the **semantics**, (i.e. meanings) of the programs.

It will be well known to all programmers that programs normally pass through several stages of development. Let us summarise them here. Firstly they are **created**, initially in the users' minds and then in some computer in source language, probably using an editor. They are then compiled into object language. This stage is known as **compile time** when the program is scanned, perhaps several times, to discover its static or lexicographic properties. Compile time errors may be reported, in which case the editor will be reinvoked to change the erroneous program to the intended one; or, if the user has been more skilful, an object program may be produced. This may be stored away in the computer's file system for subsequent combination with other compiled programs (such as library routines) during **load time**. When it has been loaded the combined package will be executed during what is known as **run time**. Alternatively the object program, if self contained (i.e. only containing reference to standard facilities – not other user defined routines) may miss out the load stage if the compiler is set up to place the object program straight into store ready for execution. Such a combination, where compile time and run time are run into one another is called a **compile and go** compiler.

Run time may take the form of the computer *directly* executing the object program if it is suitable; alternatively, it may consist of the computer **interpreting** the object code. It is sometimes convenient that the object language be different from the 'native' language of any particular computer. Many source languages' philosophies suggest very forcibly the architecture of a 'natural' machine for many to run on and the object language will be the machine code for this hypothetical machine. It is rare for the architecture underlying a source language to match that of a real computer because, sadly, hardware designers and language designers very seldom get together at the start. An impressive exception is the Burroughs 5000 and 6000 [1] series computer range where the architecture was designed to support Burroughs' own version of Algol 60 [2]. If the architectures of the real and hypothetical machine don't match we have two alternatives: we can either, as mentioned already, interpret the object program by the process whereby the real machine simulates the hypothetical one or we can pass the object code through another translation stage to turn the 'natural' machine code into code for the real computer. It can be mentioned in passing that there are interpreters which *directly* interpret source code for some languages without any compile time at all (e.g. APL [3]) but these will not concern us here.

During run time, whether interpretative or otherwise, the dynamic execution of the program takes place. At this stage we may either get run time errors or alternatively correct results may be obtained. In the former case the edit-compile-load-run cycle will have to be reinvoked; even in the latter case, it may be reinvoked if the 'correct' results are the answer to a problem which is different from the one the user intended, or if he wants to modify the program in the light of the results.

To summarise, the two main stages are compile time and run time, during which static and dynamic scanning of the programs take place respectively. Many of the interesting problems of language design and compilers become apparent when we try to separate the static aspects of the language under consideration from the dynamic ones. Can the compiler tell statically whether or not a variable name has been declared for a given usage (i.e. whether it is in scope)? This is the case for most Algol-like languages but not for LISP-like languages [4]. Can it tell what type a variable has? Can it tell what value an identifier has? Can it even tell if it is guaranteed to have *some* value?

1.2 THE PHASES AND PASSES OF A COMPILER

It is an opinion almost universally held throughout the computing community that we should think about the problems we want to solve in a modular way; that is, we should try to break down complicated tasks into easier subtasks which in turn get broken into yet simpler problems until we arrive at ones which are 'trivial' to solve.

How can we break up the process of compiling into subtasks? We shall confine ourselves in this chapter to the top level of such a refinement. The top-level subtasks we give here are common to most compilers and are known as **phases.** Later we shall see how each of the main phases breaks up into lower level subtasks.

The compiler must analyse the source program and synthesize the object program. In fact nearly all compilers perform the analysis in two distinct phases called lexical and syntactic analysis.

Lexical Analysis

The lexical phase consists of an analysis of the **microsyntax** of the source program. By analogy with spoken or written languages, this involves the collecting together of phonemes or letters to form words without any reference to the relationship of the words to one another, or to their meaning. In computer languages it means the processing of a string of characters, transforming them into a string of **basic symbols.** These include keywords (or reserved words) such as 'if', 'begin' and 'write', single symbol punctuation marks such as "(","]" and ",", operator symbols such as "+" and "*", multiple symbols of the two above kinds such as "<=", ".LE." and "::", assembly of **literals** such as "1", "3.7" and "true", and finally the collecting together of the characters in identifiers such as "x" and "mean.temperature". Writing the lexical analysis phase is not always trivial. Consider the Fortran statements:

```
DO 1 I = 1, 12
DO 1 I = 1. 12
```

and

```
IF(I(J) − I(K))1, 2, 3
IF(I(J) − I(K)) = 123
```

Are 'IF' and 'DO' keywords? In the first example 'DO' is a keyword. In the second 'DO1I' is a variable name because Fortran insists that blanks are non-significant. In the third 'IF' is a keyword, and in the last it is the name of an array being subscripted. It doesn't make the problem any easier that the subscript can be arbitrarily long and complicated.

Syntax Analysis

The second analysis phase is syntax analysis. Again by analogy with 'human' languages, this corresponds to such actions as finding the verb, subject and predicate in sentences and parsing them. In computing terms, some of the actions the syntax analyser takes are: check that in Algol like languages the *begins* and *ends* match up; make sure in Fortran that a DO statement referencing a label actually finds a statement with that label later on; and that DO loops do not overlap. The input to this phase is the string of basic symbols produced by the lexical analysis. What is the output? We shall see later that it is a **parse tree** which is an internal form of the program in a structure which allows subsequent phases to see the relationship of the parts of the program to each other and to the whole program.

Code Generation

The third important phase, that of **code generation** is synthetic rather than analytic. It takes the parse tree and traverses it. Based on the structural relationships it finds there it produces object code in at least a preliminary form.

We could stop at these three phases because they are all common to virtually every compiler but we will mention here some other optional ones. Some compilers [5] have a **prepass** phase which does some macro expansion, allowing the user the facility of making contractions of commonly used phrases in his program. We have already mentioned that a further translation phase may be written after code generation in order to convert 'hypothetical' to 'real' machine code. This too is sometimes accomplished by macro expansion. The third and last optional phase we shall mention is that of **optimization.** In environments where large programs go into heavy production use it will be advantageous to make the object programs produced as efficient in time (or possibly space) as possible. One way of solving this problem is to measure the program at run time in order to find out which parts of the program take the longest time and to hand code these sections in assembly language. A good optimizer should do this automatically. Note however a fundamental conflict; how can a compiler which only sees the static aspects of the source program measure the dynamic performance of the object program?

Optimization phases can occur at any stage of compilation: at the beginning where it is called **global** optimization and often means automatic rewriting of source code (e.g. taking unnecessary commands out of loops); in between two other phases (e.g. to optimize the tree produced by the syntax analyser); or right at the end to improve the code produced by the code generator.

The organisation of the phases built into a compiler can be one of a number of kinds. In particular, one decision the compiler writer has to take is how to organise the phases into **passes.** A multipass compiler makes complete scans over the various forms the program goes through, both internal and external. Each pass reads the output from the previous one (or the source program if it is the first pass) and produces complete output for the next pass. No pass will be invoked until the previous one is complete. For example if we were to organise the lexical analysis phase as a pass, the compiler would first completely scan the source and produce a file of basic symbols. Note that space, whether in main store or in backing store, must be found for this intermediate form of the program. The next pass which will include at least the syntax analyser will then read this file and produce its own output file.

However, in some compilers all the phases can be gathered together into one pass, and instead of storing complete files of intermediate data, the phases call each other as subroutines to ask for or provide information one piece at a time.

Thus the syntax analyser may call the lexical analyser and ask it for the next basic symbol. It may also call the code generator to emit the next piece of code.

The organisation of phases into passes may depend on the language being compiled. Some languages actually *require* several passes. For instance, if an object in a program can be used before it is declared (e.g. a jump to a label may occur before the label's definition, or a procedure call may come before the procedure declaration) then code cannot possibly be generated for the use of the object without having complete knowledge of its properties. In such cases a complete pass will have to be made to gather such knowledge and another to generate code based on that knowledge.

In some languages one cannot even perform syntax analysis properly before a complete lexical pass has been made. For instance in a language where we could define new operators and priorities for them, one would not know whether to treat an expression such as "a << b ++ c" as "(a << b) ++ c" or as "a << (b ++c)", had the user been so foolish as to leave the declarations of the priorities of "<<" and "++" until later in the program.

We should note that the situation is sometimes confused by bringing the operating system into the picture. A multi-pass compiler may be organised as a number of cooperating processes which run at least conceptually in parallel. They would have to be carefully synchronised but a good system would do this automatically be making them communicate through **pipes** (UNIX† nomenclature, see [7]) which replace those intermediate storage files which are the main disadvantage of multipass compilers. However the gain will probably be more than offset by the system overhead necessary for scheduling the processes in and out of action.

1.3 RECURSIVE DESCENT COMPILING

In this book we are going to concentrate very heavily on one particular technique and on its application to a particular language, S-algol. We shall give a brief introduction and summary of its usage in the next section. Here we talk about the method which forms the subject of this book – **recursive descent**.

This method centres around the syntax analysis phase of the compiler which is divided up into a number of **recognition** routines, each of which has the task of checking whether a particular kind of phrase is present in the input. Each recognition procedure can call upon the services of other ones to recognise the appearance of subphrases and so on. For example we will see that an S-algol program consists of a **sequence** followed by a questionmark. The central recognition routine will therefore call the sequence recognising routine and check for the appearance of the questionmark on the input stream. The sequence recogniser will, in turn, call routines to check for declarations or clauses, because a sequence is basically a list of such entities. Most of these routines will be mutually recursive, reflecting the fact that within one sequence we can find others embedded at a

† UNIX is a trademark of Bell Laboratories

lower level. In the same way, expressions can contain subexpressions, declarations include inner declarations and so on. Each of these has its own recogniser which is invoked from above when appropriate.

Some recognisers will have choices to make. In the above example of the sequence recogniser, it will have to choose between calling the recogniser for a declaration or for a clause. When such choices are to be made, decisions are always taken by looking at the input stream for the next basic symbol. We shall see that declarations in S-algol always start with one of the reserved words 'let', 'procedure', 'structure', 'forward' or 'external', and that no clauses start with any of these symbols. Hence the sequence recogniser can choose the declaration recogniser if it finds one of these, or the clause recogniser if it does not.

The task of a compiler is not however merely to *recognise* correct programs; it must also produce object code. Therefore, each recogniser will be modified or refined in order to emit code. One can notice here that the syntax tree referred to as the output of the syntax analysis phase in section 1.2 is never explicitly grown. This is because the syntax analysis phase and the code generation phase are not separated into distinct passes, but rather integrated into one another in order to understand clearly what each recogniser-emitter does. The tree is implicit in the dynamic calling structure of the recognition routines and is traversed by the code generation phase as it is built, and branches no longer of use are destroyed as the routines are exited.

The addition of code generation to the recognition routines represents a **refinement** of them. Other refinements will be introduced and these are based on error recovery and type checking. If a recogniser finds some program constructs that it doesn't expect, what should it do? Should it merely print the message: 'You have made a serious mistake.' as one early compiler was reputed to do? Or should it offer 'IEH377I' or some such terse comment to the user? Are there alternatives to these and can the compiler recover from errors?

Each recogniser must check that expressions, clauses, declarations and so on have sensible type structures. One must not, for instance, add a string to an integer if that is not allowed in the language. The type handling part of a recogniser must also be able to pass type information back to its parent recogniser.

One of the main features of the recursive descent method when used practically is that it must be able to do its recognition, type checking and code emission without 'backup'; that is, if a recognition routine A decides to call another, B, it can be sure *from the first* that, barring errors on the user's part, it has made the correct choice based on the input it has before it. This limits the kind of language which can be compiled by the method, but not too severely. We will devote the early chapters to seeing just what kind of restrictions are placed on languages by this requirement, and how to get round them. Such restrictions are called the LL(1) conditions. We will explain this term in section 4.2.

Our particular compiler will also have the property that it is one-pass in the sense discussed in the previous section but we recognise that there are multipass recursive descent compilers e.g. that for BCPL [8].

1.4 HISTORY OF RECURSIVE DESCENT AND LL(1)

For many years compiler writers have used recursive descent as an informal method, grafting on parts of other methods and using different techniques when expedient to do so. We certainly do not pretend to know about all the recursive descent compilers that have ever been written. There is little in the literature about them. Perhaps this is because the method was thought too obvious or too simple. This is not the same as saying it is trivial, because as the principle of Ockham's razor suggests, the simpler the better.

However, surveying the literature available, the following landmarks stand out.

(i) In 1968 Foster published a notable paper called 'A Syntax Improving Device' [9] (SID) in which he showed how to manipulate grammatical constructs for languages, if at all possible, into forms suitable for what is now known as the recursive descent method.

(ii) Later in the same year, Lewis and Stearns published a paper 'Syntax-directed Transductions' [10] which used the term LL(k) for the type of grammatical restriction placed on languages to allow their syntax to be scanned from left to right without backup, using a top down or recursive descent method. This placed the whole theory on a sound basis.

(iii) It is clear that the early Burroughs compilers [1] were recursive descent compilers even though they were not specifically given that description. Hoare [11] has pointed out that the early Elliott Algol [12] was also a recursive descent compiler.

(iv) In 1971 Knuth published a tutorial guide to the grammatical aspects of LL parsing called 'Top Down Syntax Analysis [13]. This lucid account deals, as does the Lewis and Stearns' paper, mainly with syntactic aspects.

(v) In the same year a group working at the Royal Radar Establishment at Malvern used Foster's SID to improve the description of the language Algol 68R [14] and automatically generate a recursive descent compiler for it.

(vi) It was 1973 before any significant paper was written about the practical aspects of compiling as a whole, using recursive descent, when Ammann published 'The Method of Structured Programming Applied to the Development of a Compiler [15]. This explains how the method is applied to writing a Pascal compiler and uses the techniques of program refinement to good effect.

1.5 INFORMAL INTRODUCTION TO S-ALGOL

We will use as our main programming vehicle the language S-algol, developed at St. Andrews University, initially as a teaching language to replace Algol W [16]. We use it in this text not only as a language to be compiled but also as the language to implement the demonstration compiler. Thus most of the later part of this book is about writing a compiler in S-algol for translating S-algol programs.

We could have used any one of a number of languages for this text such as Pascal or Algol 68. We could even have used non-Algol-like languages such as Fortran or Basic. In the former cases we felt that we would be side tracked too much into discussing the finer points of language theology; and we feel that languages of the latter class are not easily suited to systems programming of any kind (including implementation of compilers), chiefly because of their paucity of data structures.

The rest of this section is therefore devoted to giving a brief resumé of the features which make S-algol different from other Algol-like languages. We shall assume that the reader is familiar with languages of this sort.

S-algol is a block and procedure structured Algol-like language. Blocks (to use the Algol 60 terminology although they are not called that in the reference manual [17]) are delimited by **begin** and **end** or "{" and "}" and their bodies consist of an intermixed sequence of declarations and clauses. Declarations can come at any point, subject to the constraint that no declared object can be used before it has been declared. Thus the scope of a declaration is from the declaration itself to the end of the sequence in which it appears. A 'forward' declaration of a procedure may be made which specifies its parameter types and result type without giving its body, which can occur later so that mutually recursive procedures can be used.

Declarations are initialising and hence users can be sure that 'variables' have some initial value at run time. Such declarations do not specify the type of the identifier being declared, because the compiler will deduce this from the type of its initial value.

```
let x := 1                 ! has type int i.e. integer
                           ! "!" introduces comments which terminate
                           ! at the end of the line
                           ! ";" is not needed between
                           ! clauses or declarations
                           ! unless there are more than one on a line
let y := 2.7               ! has type real
let switch := x < pi       ! has type bool i.e. boolean
let name := if switch then "Tony" else "Ron"    ! has type string
let f := open ("directory")    ! has type file
```

We put quotes around the word 'variables' above because identifiers may in fact be given constant values which will not change (and this can be checked statically) during the lifetime of the sequence. This is done by placing "=" instead of ":=" after the identifier in the **let** declaration.

```
let e = 2.71828                        ! type creal i.e. constant real
let directory.name = reads             ! type cstring because
                                       ! "reads" reads a string
                                       ! note identifiers can have "."
                                       ! in them as a "letter"
let c = directory.name ++ "/myfile"    ! type cstring
                                       ! ++ is concatenation
```

Four other kinds of declaration may be made: structure class declarations, procedure declarations, forward and external declarations. Forward has been mentioned above. External is similar to forward but marks the procedure as present in a separate compilation.

Structure class declarations introduce a template which is used to create instances of structures (or records) of that shape:

```
structure identifier(cstring name; real val)
```

Pointers to such structures can be declared by a "**let**" declaration:

```
let var := identifier("x", 1.732)          ! type pntr
let const = identifier("pi", 3.14159)      ! type cpntr but its val
                                           ! field can be changed
```

The type of 'var' is pntr and types of structures are not further distinguished statically. (However one can test the structure class of a pntr dynamically by the use of the operators 'is' and 'isnt'. For instance – **if** var **is** identifier **then** . . . **else** . . .)

Procedure declarations are similar to those in most other Algol-like languages – they have a heading and a body. The simplest way to introduce them is to give some examples:

```
procedure convert(cint L,S,D -> real)
        L + S/20 + D/240                ! The body is an expression
                                        ! This is the value that is returned

procedure stack(cint val)
begin
        st(st.p) := val
        st.p := st.p + 1
end                                     ! The body is a void clause

procedure random(-> real)
begin
        seed := f(seed)
        seed                            ! The body is an expression
end                                     ! block – see below
```

All parameters of procedures *without exception* are called by value and anything *without exception* which can be declared can be passed as a parameter.

We introduced one compound data type above when talking about structures. The other is the vector. Vectors are also allocated dynamically in one of two ways:

let abc := @1 **of cint** [1, 2, 3, 4]
let xyz = **vector** 1::n, 1::n **of** 0

The first is a one dimensional vector with lower bound 1 and constant values specified individually. The second is an n × n 2-dimensional array, all of whose elements are variable and initially 0.

Vectors are to be distinguished strictly from their elements. Both vectors and their elements can be assigned to (if not originally declared as constants). Thus, with the above declarations we could later say:

abc := @2 **of cint** [2, 3, 4]

but not:

xyz := **vector** 1::n, 1::n **of** 1

and we could say:

xyz(3, 3) := 1

but not:

abc(3) := 4

The types of abc and xyz are *cint and c**int respectively. A star is added for each dimension of the vector and a "c" whenever a level is constant.

Assigning a vector (rather than its elements) is *not* equivalent to copying the elements. Such an assignment merely takes a copy of a pointer (in implementation terms) to the vector.

We have gradually strayed from declarations into the realm of clauses. Let us enumerate the kinds allowed. ":=" can be used to specify an assignment. 'if . . . . then . . . . else . . . . .' has its usual meaning. To prevent the 'dangling else' problem, there is a one-armed version of the conditional – 'if . . . . do . . . .'. There is a 'repeat . . . . while . . . . do . . . . . .' construction (where either the 'repeat . . . . .' part or the 'do . . . . . .' part but not both may be absent). This allows the test for exit to be made at the beginning, in the middle, or at the end of the loop. A fairly standard 'for . . . = ... to . . . . by . . . . do . . . .' is present (the 'by . . . .' being optional). Note the use of "=" rather than ":=". The controlled identifier is a cint (and is declared automatically by the "for" clause's appearance). The 'case' clause is of interest because the case 'labels' don't have to be compile time constants. (A clever compiler would notice if they were and compile code accordingly.) e.g.

```
case true of
x<0:      -x
x=0:      1
x<10:     x+y
default:  x
```

There are no abominations like the 'esac' of Algol 68. The default case always marks the end of the case clause.

The example above showed a case **expression**. In fact there is no difference in S-algol between expressions and other clauses. It's just that clauses executed for their side effect have conceptual type void while others have a 'regular' type. The type of the last clause in a block determines the type of the block as a whole. Thus block expressions are allowed.

A short word should be said about the primitive type string. Strings in S-algol are atomic – that is their internal structure cannot be changed by assignment nor by any other means. That is not to say that they cannot be manipulated freely. One can replace a whole string by assignment. Strings can be concatenated using the operator "++" and substrings can be taken. If S is a string then S(*m*|*n*) selects the substring starting at the m'th character of S and n characters long. Both m and n can be any integer expressions. There is a standard function 'length' which finds the length of a string. The null string "" is allowed and its length is zero.

This ends our brief exposition of some of the features of S-algol. For further details consult the references [17] and [18].

REFERENCES

[1] Creech, B. A. (1969), Architecture of the B6500, *Proceedings COINS.*

[2] Burroughs Corporation, B6700/B7700 extended algol language *Information Manual* (June 1972).

[3] Iverson, K. (1962), *A Programming Language,* Wiley.

[4] McCarthy, J. *et al.* (1965), *LISP 1.5 Programmer's Manual,* MIT Press.

[5] Kernighan, B. W. and Ritchie, D. M. (1981), *The C Programming Language,* Prentice-Hall.

[6] van Wijngaarden, A. *et al.* (1975), Revised report on the algorithmic language Algol 68, *Acta Informatica,* **5**, 1-236.

[7] Ritchie, D. M. and Thompson, K. (July 1974), The UNIX timesharing system, *CACM,* **17**, **7**, 365-375.

[8] Richards, M. (1971), The portability of the BCPL compiler, *Software, Practice and Experience,* **1**, 135-146.

[9] Foster, J. M. (May 1968), A syntax improving device, *Computer Journal,* **11**, **1**, 31-34.

[10] Lewis, P. M. II and Stearns, R. E. (1968), Syntax directed transduction, *JACM,* **15**, **3**, 465-488.

[11] Hoare, C. A. R. (February 1981), The emperor's old clothes, *CACM,* **24**, **2**, 75–83.

[12] Hoare, C. A. R. (1962), The Elliott algol programming system, *Introduction to Systems Programming,* 156–165, Academic Press.

[13] Knuth, D. E. (1971), Top down syntax analysis, *Acta Informatica,* **1**, 79–110.

[14] Currie, I. F., Bond, S. G., Morison, J. D. (1971), Algol 68R, its implementation and use, *Proceedings IFIP Ljubljana* **3**, 43–46.

[15] Ammann, U. (1973), The development of a compiler, *Proc. Int. Symposium on Computing,* 93–99, North Holland.

[16] Wirth, N., Hoare, C. A. R. (June 1966), A contribution to the development of algol, *CACM,* **9**, **6**, 413–431.

[17] Morrison, R. (1979), *S-algol Reference Manual,* St. Andrews University Computer Science Department Report CS/79/1.

[18] Cole, A. J., Morrison, R. (1980), *An Introduction to S-algol Programming,* St. Andrews University Computer Science Department Report CS/80/1.

CHAPTER 2

Mathematical Preliminaries

2.1 INTRODUCTION

This book uses very little mathematics, but one idea which crops time and time again is the concept of **closure**. We shall describe this more formally later but for the moment we can give an informal explanation of the ideas central to it. In computing we deal with operations which are being carried out; the computer changes from one state to another. Often we are interested in following a computation through a sequence of such state changes. The means we use to change from a single state-changing operation to a sequence of operations carried out one after the other is a closure operation which generates a 'super' state change corresponding to the sequence of 'primitive' state changes. This idea of moving from a single entity, such as a state change, to a sequence of entities appears in other ways. For instance in data structures in computing we frequently have one primitive structure pointing at another. If this in turn points at a third structure and so on we again see closure in operation by allowing the pointers to be followed to any distance we like. Here we have a **relationship** between structures (A is pointed at by B) rather than an operation which changes something and we are finding a new 'super' relationship (A can be reached from B by following pointers any number of times) which is the closure of the original relationship.

Closure also appears in ordered sets. We shall be concerned with sets later in this text, especially ordered sets of characters of some alphabet which are called **strings** in many programming contexts and which potentially form **sentences** in some language, usually a programming language. The idea of concatenating any number of characters together to form strings of any length is a closure of the fundamental idea of concatenating two primitive characters.

Let us examine this in more detail and with mathematical formality. An **alphabet**, A, is a finite set of symbols sometimes called **letters**. By a string of length k we mean an ordered set of letters – that is a member of $A^k = A \times A \times \ldots\ldots \times A$, the Cartesian product of A with itself k times. Instead, however, of writing a string of letters in the conventional mathematical way for an ordered set i.e. (a, b, c, ...), we often prefer to place the letters in **string quotes**, thus: "abc.....". We can also conceive of a unique string of length zero – the **null string** which we shall write λ or "". If we define A^0 to be the set consisting of λ alone, then a string (of any length) is a member of the infinite union:

$$\bigcup_{n=0}^{\infty} A^n \tag{1}$$

This union is written A* and is called the **reflexive transitive closure** of the alphabet A under the operation of Cartesian product $-\times$. The "*" in A* is called the Kleene star after the logician who defined it [1]. We sometimes just call A* the closure of A, but there is another kind of closure used when we specifically want to exclude the empty string, the **transitive closure** defined by:

$$\bigcup_{n=1}^{\infty} A^n \tag{2}$$

and written A^+. This set is the set of all non-empty strings over the alphabet A.

We can define an operation called **concatenation** which takes two strings from A* and produces another by placing the two ordered sets end to end, juxtaposing them. This defines an algebra over A* with λ as the unit element since for any string $s \in A^*$:

$$s \,.\, \lambda = \lambda \,.\, s = s$$

where "." is the concatenation operator. We quite often miss out the "." and just write, for instance, "st" instead of "s.t". Concatenation is associative but not commutative.

The essence of the term 'closure' is that it gives the smallest set containing a given basic set and closed under certain operations – i.e. if the operations are carried out on members of the set the resulting object is still in the set.

In the above case the basic set has only one object, the null string λ, and the allowed operations are those of concatenation with any letter of the supplied alphabet.

2.2 RELATIONS

Another place in which closure appears is in another algebra – that of **relations**. We have already seen an example of a relation informally, the 'is pointed to by' relation between data structures. Other common relations occurring in mathematics and later on in this book are 'is the greatest divisor of', 'is less than' and 'can come at the start of'. Some relations are so common that we give them special symbols e.g. "<".

It is necessary to know what kind of object is being related to what. Thus in the case of 'can come at the start of', do we mean horses at the start of the field in a race; or perhaps breakfast at the start of the day? In fact in this book we mean something more like the statements that '**begin** can come at the start of a clause in S-algol'; or that 'a declaration can come at the start of a program'. We shall see more of this particular relation in sections 4.2 and 4.3. The point is however, that when a relation is defined between objects we need to know what sets the objects belong to.

More formally a relation between two sets S and T is merely a subset of their Cartesian product S × T, each member of the subset representing a pair of objects lying in the relationship.

Example 2.2.1

Let $S = T = \{1, 2, 3\}$

Then the 'less than' relation can be defined as the set

$U = \{(1, 2), (1, 3), (2, 3)\}$

though we more usually write

$1 < 2 \quad 1 < 3 \quad 2 < 3$

and, of course, for other elements in $S \times T - U$ such as (2, 2) we write

$2 \nless 2$

Example 2.2.2

Let S = T = the set of divisors of 12

Then the 'is a direct divisor of' relation contains the elements

$\{(1, 2), (1, 3), (2, 4), (2, 6), (3, 6), (4, 12), (6, 12)\}$

In plain English 'a is a direct divisor of b' means that 'a is less than and divides b' (another relation) but that 'no multiple of a except b itself divides b' (yet another relation).

We should point out that relations can be generalised to subsets of Cartesian products of *any* number of sets but here we shall not use more than two and they will quite often be equal to one another as in the above examples.

Another way of defining a relation between S and T is to say that it is a mapping from S × T to the set {true, false}. The mapping takes the value true if the arguments lie in the relational subset and false otherwise. It is often best to think of a relation in this way if we write it as an infix operator e.g. "$a < b$" can be considered to have value true or false.

2.3 DIGRAPHS

One picture is worth a thousand words; and it is therefore useful to give pictures of relations (especially when they are finite). The **digraph** of a relation is a picture of the two sets involved with arrows connecting the pairs of objects that are related (i.e. are in the subset of the Cartesian product). Sometimes we shall abbreviate 'digraph' to 'graph'. The reader should understand however that there is a difference which need not concern us here. See Berge [2] or Wilson [3] for further details.

Example 2.3.1
The relationship 'is a town in' between S = the set of towns and T = the set of countries looks like the example in Fig. 2.1.

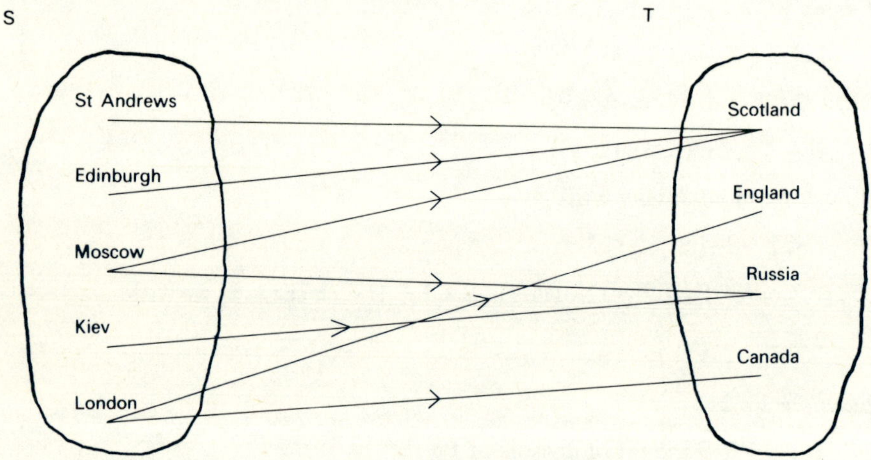

Fig. 2.1

Only some of the towns, countries and relationship arrows are shown.

If S = T (as is very often the case), then we only need to draw one set and the arrows join elements of that set.

Example 2.3.2
Let S = T = the set of integers and let the relationship be 'is the predecessor of'. The graph is as in Fig. 2.2.

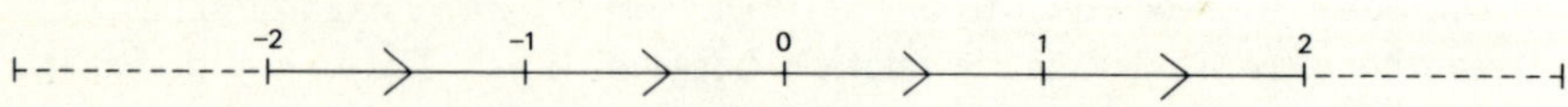

Fig. 2.2

Note that the graph of the relationship 'is less than' is much denser. We normally only draw graphs of finite relations.

Example 2.3.3
Let S = T = the set of humans and let the relationship be 'was the father of'.

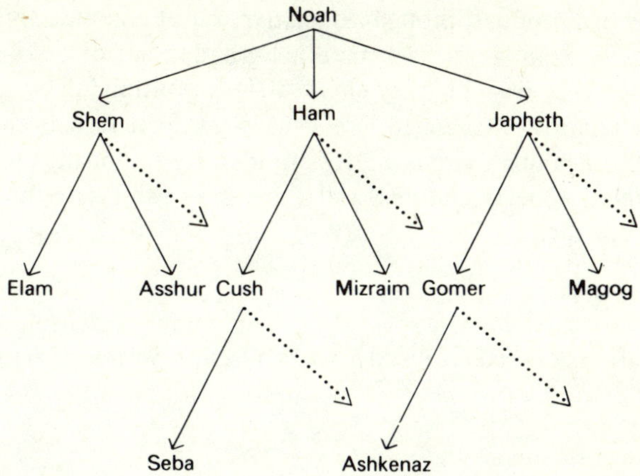

Fig. 2.3

2.4 PROPERTIES AND ALGEBRA OF RELATIONS

If A and B are two relations between S and T then we can define the following concepts:

(i) A *includes* B if for all $s \in S$ and $t \in T$ sBt implies sAt. For instance "$\leqslant$" includes "$<$" where $S = T =$ the set of integers.

(ii) A is the *transpose* of B if for all $s \in S$ and $t \in T$ sAt if and only if tBs. For instance 'is a parent of' is the transpose of 'is a child of' over the set of people.

(iii) A is *reflexive* if $S = T$ and for all $s \in S$ sAs is true. For instance the equality relation "$=$" over any set is reflexive. So is "$\leqslant$" over the set of integers.

(iv) A is *transitive* if $S = T$ and for all $r, s, t \in S$ rAs and sAt imply rAt. For instance the 'is a descendant of' relation over the set of people.

How can these be interpreted graphically? If A includes B then every arrow on B's digraph will be present on A's which may have others besides. If A is the transpose of B then their digraphs will be the same but with the directions of the arrows reversed. A reflexive relation will have 'loop' arrows starting and finishing at every element of the set. A transitive relation will be such that if there is a path (sequence of arrows all pointing in the forward direction) along several arrows from one element to another then there will be a *direct* arrow from one to the other.

We can impose an algebra on relations by defining a product and a sum.

If A is a relation between R and S and B is a relation between S and T, we can define the product relation AB between R and T by: r AB t if and only if there exists an element s of S such that rAs and sBt. As an example – if A is 'is the mother of' and B is 'is a parent of' then AB is 'is a grandmother of'.

Note that this product, though associative, is not commutative. For instance BA in the above example is 'is a maternal grandparent of'. Note also that the equality relation acts as an identity element since multiplying by it on the left or right leaves a relation unchanged. We usually write it as I. It should be noted that technically speaking there is a different identity or equality relation for each set. If A is a relation between sets S and T and if I_S and I_T are the corresponding identity relations then:

$$I_S A = A = A I_T$$

For a relation A between S and S we can define **powers** of A by the following definition:

$$A^0 = I$$

$$A^{n+1} = A^n A \quad n \geqslant 0$$

Note (and prove!) that A^i always commutes with A^j and their product is A^{i+j}.

Graphically the powers of a relation can be thought of as follows: If there is a path of length k arrows from s to t in the digraph of A, then there will be a direct arrow from s to t in the digraph of A^k.

We can also define a sum of two relations A and B between the same sets S and T written A + B by: s A + B t if and only if sAt or sBt. This operation is commutative and associative. As an example, if S = T = the set of integers, then "$<$" + "$=$" is "$\leqslant$". Note that the sum of two relations thought of in their strict sense as sets is merely their union.

2.5 CLOSURE OF RELATIONS

We are now coming to the most important part of our exposition of relations. We have been selective in what we have said about them, (any standard textbook of algebra, such as Birkhoff and MacLane [4] will give a fuller treatment), but we shall finish by defining two kinds of closure on relations which will be used extensively in the next two chapters. First the **transitive closure** of a relation A between S and S, written A^+, is defined by: s A^+ t if and only if s A^k t for some $k > 0$. Graphically this means that there is a path of *some* length from s to t. Another way of expressing this is:

$$A^+ = A^1 + A^2 + \ldots\ldots\ldots$$

$$= \sum_{i=1}^{\infty} A^i \tag{3}$$

It is useful to realise that in calculating the transitive closure of a relation on a *finite* set (of size k, say), the summation (3) terminates after a finite number of terms. Intuitively this is because in the graph of the relation, if there is a path between two elements there must be a path (without loops) of length at most k−1 because otherwise we would run out of elements to pass through.

It is sometimes necessary to define a further closure called the **reflexive transitive closure** of a relation written A^*. This is merely an extension to A^+ obtained by adding in an extra term $I = A^0$. Thus:

$$A^* = \sum_{i=0}^{\infty} A^i \tag{4}$$

Compare equations (3) and (4) with (1) and (2) in section 2.1. It can be proved (and it is just as well for the sake of nomenclature) that the transitive closure of a relation is transitive and that the reflexive transitive closure is reflexive.

We end this section with some examples of closures: "$<$" is the transitive closure of 'is the predecessor of'; 'is an ancestor of' is the transitive closure of 'is a parent of'; and 'is a divisor of' is the reflexive transitive closure of 'is a direct divisor of'.

2.6 BOOLEAN MATRIX REPRESENTATION

The examples given in this book are not exactly trivial but they are all very simple and designed merely to show the problems and their solutions. Usually when presented with the digraph of a relation, its closures can be 'read off' merely by looking at the diagram and following the pointers. However sooner or later all this must be applied to a 'real' problem. We will see later that, in order to demonstrate a computer language's suitability for treatment by the recursive descent method, we need to calculate closures of finite but large relations and to do this by hand is messy and error prone. It is therefore advisable to develop computational methods for closure calculation.

We have already seen one model of relations – the digraph picture representation. Now we require a model suitable for storage and manipulation in a computer. The functional representation of a relation suggested at the end of section 2.2, where it is given as a mapping from the Cartesian product of the relevant sets to {true, false}, suggests that we might represent a relation by a function. However it is difficult to 'read in' a function to a general program designed to process *any* relation. Luckily a mapping from $S \times T$ can be represented by a boolean matrix with elements of S ranged down the left hand edge and those of T along the top to be used as indices. The value of the mapping applied to a particular pair (s, t) is found at the intersection of the row indexed by s and the column indexed by t.

If A is a relation we will represent it by matrix M(A). Let us put this into practice by showing the matrix for the 'is a direct divisor of' relation given in Example 2.2. Its digraph is as follows:

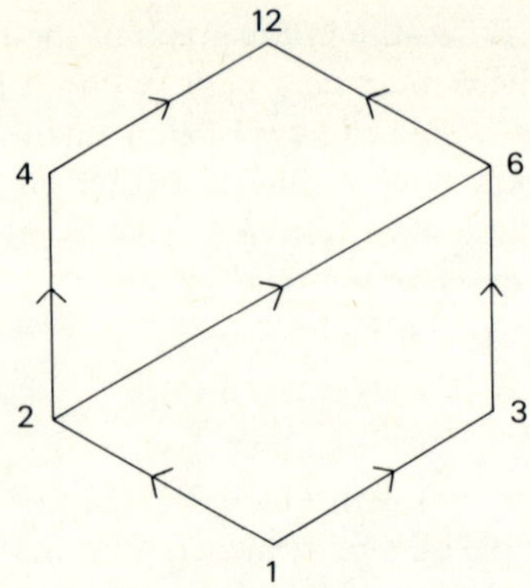

Fig. 2.4

Representing "true" by a "*" and "false" by a blank space, the matrix representation is:

M(A) =

	1	2	3	4	6	12
1		*	*			
2				*	*	
3					⊛	
4						*
6						*
12						

The circled * represents, for instance, that there is an arrow from 3 to 6. The matrices will not always in general be square. It will depend on the sizes of S and T. But in most cases of interest to us S = T. Note that such matrices overcharacterize the relation since we can choose the elements of S and T to be taken in any order and each time get a different matrix representing the same relation.

2.7 CALCULATION OF CLOSURES

In order to use the matrix representation to calculate closures, we have to be able to find the sums given in equations (3) and (4) in section 2.5. This means that we need to find matrices representing products of relations, in particular powers, and matrices specifying sums of relations.

Let us look at the latter case first. The sum of two relations is obtained by seeing if either (or both) of the relations is true for each particular pair of elements of the sets. Thus to add two relations we merely take the elements of the corresponding matrices and 'or' them together element by element. Thus:

$$M(A + B) = M(A) \vee M(B)$$

For the product of two relations things are not much more difficult. Given elements r and t and wishing to see if r AB t, we have to find out if there is any element s such that rAs and sBt. We therefore have to look at the row indexed by r in M(A). This gives the relationships of r with all the possible candidates s as we move along the row. If we simultaneously scan the t indexed column of M(B), we can see if the relationship s B t holds. This means that we must calculate a 'dot product' of the row and column in a very similar manner to 'ordinary' matrix multiplication but with addition being replaced by the operation 'or' and multiplication by 'and'.

As an example let us calculate $M(A^2)$ where A is as in Fig. 2.4 and M(A) as shown below that. The product of M(A) with itself is then:

$$M(A^2) = \begin{array}{c} \\ 1 \\ 2 \\ 3 \\ 4 \\ 6 \\ 12 \end{array} \begin{array}{c} \begin{array}{cccccc} 1 & 2 & 3 & 4 & 6 & 12 \end{array} \\ \left[\begin{array}{cccccc} & & & * & * & \\ & & & & & * \\ & & & & & * \\ & & & & & \\ & & & & & \\ & & & & & \end{array}\right] \end{array}$$

This relation represents all the paths of length 2 in the graph of A.

If we 'sum' M(A) and $M(A^2)$ we get:

$$M(A + A^2) = \begin{array}{c} \\ 1 \\ 2 \\ 3 \\ 4 \\ 6 \\ 12 \end{array} \begin{array}{c} \begin{array}{cccccc} 1 & 2 & 3 & 4 & 6 & 12 \end{array} \\ \left[\begin{array}{cccccc} & * & * & * & * & \\ & & & * & * & * \\ & & & & * & * \\ & & & & & * \\ & & & & & * \\ & & & & & \end{array}\right] \end{array}$$

and this represents all the paths of length 1 or 2 in the graph of A.

Note that this adding of a matrix to another can only contribute new true elements to it – none can be removed. This is another way of saying that the sum:

$$A + A^2 + \ldots\ldots\ldots$$

terminates for finite relations; because the corresponding finite matrix will either become full up with true elements or settle down to a steady state earlier than that. Remember that it will always terminate at A^{n-1} at worst where A is a relation over a set of size n.

The 'direct divisor' relation A settles down after $M(A^3)$ is added giving:

$$M(A^+) = \begin{array}{c} \\ 1 \\ 2 \\ 3 \\ 4 \\ 6 \\ 12 \end{array} \begin{array}{c} \begin{array}{cccccc} 1 & 2 & 3 & 4 & 6 & 12 \end{array} \\ \left[\begin{array}{cccccc} & * & * & * & * & * \\ & & & * & * & * \\ & & & & * & * \\ & & & & & * \\ & & & & & * \\ & & & & & \end{array}\right] \end{array}$$

To get $M(A^*)$ all we need do is add true elements all the way down the diagonal to make the relation reflexive.

When calculating $M(A^*)$ or $M(A^+)$ for a large relation A, efficiency will be very important. A single matrix multiplication of $n \times n$ arrays requires $O(n^3)$ operations to be carried out. If we calculate $M(A^*)$ in the 'direct' way by computing $M(I)$, $M(A)$, $M(A^2)$, ... $M(A^{n-1})$ we have to do $O(n)$ matrix multiplications, so the whole process takes a time $O(n^4)$. If we notice, however, that:

$$M(A + A) = M(A)$$

then we can calculate instead the sequence:

$$M(I + A)$$

$$M((I + A)^2) = M(I + A + A^2)$$

$$M(((I + A)^2)^2) = M(I + A + A^2 + A^3 + A^4)$$

.

.

.

.

then we will only need about $\log_2 n$ matrix multiplications and so the whole process is $O(n^3 \log n)$ in time.

In fact there is an even faster method due to Warshall [5]. This calculates the transitive closure of A (from which the reflexive transitive closure may easily be obtained) as follows:-

```
! Read or calculate bool matrix A (n × n)
for i = 1 to n do
    ! Each time round the loop add a new node
    ! (number i) to the transitive closure graph

    for j = 1 to n do
        ! Find all arrows leading into node i
        if A(j, i) do
            ! If there is an arrow from
            ! node j to node i, find all
            ! those out of node i

            for k = 1 to n do
                ! and make a direct
                ! path arrow from node j
                ! to node k

                A(j, k) := A(j, k) or A(i, k)

! Now A contains the transitive closure matrix
```

This method is $O(n^3)$ in time since each loop is executed a maximum of n times. Note that the inner loop is perfectly suited to very fast parallel computation which can be partially achieved on most conventional computers by holding the columns of the matrix as bit patterns and 'or–ing' whole words together at a time.

2.8 SUMMARY

In this chapter we have introduced a small number of mathematical concepts needed in later chapters. These have included strings, relations and graphs. We have directed the development of these subjects towards the pivotal topic of closure which will be extensively needed in Chapters 3 and 4, when we find out whether certain grammars are suitable for describing languages which can be compiled using the recursive descent technique.

REFERENCES

[1] Kleen, S. C. (1956), Representation of events in nerve nets and finite automata, *Automata Studies,* Princeton University Press, 3–42.
[2] Berge, C. (1973), *Graphs and Hypergraphs,* North Holland.
[3] Wilson, R. J. (1972), *Introduction to Graph Theory,* Longman.
[4] Birkhoff, G. and MacLane, S. (1953), *A Survey of Modern Algebra,* Macmillan.
[5] Warshall, S. (1962), A theorem on boolean matrices, *JACM,* **9**, **1**, 11–12.

CHAPTER 3

Grammatical Preliminaries

3.1 GRAMMARS AND LANGUAGES

Before we can write a compiler for a computer language, we need a precise definition of that language. We must therefore first have languages in which such definitions may be given. Languages which discuss others in this way are called **metalanguages**. A language defined or considered by a metalanguage is a **subject** language.

Initially we shall use the mathematics of set theory as our metalanguage but we shall 'humanise' this in practice to a more palatable form using a more intuitive metalanguage called BNF. This will be described in more detail in section 3.3.

First, however, let us see in very general form how set theory can be used to define languages. Intuitively a language is a set (usually infinite) of texts expressible in that language. Such texts are known to computational linguists as **sentences** of the language. Thus the sentences of a subject language are a subset of all the texts that could possibly be written using the letters of the alphabet chosen for writing the language. We must somehow separate out the legal texts of the language from the ungrammatical ones. To do this we can use a **grammar** to specify the syntactic rules of a language.

A grammer (also known sometimes as a **syntax**) consists of four components:-

(i) A finite set T (called an **alphabet**) of symbols which form the basic characters or groups of characters which can be strung together to form texts of the language under consideration. Such symbols are called **terminal symbols.**

(ii) Another finite alphabet of **non-terminal symbols**, N. If we are going to analyse sentences, we must have some way of naming parts of sentences (phrases). Non-terminals can be thought of as variables whose values are subphrases of a whole sentence. Alphabets T and N must be disjoint. We must always be able to tell whether a symbol is a terminal one or not.

(iii) A specially designated member of N called the **distinguished symbol** or **start symbol** S. This can be used for naming whole sentences.

(iv) A set, P, of **productions.** We shall see that to generate a legal string of terminal symbols which is a sentence we must successively transform strings of terminals and non-terminals which describe sentences in partially synthesised form.

As an example, consider the synthesis of a person's name. We might carry out the transformation:

⟨name⟩ =⟩ ⟨forenames⟩ ⟨surname⟩
=⟩ ⟨firstname⟩ ⟨middlenames⟩ ⟨surname⟩
=⟩ David ⟨middlenames⟩ ⟨surname⟩
=⟩ David ⟨surname⟩
=⟩ David Smith

Here the members of the non-terminal language N appear as entities in angled brackets and other elements are members of T. The relationship "=⟩" shows successive mutations starting with the distinguished symbol, in this case ⟨name⟩, and ending up with the sentence 'David Smith' of the simple language of names.

The rules which tell us which transformations are legal are known as productions or production rules. Each production is a pair of strings P and Q each of which can contain members of the alphabets T and/or N. If (P, Q) is such a pair we are essentially saying that a transformation which allows the replacement of P by Q is allowable. With this in mind we often write "P —⟩ Q" for the pair (P, Q). "P ::= Q" can also be used. Thus:

⟨firstname⟩ —⟩ David
⟨firstname⟩ —⟩ Sue
⟨forenames⟩ —⟩ ⟨firstname⟩ ⟨middlenames⟩
⟨middlenames⟩ —⟩
⟨middlenames⟩ —⟩ ⟨middlenames⟩ ⟨midname⟩

are some of the productions of the small example language of names. Note that the right hand side of the "—⟩" can be empty. In this case ⟨middlenames⟩ is to be replaced by nothing at all – λ the **empty string** – in the transformation.

We place one important restriction on productions "P —⟩ Q". P *must* contain at least one non-terminal. Thus no transformation can replace a subphrase consisting only of terminals by something else. This, indeed, is why they are known as terminals.

More formally the rule of substitution can be stated as follows: the relationship "V =⟩ W" holds (where V and W belong to $(N \cup T)^*$) if V and W can be decomposed into substrings:

$$V = XV'Y$$
$$W = XW'Y$$

and there is a production V′ —⟩ W′.

For example, in the series of transformations given above, the following step occurs:

⟨firstname⟩ ⟨middlenames⟩ ⟨surname⟩
=⟩ David ⟨middlenames⟩ ⟨surname⟩

Here V′ = ⟨firstname⟩, W′ = David, X is empty and Y = ⟨middlenames⟩⟨surname⟩.

Given these four elements of a grammar G, we can define the language L(G) **produced by** G as those terminal sentences generated by successive uses of "=⟩", starting with the distinguished symbol (i.e. formed by "$\overset{*}{=}\rangle$", the reflexive transitive closure of "=⟩").

More formally

$$L(G) = \{ s \in T^* \mid S \overset{*}{=}\rangle s \}$$

The method used here to generate sentences by means of a grammar is called the **phrase structure** method and this particular type of grammar is a **phrase structure grammar.**

3.2 CHOMSKY'S STRATIFICATION

The definition of a language given in the last section was very general and allowed a very large class of grammars to be used. In fact we need not use grammars as powerful as this in this text.

Noam Chomsky [1] has categorised grammars into four classes, each one essentially a subset of the previous one. The types of grammars he describes are restricted by only allowing productions of certain types. The four classes are as follows:-

0 A Chomsky type 0 grammar is the most general type. It is sometimes called a **semi-Thue** grammar. It allows productions to be as complicated as needed, and this type of grammar is as described in the last section. We will not need grammars with this unrestricted power in this text.

1 We can restrict the generality of Type 0 grammars to Type 1 or **context sensitive** grammars by insisting that the production rules are all of the form:-

PAQ —⟩ PBQ

where P and Q are (possibly empty) strings of $(N \cup T)^*$, A is a single non-terminal, and B is any non-empty string of $(N \cup T)^+$. What we are doing here is allowing transformations in which A is replaced by B *in the context of* P and Q. P is called the **left context** and Q the **right context.**

Once again this type of grammar is in general too powerful for our needs; or, to be more honest, it does not provide a suitable framework around which to build an efficient compiling method. In fact, to describe most useful computer languages' syntax completely, we *would* need a context sensitive grammar or perhaps even a type 0 grammar. Intuitively the illegality of the program

```
let a = 1
write b
?
```

is based on the fact that the occurrence of "b" takes place in the *wrong context,* one in which only "a" has been declared – but it is neither easy to see (a) how to reflect the declaration rules needed to prevent this sort of thing in an appropriate type 1 grammar nor (b), how to write a compiler based on such a grammar. In fact some work has been done in this area but not using context sensitive grammars as defined here but rather **Affix** grammars [2] and **Attribute** grammars [3]. Another approach is the **two-level** grammars of van Wijngaarden [4] used to describe Algol 68 [5] though it would be very difficult to base a compiler on this method of syntax specification.
In this book, most of the contextual constraints put on a language will be expressed in an informal manner. (However the **type rules** which we shall describe in section 9.2 are a useful contextual device for limiting a language to correctly typed expressions).

2 We therefore need a further restriction of grammars. Chomsky's type 2 category is also called the **context free** group of grammars. Here the productions can only be of the form

A –⟩ B

where A ϵ N and B is any string of symbols in (N U T)*. (There are problems if B is empty but let us neglect that for the moment – see sections 4.2 and 4.3). Note that these rules are similar to Type 1 rules except that we are not allowed to place any context sensitive constraints P and Q around A and B.
This type of grammar is the most important from our point of view which is why we devote the whole of the next section to it.

3 To complete our description of Chomsky's hierarchy we describe the Type 3 or **regular** (or right linear) grammars. Here productions are very restricted indeed. They can only be of the following types:

A –⟩ xB
A –⟩ x

where A and B are non-terminals and x is any terminal symbol. It can be shown that this kind of grammar can be useful for describing a language at its lexicographic level, where groups of letters such as "b", "e", "g", "i", "n" are taken together to form basic **lexemes** of the language. We talk more about lexical analysis in Chapter 7 where we relate it to regular grammars. More details about using regular grammars to help to write lexical analysers can be found in texts such as Gries's book [6].

3.3 CONTEXT FREE GRAMMARS

As we pointed out in the last section, context free grammars will be our primary tool for describing object languages.

Let us make some useful conventions in order that we do not have to keep qualifying sentences with such phrases as '. . . . . .where A is a non-terminal'. We shall talk about context free grammars using *two* conventions in fact: one when we are looking at their theoretical aspects to give fairly trivial but pointed examples in this and the next chapter, and the other to be used in practice when we describe real languages.

Convention 1

The first, theoretically used, convention is that we shall consistently use capital letters to denote non-terminals and small letters and other characters such as "(", "+", ... to denote basic symbols. Unless otherwise stated, "S" will always be reserved for the distinguished symbol.

For example the following is a grammar which describes a small subset of the expressions available in many programming languages. We shall use it from time to time in examples and shall refer to it as grammar G, and to the language it describes as language L.

Non-Terminals:

S (Distinguished symbol)
E (Expressions)
T (Terms)
F (Factors)
U (Units)

Terminals:

+,*,(,),0,1,2,3,4,5,6,7,8,9

Productions:

S —⟩ E
E —⟩ T
E —⟩ E + T
T —⟩ F
T —⟩ T * F
F —⟩ U
F —⟩ (E)
U —⟩ 0
U —⟩ 1
U —⟩ 2
.
.
.
U —⟩ 9

As pointed out in section 3.2 above, the left hand side of a context free production must consist of a single non-terminal. We make a further addition to the convention that if several production rules have identical left sides then they may be combined by placing a vertical bar, "|", between their right hand sides. Thus the rules of grammar G can be shortened to:

S –⟩ E
E –⟩ T | E + T
T –⟩ F | T * F
F –⟩ U | (E)
U –⟩ 0 | 1 | 2 | 3 | 4 | 5 | 6 | 7 | 8 | 9

Convention 2

The second convention which we shall use in practical cases is called **BNF** which stands for Backus Naur Form or Backus Normal Form. Backus and Naur were both involved in producing the famous Algol 60 Revised Report [7]. Naur was the editor and Backus the inventor of a notation now known as BNF which was used in this report to describe Algol's syntax.

In BNF, non-terminals are represented by meaningful names or phrases enclosed in angled brackets "⟨" and "⟩". The "–⟩" between the pair of elements of a production is replaced by ": :=". The "|" notation as defined above in convention 1 is also used and has the same meaning. Thus the following grammar (or set of productions – we shall often use the terms synonymously when, as with both these conventions, it is obvious what the terminals, non-terminals and distinguished symbol are) is a BNF version of grammar G:

⟨S⟩ : := ⟨Expression⟩
⟨Expression⟩ : := ⟨Term⟩ | ⟨Expression⟩ + ⟨Term⟩
⟨Term⟩ : := ⟨Factor⟩ | ⟨Term⟩ * ⟨Factor⟩
⟨Factor⟩ : := ⟨Unit⟩ | (⟨Expression⟩)
⟨Unit⟩ : := 0 | 1 | 2 | 3 | 4 | 5 | 6 | 7 | 8 | 9

The result is, of course, more long-winded than convention 1 but with careful choice of syntactic variable names, it will have a much more transparent meaning. We will use a slight extension of BNF in this book for reasons of brevity. Two new additions to the convention are introduced. If a part of the right hand side of a production is enclosed in square brackets "[" and "]", this means that it is optional whether that part has to appear at all. Thus

⟨somevar⟩ : := α [β] γ

where α and γ both belong to $(N \cup T)^*$, and β belongs to $(N \cup T)^+$, is equivalent to

⟨somevar⟩ : := $\alpha\gamma$ | $\alpha\beta\gamma$

If, in addition, an asterisk, "*", (the Kleene star again) is placed after the square brackets, it means that the entities within can appear *any* number of times (including zero). Thus:

⟨somevar⟩ : := α [β] * γ

has the same effect as

⟨somevar⟩ : := α ⟨betaplus⟩ γ | $\alpha\gamma$
⟨betaplus⟩ : := β [⟨betaplus⟩]

In fact in most useful cases γ is empty.

Language L may be described (with a little obvious transformation of grammar G) by:

⟨S⟩ : := ⟨Expression⟩
⟨Expression⟩ : := ⟨Term⟩ [+ ⟨Term⟩] *
⟨Term⟩ : := ⟨Factor⟩ [⟨times⟩ ⟨Factor⟩] *
⟨Factor⟩ : := ⟨Unit⟩ | (⟨Expression⟩)
⟨Unit⟩ : := 0 | 1 | 2 | 3 | 4 | 5 | 6 | 7 | 8 | 9
⟨times⟩ : := *

(Note how "*" is playing two rôles here – one as a basic symbol and one as a **metasymbol** – a symbol of the metalanguage, not the subject language. Something similar must obviously be done for "[", "]", "|", "⟨" and "⟩" if they appear in the subject language).

We will see later that this iterative way of specifying repeating groups (rather than the recursive way that 'pure' BNF usually uses) has a direct reflection in the way we code recognition procedures for syntactic categories involving it (see section 6.3) – using **while** loops rather than calling the procedures recursively. It also helps to solve a rather tricky grammar transformation problem which we shall discuss in section 4.6.

As we hinted earlier in this chapter, we shall impose some context sensitive restraints on the languages we discuss, using what we call the type rules. These will be discussed further in section 9.2.

3.4 SENTENCE GENERATION AND RECOGNITION

The transformational grammars described here were originally designed by Chomsky to be used by linguists. As we have seen, their idea is to start with the distinguished symbol and, by successive transformations, mutate it into a sentence consisting only of basic symbols. Thus we can, by choosing different sequences of transformations, **generate** different sample sentences of the language under consideration.

There is another logical way of considering such a succession of transformations, by thinking of the sequence *backwards*; that is starting with the sentence and transforming it step by step into the distinguished symbol. Such a process is, of course, no different in principle from the generative one. But there is a psychological difference in that we think of a given sentence as **recognised** as a legal one rather than as generated (possibly arbitrarily) from the distinguished symbol.

When a compiler attempts to parse a sentence (program), it may in fact use either of the above processes and at this stage it becomes apparent that the difference, to a computer, is no longer just psychological because the kinds of programs used for generative parsing are very different from those for recognitive parsing. The technical terms for these methods are top down (generative) and **bottom up** (recognitive). Of course we need hardly say that top down synthesis of a sentence is *not* done arbitrarily in practice. At each stage the process is guided by the form of the particular program being compiled, and care is taken to make sure that that is the one actually generated.

The major part of this book is about a particular top down method (recursive descent) but we shall discuss briefly some of the other methods available, including bottom up processes, later in this chapter.

3.5 DERIVATIONS

For the moment however let us discuss the transformation process itself without worrying about whether it runs backwards or forwards. A sequence

$$\alpha_0 \Rightarrow \alpha_1 \Rightarrow \ldots\ldots \alpha_n$$

is called a **derivation** of α_n from α_0 (which we write $\alpha_0 \overset{*}{\Rightarrow} \alpha_n$ so that "$\overset{*}{\Rightarrow}$" is the "is derived from" relation). Its single steps $\alpha_i \Rightarrow \alpha_{i+1}$ $(0 \leqslant i < n)$ are called **direct derivations.** Thus the sentences of a language are all derivations from the distinguished symbol. The converse is not true since non-terminals may be present. If they are, we have what are called **sentential forms** which are half-way stages in derivations between the distinguished symbol and the ultimately recognised sentence.

Consider the following sentence of the language L:

1 + 2 * 3

We know that it is a sentence of L because of the transformation sequence:

$$\begin{aligned} S &\Rightarrow E \\ &\Rightarrow E + T \\ &\Rightarrow T + T \\ &\Rightarrow F + T \\ &\Rightarrow U + T \\ &\Rightarrow 1 + T \\ &\Rightarrow 1 + T * F \\ &\Rightarrow 1 + F * F \\ &\Rightarrow 1 + U * F \\ &\Rightarrow 1 + 2 * F \\ &\Rightarrow 1 + 2 * U \\ &\Rightarrow 1 + 2 * 3 \end{aligned} \qquad (5)$$

In fact, however, we could have used the sequence:

```
S =⟩ E
  =⟩ E + T
  =⟩ E + T * F
  =⟩ E + T * U
  =⟩ E + T * 3
  =⟩ E + F * 3
  =⟩ E + U * 3
  =⟩ E + 2 * 3
  =⟩ T + 2 * 3
  =⟩ F + 2 * 3
  =⟩ U + 2 * 3
  =⟩ 1 + 2 * 3                                   (6)
```

or indeed any one of a whole host of other transformation sequences. The reader might like to work out how many legal derivations of ″1 + 2 * 3″ there are using grammar G. The answer is 2,100. Which one should we choose? Does it matter? One is initially tempted to say that it does, until one notices that in each such sequence the same transformations are carried out in the same places but in a different order. They are all the 'same' parse in some sense.

3.6 AMBIGUITY AND SYNTAX TREES

Before we tighten up this notion, let us consider a related question. Why did we use grammar G to describe language L? On the face of it, the following productions (grammar G′) would have served our purpose just as well:

```
S −⟩ E
E −⟩ 0 | 1 | 2 | 3 | 4 | 5 | 6 | 7 | 8 | 9 |
     E + E | E * E | ( E )
```

The answer is that, although G′ and G describe the same language L (prove it!), different derivations of the same sentence using the productions of G′ sometimes use sequences of transformations either entirely different or used at different places in the sentence rather than just in a different order.

To make this clear, consider the following example. The sentence ″1 + 2 * 3″ can be derived using G′ by:

E =⟩ E+E =⟩ 1+E =⟩ 1+E*E =⟩ 1+2*E =⟩ 1+2*3 (7)

or by

E =⟩ E*E =⟩ E+E*E =⟩ 1+E*E =⟩ 1+2*E =⟩ 1+2*3 (8)

Although we *have* used the same productions in a different order here, they are being used at different points in the sentence. The use of E —⟩ E * E in derivation (7) represents a multiplication of "2" by "3" and in (8) of "1+2" by "3". Our intuition tells us that the first is the 'correct' derivation because that is the way we group multiplication and addition, and there is something 'wrong' with grammar G′, in that it allows the second derivation(8) at all. Such 'wrong' derivations cannot occur with grammar G and we see that its hierarchical nature *forces* the correct grouping of expressions into sums of terms which are, in turn, products of factors. In fact, the grammar G also imposes left associativity on the operators "+" and "*" by specifying:

E —⟩ E + T
T —⟩ T * F

rather than

E —⟩ T + E
T —⟩ F * T

We shall see that the former (which are called **left recursive** productions because the left hand side appears as the leftmost component of the right hand side) cause some problems for our method of parsing.

How can we capture this **ambiguity** of grammar G′ in a more rigorous sense? Consider derivations (5) and (6) again. There is something special about them. In (5) we always picked the leftmost non-terminal for expression, using a suitable production rule, and in (6) the rightmost non-terminal was used. Those particular derivations are hence known as **leftmost** and **rightmost derivations.** We say that a grammar is **ambiguous** if there exist sentences with more than one leftmost derivation. (We could have substituted 'rightmost' with the same effect.) Now consider the two derivations (7) and (8). These are both leftmost derivations and hence grammar G′ is ambiguous.

Above, we stated it as a fact that G was unambiguous. We will not enter here into the complicated but tedious proofs of how the ambiguity or unambiguity of particular grammars can be made. Suffice it to say that it is unsolvable for a *general* context free grammar although individual grammars may be proved. The reader is referred to [8] for further discussion of such points.

Another way of looking at ambiguity is to consider parse trees. We will not define these rigorously but appeal to the reader's intuition. For a tight definition see [8]. A parse tree or **syntax tree** is a tree structure labelled with terminals or empty at its tips and non-terminals at its other nodes, with, in particular, S labelling the root. The idea is that when a production, say "A —⟩ $\alpha\beta\gamma\ldots$" is used in a derivation (where α, β and γ are terminals or non-terminals), a corresponding subtree:

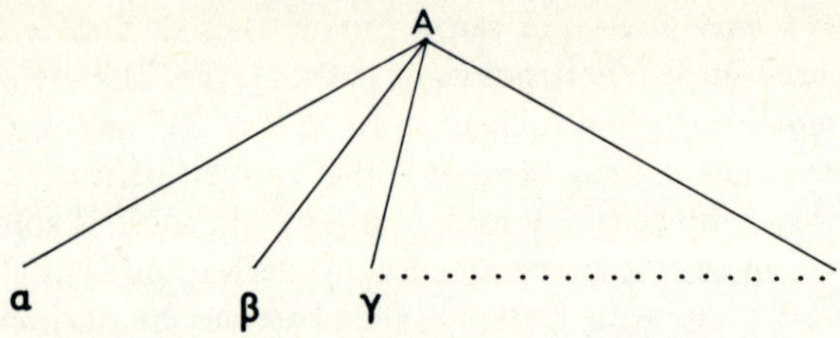

Fig. 3.1

of the final parse tree is created. Thus the steps of derivation (5) grow successive trees:

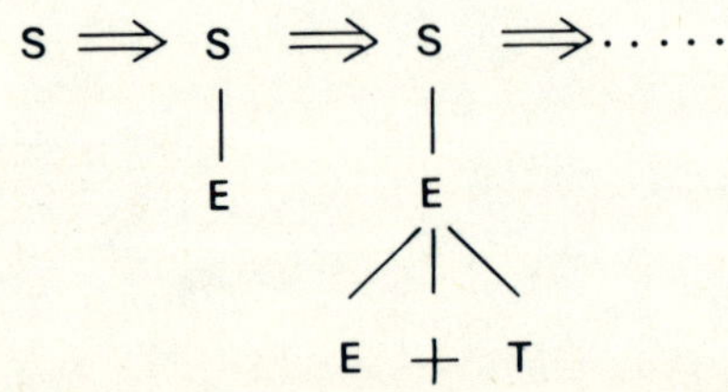

Fig. 3.2

until we end up with

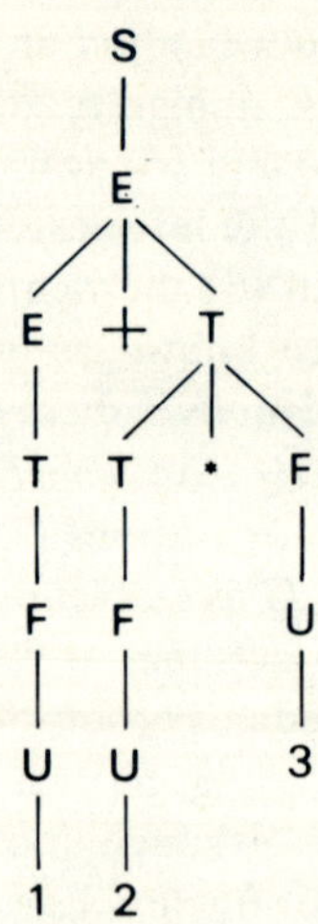

Fig. 3.3

Steps of derivation (6) will grow the *same final tree,* but the intermediate trees will be different since the nodes are developed in a different order. We could in fact have defined ambiguity with reference to these trees. If every sentence generated by a grammar has only one parse tree, the grammar is unambiguous.

So we should expect grammar G′ to admit different parse trees of some sentences; and so it does. Derivations (7) and (8) correspond to the trees:

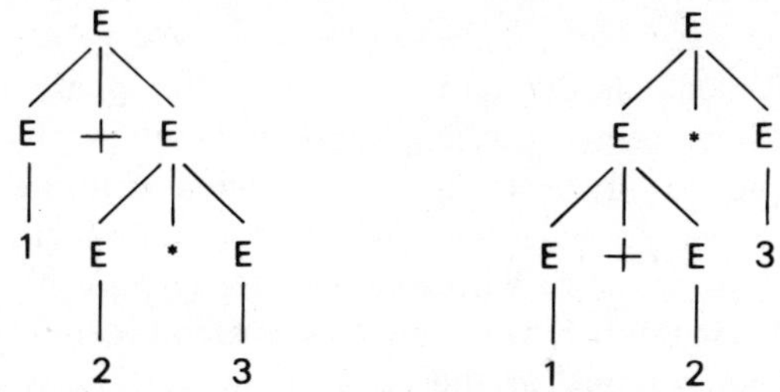

Fig. 3.4

Besides their having the nasty effects mentioned above, there is another reason why we would like to get rid of ambiguous grammars; no ambiguous grammar is a suitable foundation from which to build a recursive descent compiler. We shall see this in Chapter 4 where we introduce LL(1) grammars upon which recursive descent parsing is based. There it will be shown that no ambiguous grammar is an LL(1) grammar.

3.7 A GENERAL TOP DOWN METHOD

The basic problems of compiling are the building of the unique syntax tree from a legal sentence, and the subsequent traversal of the tree attaching meaning or **semantics** to it either by directly 'executing' the tree, interpreting it, or by generating code for subsequent execution by a computer or interpreter. This is done by traversal of the tree, visiting its nodes in some appropriate order. Note however that the tree need never be built explicitly. The dynamic structure of the parsing algorithm may reflect the structure of the tree and be its only model of existence. The semantic walk-through of the tree may well take place at the same time as it is being built. This is the approach that recursive descent compilers take. Chapters 6 and 7 discuss this in more detail.

We shall leave the semantics part of the problem – the breaking down of the tree – until Chapter 12. We shall however look in some detail at how a top down analyser, faced with an arbitrary grammar, might try to build a tree from a sentence. This will give us some insight into the problems to be faced.

We have seen that an unambiguous grammar gives rise to a single leftmost derivation for any sentence of its language, and informally that such derivations will be in one-to-one correspondence with parse trees. Our problem in growing the parse trees (or merely recognising the correctness of the sentence by doing so implicitly) can therefore be reduced to that of finding a leftmost derivation.

We should therefore try to imagine a top down parser at some stage having before it some sentential form that is one of the steps in the derivation. This form will consist of terminals and non-terminals in general. It starts by being the distinguished symbol and ends up by being the sentence which is being parsed. Since we are building a leftmost derivation, it is always the leftmost non-terminal which is the current candidate for expansion using some production rule. Naturally the main part of the problem for the parser is to choose the correct rule. Note that all the terminals up to this point must match some initial substring of the sentence string which is being parsed. We can consider this string as being steadily eaten into by being read into the computer one terminal at a time. As the parse proceeds, new terminals appear at the left of the derivation and are matched with terminals read in. At this stage they can be discarded from the sentential form the parser is considering; so that it always has the leftmost non-terminal at the start of the section of sentential form it is working on ready to match against the next section of input. This non-terminal is called the **target, goal** or **active symbol.**

If at any moment a match fails, this means that the parsing process has taken a wrong turning at some previous stage (or that the input string is in error and is not a sentence). This mismatch is not only caused if terminal symbols at the left hand ends fail to correspond, but if either of the strings runs out of symbols. A parse only succeeds if both strings run out simultaneously. In the case of a mismatch, we must **backtrack** to the last position where a choice (of which production to apply) was made, 'unreading' all the input symbols which have been read since then, restoring the fragment of the current sentential form to its previous state, and 'undoing' any semantic actions of code generation or direct execution that may have been carried out while searching down the blind alley the parser has found itself in. We must also 'unbuild' at least part of the syntax tree if we have been doing this explicitly.

This obviously presents real problems as 'unreading' and 'undoing' are very unnatural processes for a computer. What we would like is for the parser to be oracular, to be able to tell merely by looking at the input on hand what is the correct path to follow. Obviously this will only be possible for certain classes of grammar. Our job in Chapter 4 will be to see which classes behave in this **deterministic** way.

It should be mentioned at this stage that backtracking is a fairly well used technique in the field of combinatorics and Floyd [9] has written an interesting paper on how to do it by making algorithms run backwards; but most of these problems have solutions whose time taken is exponential relative to the length of the input. Ideally we would like to parse long programs in a time proportional to their length.

Will the method described above always work? If not, what modifications do we have to make to it to convert it into one that does?

Let us try an example. In the following, the left hand column represents the still-to-be-matched part of the sentential forms under consideration. The right hand column shows successive states of the input. Its left hand character represents the next one to be read. Our starting position is:

1. S 1 + 2 * 3

Our ground rules say that we must now choose a rule to substitute S, being the leftmost (and only) non-terminal and hence the target. In this case there is only one rule "S —⟩ E" so we move to our next position:

2. E 1 + 2 * 3

Simultaneously the tree, if we are growing it explicitly, will extend to:

Fig. 3.5

At this stage we have a choice of rules to apply. We could either use "E—⟩ T" or "E —⟩ E + T". We now note the first dangerous trap the general parser may fall into. The compiler has very little to go on when making its choice, except the next few input symbols and these do not obviously help. In such a case it will have to choose the rules one by one in some consistent order, backtracking occasionally to try another. If the rule "E —⟩ E + T" is the parser's regular first choice, it will get into a loop:

```
E + T           1 + 2 * 3
E + T + T       1 + 2 * 3
E + T + T + T   1 + 2 * 3
.               .
.               .
.               .
```

Perhaps we might circumvent this by arranging for such left recursive productions to be placed at the end of the choices to be made. This would have to be done for *mutually* left recursive rules as well such as:

```
A —⟩ B | C D
C —⟩ E | A F
```

For our particular grammar this is an easy task, but it is clear that, in the general case, it may be quite difficult to order the alternatives appropriately.

Let us continue our parse with the left recursive rules placed at the end. The next few steps are:

```
3.   T   1 + 2 * 3
4.   F   1 + 2 * 3
5.   U   1 + 2 * 3
```

It should be noted that we *can* use the input symbol "1" here to choose between "F —› U" and "F —› (E)" because the latter definitely starts with "(", which will not match. Similarly we *must* now choose "U —› 1" to give

6. 1 1 + 2 * 3

whereupon the leading (matching) symbols may be dropped in both columns to give

7. λ + 2 * 3

where λ represents the empty string. We now have a mismatch because the sentential form in the left hand column has run out (there is no target symbol) so we must backtrack to the last choice point which was the move from step **3** to step **4.** (In fact a parser will probably have to backtrack through *all* the stages, 'discovering' at each one that there is no further choice available.) So we undo everything we have done back to step **3** and continue with:

8. T * F 1 + 2 * 3
9. F * F 1 + 2 * 3
10. U * F 1 + 2 * 3
11. 1 * F 1 + 2 * 3

Again we have a mismatch. The initial "1 *" of the sentential form does not correspond to "1 +". So we must backtrack again. This time we go back to step **8** and continue with

12. T * F * F 1 + 2 * 3
. .
. .
. .

We note that we are again caught in the loop caused by left recursion. So we see that the simple act of ordering the rules is *not* sufficient to eliminate loops. Somehow we must *remove* the left recursion. Luckily this is always possible and we give an algorithm for it in section 4.5.

Even if we do remove the left recursion, it must be fairly clear to the reader that the above is going to be very inefficient indeed. We have only used the example to reinforce the desire for a deterministic algorithm and we need consider this 'general' method no further. A complete algorithm for any non-left recursive grammar is given in detail in Aho and Ullman [8].

We shall, in the next chapter, look at some techniques which can transform grammars (in some cases) into ones that admit deterministic parsing in the sense that the parser will, by looking only at the next input symbol, be able to decide which production to apply next in the parse.

3.8 BOTTOM UP METHODS

It is only fair that we should, before moving on to the particular method we have chosen as the subject of this book, give a brief summary of some bottom up methods of parsing which are often used in compilers. These are very popular with those who advocate **automatic parser generators** where, from a stylised form of syntax and semantics a compiler is generated. They are usually **table driven** in that, from the grammatical rules, a table is built which is used to control a central parsing loop. (Table driven methods are also available for top down methods).

Bottom up methods work in general on the **shift-reduce** principle (Floyd [10]). Since we build the syntax tree from the bottom up, we will have, at any moment, a list of subtrees representing parts of the whole syntax tree. Practical parsers nearly always scan the input from left to right, so the subtrees we have formed will be from the left hand part of the whole tree.

For instance, with grammar G and the input "1 * 2 + 3 * (4 + 5)" we might at some stage have formed the subtrees:

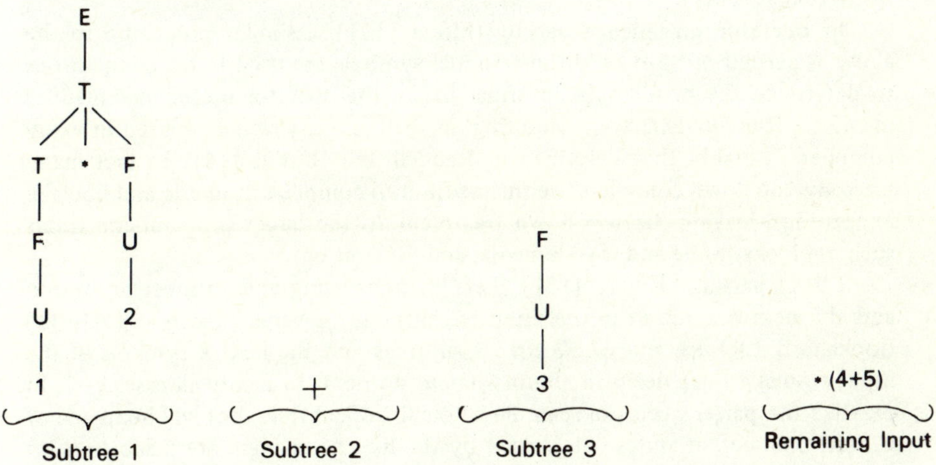

Fig. 3.6

As the parse proceeds there are at any moment two main alternatives from which the parser has to choose. Firstly it could **shift** a symbol from the remaining input over to the list of subtrees where it will form a new primitive subtree by itself at the right hand end of the list of subtrees. Secondly it could collect one or more of the trees at the right hand end of the list together and **reduce** them to a single subtree by using a production rule and making a new node with its left hand non-terminal as its label. The parser may have to choose which production to use. Such a collection of subtrees is called a **handle** since it is a collection of objects that we grasp together into one by the reduction. In general a parser will shift until the right hand end of the list of trees contains a handle and then reduce it.

In the above example a parser would probably shift the "*" and "(" and "4" and then reduce the "4" successively to "U", "F", "T" and "E" before continuing by shifting "+" and so on. We will not go into the details here.

As with top down methods, it is easy to see that a *general* shift-reduce parser will have severe backtracking problems. So the methods used in practice are again deterministic.

The differences between the various methods lie in what information is used to decide between shifting and reduction and, if the latter, which rule to apply.

In **simple precedence** parsing (Wirth and Weber [11]) only the single symbol at the left hand end of the input and the single symbol at the root of the rightmost subtree of the list are used to decide whether to shift or reduce. A **precedence table** is built to allow these to be compared. When a handle is to be reduced, its left hand end is found by a series of similar comparisons between adjacent roots of the trees at the right hand end of the list. This determines which rule to use (because no two are allowed to have identical right hand sides, which is a severe restriction at times).

In **operator precedence** parsing (Floyd [12]), a similar procedure to the above is carried out but only the terminal symbols are used in the comparisons to determine the handle. An informal use of the operator precedence method manifests itself in Dijkstra's 'shunting' algorithm [13] which is used in many compilers, notably that described in Randell and Russell [14]. In fact many basically top down compilers use this method to compile arithmetic and boolean expressions, leaving the top down treatment to the larger program constructs such as blocks, **while** and **if** statements, and declarations.

LR(k) parsing (Knuth [15]) (Left to right using a Rightmost derivation and the next k symbols in the input stream) and its variants such as LALR(k) (lookahead LR) use the *whole list* of subtrees and the next k symbols of the input to make their decision about what to do next. In nearly all cases k=1. In practice the parser need not scan the whole list of subtrees, but will be in one of a finite number of **states** determined by the list. As changes are made to it by shifting and reducing, the parser changes state so as to reflect the contents of the list; and it is this state plus the next k symbols which are used to determine the next move. The calculation of the tables which have to be looked up to do this is very complicated and in non-trivial cases is best done by a custom built compiler generator program such as YACC [16]. It is too difficult a task for manual calculation. For further details and discussion of these techniques the reader is referred to Gries [6], Aho and Ullman [8] and [17] and Bornat [18].

3.9 SUMMARY

In Chapter 3 we have seen how grammars, in particular context free grammars, can be used to define languages by generative or recognitive techniques which involve the construction of a derivation or a parse tree. We gave two conventions used in the book to describe grammars. We indicated the dangers of ambiguity and informally gave a 'general' algorithm for non-left recursive grammars which was seen however to be highly inefficient. This led us to a desire for deterministic methods. Finally we summarised some bottom up methods sometimes used in the syntax analysis phase of compilers.

REFERENCES

[1] Chomsky, N. (1959), On certain formal properties of grammars, *Information and Control,* **2**, **2**, 137–167.

[2] Koster, C. H. A. (1971), A compiler-compiler for affix grammars, Mathematisch Centrum Amsterdam report MR 127/71.

[3] Pagan, F. C. (1981), *Formal Specification of Programming Languages,* Prentice-Hall.

[4] van Wijngaarden, A. (1965), Orthogonal design and description of a formal language, Mathematisch Centrum Amsterdam Report MR 76.

[5] van Wijngaarden, A. *et al,* (1975), Revised report on the algorithmic language algol 68, *Acta Informatica,* **5**, 1–236.

[6] Gries, D. (1971), *Compiler Construction for Digital Computers,* Wiley.

[7] Naur, P. *et al,* (January 1963), Revised report on the algorithmic language algol 60, *CACM,* **6**, **1**, 1–17.

[8] Aho, A. V. and Ullman, J. H. (1972), *The Theory of Parsing, Translation and Compiling,* Prentice-Hall.

[9] Floyd, R. W. (1967), Nondeterministic algorithms, *JACM,* **14**, **4**, 636–644.

[10] Floyd, R. W. (1961), A descriptive language for symbol manipulation, *JACM,* 8, 4, 579–584.

[11] Wirth, N. and Weber, H. (January 1966), EULER – A generalization of algol and its formal definition, Part I, *CACM,* **9**, **1**, 13–23.

[12] Floyd, R. W. (1963), Syntactic analysis and operator precedence, *JACM,* **10**, **3**, 316–333.

[13] Dijkstra, E. W. (1961), Making a translator for algol 60, *A.P.I.C. Bulletin,* 3–11.

[14] Randell, B. and Russell, L. J. (1964), *Algol 60 Implementation,* Academic Press.

[15] Knuth, D. E. (1965), On the translation of languages from left to right, *Information and Control,* **8**, **6**, 607–639.

[16] Johnson, S. C. (1975), YACC – yet another compiler-compiler, Bell Laboratories, New Jersey.

[17] Aho, A. V. and Ullman, J. H. (1977), *Principles of Compiler Design,* Addison-Wesley.

[18] Bornat, R. (1979), *Understanding and Writing Compilers,* Macmillan.

CHAPTER 4

Testing and Manipulating Grammars

4.1 THE NEED FOR DETERMINISTIC METHODS

We spent some time in section 3.7 showing first that a top down method was not as general as it might have seemed and even then, when modified to deal with grammars with no left recursive productions, that it would be grossly inefficient because of the amount of backtracking involved. We concluded that a deterministic method of some kind would be desirable. We can emphasise the inefficiency of the method by pointing out that actions associated with the 'pure' parsing, the tree building part, may well be interleaved with semantic actions based on the structure of the tree itself. For instance, code may be generated (which may write material to an output file) and entries may be made in a highly structured symbol table (see Chapters 10 and 11). Not only must these actions be 'undone', but in many cases they may have to be 'done' again!; and sometimes almost immediately. For instance if we have two productions which describe a conditional construct as follows:

C —› **if** B **then** C **else** C | **if** B **do** C

and a sentence containing the phrase

if complicatedbooleanexpr **do** someclause

is parsed and if further the parser tries the '**if**. .**then**. .**else**' production to start with, it will fail when **do** and **then** cause a mismatch. It will then have to back up. Now the "complicatedbooleanexpr" may involve compiling a whole block together with local declarations, possibly including those of procedures. Not only must all the work done when parsing be unravelled but, when we try the second alternative, *exactly the same work as before* has to be carried out again. In section 4.4 we will see how 'factorisation' can be used to overcome this particular problem in appropriate cases. However it should by now be abundantly clear that a deterministic method is desperately needed. We shall now outline one.

4.2 LL(1) GRAMMARS

We have seen that the trouble which gives rise to non-determinacy and backtracking in top-down syntax analysis shows itself at one place only – that is when a parser has to choose between several alternative productions with the same left hand side. What information is available to help it make the right choice? The answer would appear to be – only the input sequence to hand at that time. We have indicated that methods which have to back up must 'unread' any input which has been scanned ahead of time. *Any* method therefore that looks ahead in this way, even a deterministic one, will only work well if we provide some sort of **buffer** internal to the compiler where input can be examined. Conceptually this buffer represents the first few terminals of the input, the rest of which is still in 'the outside world'. In practice, it is an advantage for efficiency and ease of access that this buffer be of fixed length. A top down parser which can make a deterministic decision about which alternative to choose when faced with one, if given a lookahead buffer capable of holding k terminals, is called an **LL(k) parser.** The first L stands for 'Left to right scanning', the second for 'using a Leftmost derivation' and the k says how many terminals of lookahead are allowed. In practice k is usually 1. The grammar that an LL(k) parser scans is an **LL(k) grammar** and any language that has an LL(k) grammar description is an **LL(k) language**.

The technique described here first appeared in the computing literature in papers by Foster [1] and later received a more theoretical treatment by Lewis and Stearns [2] who coined the term **LL(k)**. Knuth [3] gives a good tutorial treatment based on some lecture notes.

The intelligent reader may take exception to at least one of the statements we made above, though we were careful to qualify them! That was to the effect that the only information we had at hand which should help the parser make a choice of alternatives was the next few terminals in the input. We could also however draw on information embedded in the history of the parse done so far. If we do this we obtain strong LL(k) parsers, grammars and languages. We shall pursue this no further here except to say that when k=1, there is no difference between LL(1) and strong LL(1) parsers. The interested reader can find further reference in Backhouse [4] and Rosencrantz and Stearns [5].

In which cases then can we say that a grammar is LL(1)? When a given target symbol, A, is due for expansion and several alternatives are available:

$$A \rightarrow \alpha_1 \mid \alpha_2 \mid \ldots\ldots \mid \alpha_n$$

we must be able to choose one of the α_i uniquely merely by looking at the next input symbol. The set of α_1 must therefore partition the terminal symbols into (*disjoint*) sets and by selecting the set in which the lookahead input symbol lies we select the corresponding α_i to substitute for A. These sets are called (after Griffiths [6]) the **director sets** for the production, written $D(A \rightarrow \alpha_i)$. In fact there will be an extra set in the partition such that, if any of its members turns up on the input, the parser will immediately know that an error has occurred.

As a first approximation to calculating the director sets, it is obvious that if $\alpha_i \overset{*}{=}\rangle\, t\gamma$, where t is some terminal, then t ϵ D(A —⟩ α_i) because then A $\overset{+}{=}\rangle\, t\gamma$ is a valid derivation which could occur. Let us define a relationship "⟨⟨" between symbols of (N ∪ T) such that β ⟨⟨ α holds if there is a production α —⟩ β. . . . (i.e. β is the first symbol on the right hand side). For obvious reasons we can call this relation 'can immediately start'. If we form its reflexive transitive closure we get "⟨⟨*", the 'can start' relation. Forming "⟨⟨*" for the symbols of a particular grammar is going to be of considerable help to us in calculating the director sets. For a particular symbol α, those symbols β in the relationship β ⟨⟨* α form what is known as the **start set** of α, START(α). Obviously if α is a terminal, then START(α) = {α}; but in other cases the set START(α) will be larger.

If we consider one of the alternative productions, in particular A —⟩ α_i, and suppose:

$$\alpha_i = \beta_1 \beta_2 \ldots\ldots \beta_r$$

then it is clear that any terminal belonging to START(β_1) also belongs to D(A—⟩α_i).

As an example, let us calculate the start sets of grammar G. The digraph of the "⟨⟨" relation is:

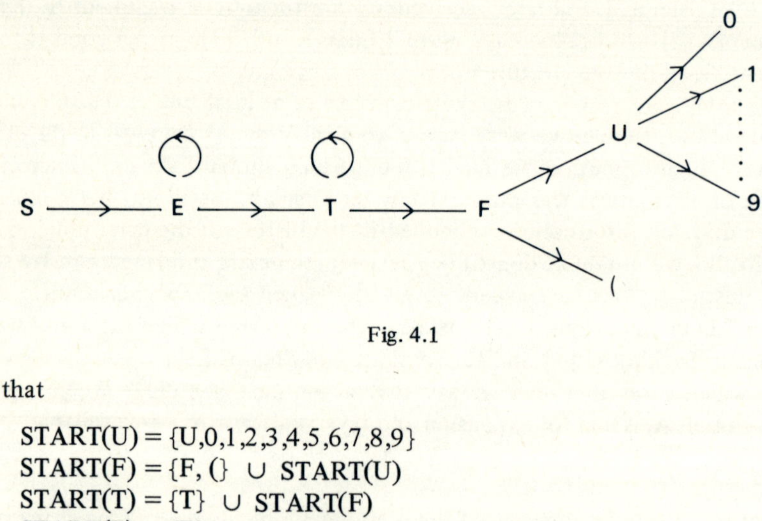

Fig. 4.1

so that

START(U) = {U,0,1,2,3,4,5,6,7,8,9}
START(F) = {F, (} ∪ START(U)
START(T) = {T} ∪ START(F)
START(E) = {E} ∪ START(T)
START(S) = {S} ∪ START(E)

As mentioned above, the director set of a production contains, at least, the terminals in the start set of the first symbol on its right hand side. It is therefore easy to see that G is not an LL(1) grammar because for instance D(E —⟩ T) and D(E —⟩ E + T) are certainly not disjoint. The terminals in the start sets for T and E are the same.

In fact, we can go further and say that *no* grammar with left recursive rules is LL(1) because D(A —⟩ Aγ) contains *all* the terminals in START(A) which will include some from the director sets of other alternatives and consequently these will not be disjoint. (Note that in a 'sensible' grammar there *will be* alternatives to this rule because otherwise it recurses infinitely.)

4.3 FIRST AND FOLLOW RELATIONS

But are the terminals in the start sets of β_1 the only members of D(A —⟩ α_i)? Suppose t is the next terminal in the input. Consider the following trees (Figs. 4.2–4.4) which show the different ways in which a parse could proceed if A —⟩ α_i were the correct production to use:

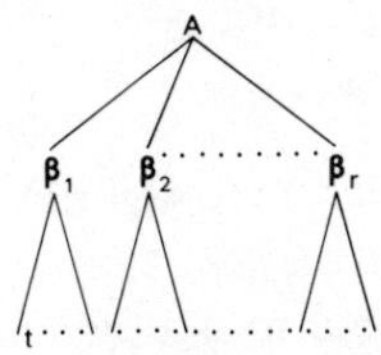

Fig. 4.2

This is the case we have already dealt with where t ϵ START(β_1). But any of the following could also be the case:

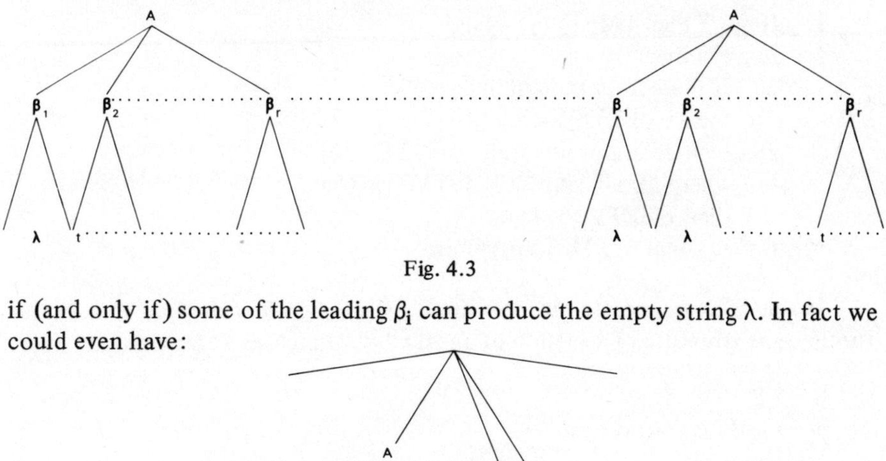

Fig. 4.3

if (and only if) some of the leading β_i can produce the empty string λ. In fact we could even have:

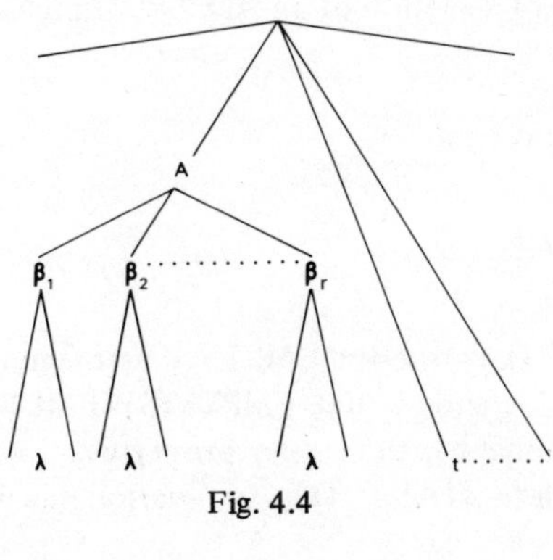

Fig. 4.4

Leave this last category for the moment. In the other cases we will have to augment D(A —⟩ α_i) by the terminals in START(β_2), START(β_3). . . . . until we come to a β_j which cannot produce the empty string.

To formalise the solution to this problem we have to extend the function START, which can only have as arguments members of (N ∪ T), to a function FIRST which can take a whole string $\beta_1\beta_2\beta_3 . . . . \beta_r$ of (N ∪ T)* and find out which terminals can start it. Then a better approximation to D(A —⟩ α_i) is FIRST(α_i). We can calculate this with the (recursive) definition:

FIRST(λ) $= \phi$
FIRST($\gamma\delta$) = terminals of START(γ) ∪ FIRST(δ)
if $\gamma \overset{*}{=}\rangle \lambda$
FIRST($\gamma\delta$) = terminals of START(γ)
otherwise

where $\gamma \in$ (N ∪ T) and $\delta \in$ (N ∪ T)*. Algorithm for calculating FIRST can be based on this definition.

Note that we need to be able to determine when a derivation $\gamma \overset{*}{=}\rangle \lambda$ exists. In such a case we say that γ has the **EMPTY** property and write EMPTY(γ) = true. This can be worked out from the definition of "=⟩"; and an algorithm based on the following description then applies:

1. If $\gamma \in$ T then EMPTY(γ) =false
2. If $\gamma \in$ N then
   2a. If there is a production "γ —⟩ λ"
   then EMPTY(γ)=true
   2b. If there is a production "γ —⟩ $\delta_1 . . . \delta_k$"
   where for all $1 \leqslant i \leqslant k$ EMPTY(δ_i)=true
   then EMPTY(γ)=true
3. For all other γ, EMPTY(γ)=false

Let us take a concrete example at this stage. Consider the following syntax for the type structure of a section of an Algol-like language – grammar H:

S —⟩ T
T —⟩ L B | L C array
L —⟩ long | λ
C —⟩ B | λ
B —⟩ real | integer

We can see that EMPTY(L)=true and EMPTY(C)=true immediately but the further application of the rules shows that EMPTY(S)=EMPTY(T)=EMPTY(C)=false (and of course no terminal has the empty property).

We can also calculate START. The "⟨⟨" relation has the graph:

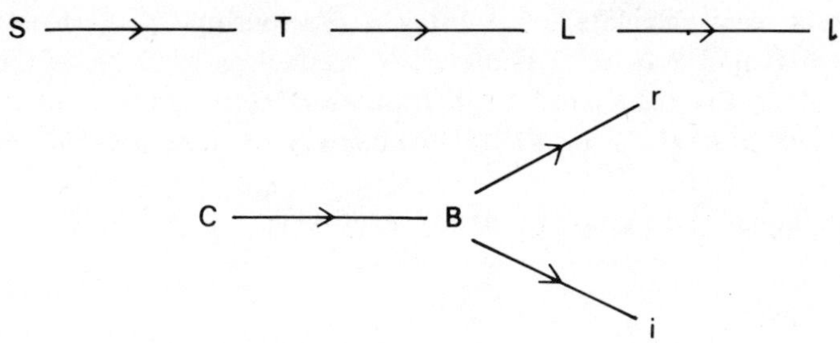

Fig. 4.5

so the start sets (*restricted to terminals*) are:

START(S) = START(T) = START(L) = {1}
START(C) = START(B) = {r,i}

We can now find FIRST for each of the right hand sides:

FIRST(T) = START(T) = {1}
FIRST(L B) = START(L) ∪ FIRST(B)
(since EMPTY(L)=true)
= {1} ∪ START(B)
= {1,r,i}
FIRST(L C array) = START(L) ∪ START(C) ∪ {a}
(since EMPTY(L) = EMPTY(C) = true)
= {1,r,i,a}
FIRST(long) = {1}
FIRST(λ) = ϕ
FIRST(B) = START(B) = {r,i}
FIRST(real) = {r}
FIRST(integer) = {i}

We can see that this grammar is not LL(1) because D(T —〉 L B) and D(T —〉 L C array) have FIRST(L B) and FIRST(L C array) as subsets respectively.

Let us now complete the calculation of the director sets by seeing what we must do for the case exhibited in Fig. 4.4 where a right hand side of an alternative $\overset{*}{=}\rangle$ λ. An example of this category occurs in grammar H if either L or C is the target nonterminal. In both sets of productions one of the right hand sides $\overset{*}{=}\rangle$ λ (in fact = λ in this case).

By looking at Fig. 4.4 we see that, when $\alpha_i \overset{*}{=}\rangle \lambda$, A —〉 α_i will be the correct choice if and only if the terminal t can *follow* A. So in cases where $\alpha_i \overset{*}{=}\rangle \lambda$, we must calculate a new function FOLLOW(A) which will augment D(A —〉 α_i) for such cases.

We can calculate FOLLOW in the following way. Firstly calculate a FINISH set for each member of (N ∪ T) in an exactly analogous fashion to the way

START sets were calculated, but using a relationship "⟩⟩" (can immediately finish) such that β ⟩⟩ α holds if there is a production α —⟩ . . . . β (i.e. β is the last symbol on the right hand side), forming ⟩⟩* (can finish) and then, for a given symbol, α, of (N ∪ T), FINISH(α) consists of those β in the relationship β ⟩⟩* α.

For grammar H the graph of the "⟩⟩" relation is:

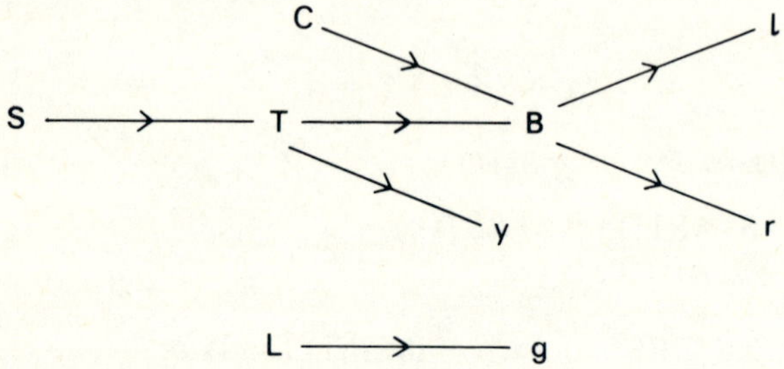

Fig. 4.6

so that:

FINISH(B) = { B,l,r }
FINISH(C) = { C,B,l,r }
FINISH(T) = { T,B,l,r,y }
FINISH(S) = { S,T,B,l,r,y }
FINISH(L) = {L,g}

FINISH for a terminal is merely the set whose only member is that terminal. (In fact we shall not need *all* these sets; we only need FINISH for non-terminals A such that EMPTY(A) = true.) Having calculated the FINISH sets we can finally calculate FOLLOW by the following means. Consider every position on the right hand side of a production where two symbols of (N ∪ T), α and β, come side by side. Then for each symbol $\gamma \in$ FINISH(α), all the members of FIRST(β) belong to FOLLOW(γ).

For grammar H, the production "T —⟩ L B" gives rise to FOLLOW(L) (and FOLLOW(g)) both containing START(B) = {r,i} as subsets. "T —⟩ L C array" gives rise to FOLLOW(L) containing START(C array) = {r,i,a} and to FOLLOW(C) (and FOLLOW(B)) containing START(array) = {a}. Various other members of FOLLOW sets can be calculated but we are not particularly interested in these. We only want to know about FOLLOW(L) and FOLLOW(C) which are thus {r,i,a} and {a} respectively, because these are now the director sets D(L —⟩ λ) and D(C —⟩ λ). In fact we have all the director sets for H now. They can be summarised as follows:

D(S —› T) = {1}
D(T —› L B) = {1,r,i}
D(T —› L C array) = {1,r,i,a}
D(L —› long) = {1}
D(L —› λ) = {r,i,a}
D(C —› B) = {r,i}
D(C —› λ) = {a}
D(B —› real) = {r}
D(B —› integer) = {i}

There remains one point to clear up. What happens if an LL(1) parser is looking for the next symbol to check against a director set and *there isn't one* because we have come to the end of the input. This will, in most cases, indicate an error condition, but it is just possible that the parse is finishing off with an empty subtree of the parse tree:

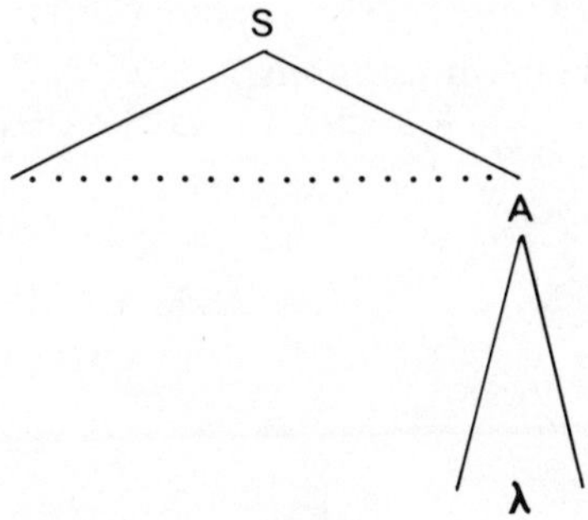

Fig. 4.7

In this case we will be looking for D(A —› . . . . . .) and trying to see if the current input symbol lies in it. We can get over this problem by adding a special **end of file** symbol "⊣" which we treat as an extra terminal to our grammar. The reader may have wondered why our grammars have always had an isolated production (for instance S —› T in H) for the distinguished symbol. The reason now becomes clear. If we add "⊣" at the end of this rule (to give S —› T⊣ in H) we can treat it as an extra terminal which is considered to be present when an end of file condition obtains. Readers should note the "?" which comes at the end of S-algol programs. This is serving the purpose of an end of file marker. As an example of where this really matters see grammar H‴ in the next section.

4.4 FACTORISATION AND SUBSTITUTION

The grammars we have exhibited as test cases so far have *not* been LL(1). This chapter has, so far, been devoted to testing for the LL(1) condition. Can we do anything about it if a grammar is *not* LL(1)? Can we transform it into an **equivalent** grammar (one that recognises the same language) which *is* LL(1)?

Unfortunately the answer to this question is 'not in every case'. For instance no ambiguous grammar is LL(1), because it admits at least two left parses of some strings and the LL(1) conditions would direct a parser deterministically to exactly one. The process of 'disambiguating' a grammar is in general unsolvable (see Aho and Ullman [7]) and informally we can see that in such cases the process of making a grammar LL(1) will similarly be unsolvable. However, we must not lose hope. In certain cases there are special techniques which may work. One of these is **factorisation.** Take the example we gave at the start of section 4.1:

C —⟩ **if** B **then** C **else** C | **if** B **do** C

We see that both productions start with the same subphrase ″**if** B″. Indeed it is exactly this that causes a grammar containing these productions not to be LL(1). But we can factor the subphrase out to give:

C —⟩ **if** B T
T —⟩ **then** C **else** C | **do** C

and this has no conflicts in the director sets.

Can we do anything to grammar H? The obvious transformation changes it into H′ as follows:

S —⟩ T
T —⟩ L X
X —⟩ B | C array
L —⟩ long | λ
C —⟩ B | λ
B —⟩ real | integer

This, unfortunately, is still not LL(1) because the director sets for ″X —⟩ B″ and ″X —⟩ C array″ both contain {r,i} as a subset. This is because ″C —⟩ B″. We can use another technique here prior to further factorisation and that is **substitution.** If we substitute the possible right hand sides for C wherever it appears we get H″:

S —⟩ T
T —⟩ L X
X —⟩ B | B array | array
L —⟩ long | λ
B —⟩ real | integer

and we can now carry out factorisation of B in X to give H‴:

S —⟩ T
T —⟩ L X
X —⟩ B Y | array
Y —⟩ λ | array
L —⟩ long | λ
B —⟩ real | integer

This grammar is indeed LL(1) as the reader should verify by calculating the director sets. (S —〉 T will here need to be modified to S —〉 T ⊣ and we will find that D(Y —〉 λ) = {⊣}.)

4.5 LEFT RECURSION AND ITS ELIMINATION

We pointed out in section 4.2 that no grammar with sensible left recursive productions could be LL(1). We shall give here a method of transforming left recursive grammars into ones without left recursion.

First we need to be able to *detect* left recursion when it arises. When the recursion is direct it is obvious, but sometimes (though very seldom in practice – in fact the authors have never seen a 'real life' case) the recursion can be indirect or mutual. We may get for instance:

A —〉 B | C
B —〉 A | D

Such mutual recursion can be detected by calculating the "$\langle\langle^+$" transitive closure (which will probably be done anyway while calculating "$\langle\langle^*$" en route to the START sets). If a non-terminal A exists such that A $\langle\langle^+$ A then it is involved in a left recursive loop, direct or otherwise.

Let us look at the direct left recursive case first as this is the one that nearly always occurs. In its most general form we will have rules of the form:

A —〉 $A\alpha_1$ | $A\alpha_2$ | . . . . . $A\alpha_i$ | β_1 | β_2 | . . . . . β_k

where none of the β's start with A. By 'collecting like terms' and factorising we can rewrite this as:

A —〉 A X | Y
X —〉 α_1 | α_2 | . . . . . α_i
Y —〉 β_1 | β_2 | . . . . . β_k

so that A —〉 A X | Y is the general recursive case to be solved. By 'expansion' we see informally that this is equivalent to:

A —〉 Y | Y X | Y X X | Y X X X | . . . .

which can be rewritten as

A —〉 Y Z
Z —〉 λ | X Z (9)

neither of which is left recursive. This, then, is a general solution to direct left recursion.

For indirect left recursion we shall pick an (artificial) example and show how to solve it. From this the reader should be able to manufacture a general method.

Example 4.1

A —〉A x | B y | z
B —〉A p | B q | r (10)

Choose one of the left recursive non-terminals, say A. 'Solve' the equation involving A to remove the direct left recursion using the method given above in (9). This gives first:

A —〉A x | Y
Y —〉B y | z

and then

A —〉Y Z
Z —〉λ | x Z

which can be re-expanded to:

A —〉B y Z | z Z
Z —〉λ | x Z

which has now removed the direct left recursion in A. We now substitute for A in the second equation of (10) to give:

B —〉B y Z p | z Z p | B q | r
Z —〉λ | x Z

Gather like terms to give:

B —〉B X | Y
X —〉y Z p | q
Y —〉z Z p | r
Z —〉λ | x Z

The first equation is the only (now direct) left recursive rule remaining and this can be solved as in (9). We will not go into the details.

If this seems to be messy, it is; but we doubt if the reader will ever come across it in practice. Readers who are skilled in linear algebra will recognise an analogy with Gaussian elimination [8] in the solution of linear equations in several unknowns. Foster [1] bases his original method on this and gives an elegant *general* solution which *automatically* converts the input grammar to an equivalent LL(1) form if it can.

As a more realistic example take the grammar G which we used extensively in the last chapter and remove its (direct) left recursion.

E —〉E + T | T

becomes

E —〉T E′
E′ —〉λ | + T E′

and

T —〉T * F | F

transforms to

T —〉FT′
T′ —〉λ | * F T′

to give a complete grammar:

S —〉E
E —〉T E′
E′ —〉λ | + T E′
T —〉F T′
T′ —〉λ | * F T′
F —〉(E) | U
U —〉0 | 1 | 2 | 3 | 4 | 5 | 6 | 7 | 8 | 9

which is LL(1). The reader should verify this by calculating the director sets as an exercise.

4.6 CHEATING

The reader may object to the transformations we have given to eliminate left recursion for the reason we gave in section 3.6 – that the original grammar G imposed left associativity on the operators "+" and "*". If we examine the syntax tree of "1 + 2 + 3" using the transformed grammar we have:

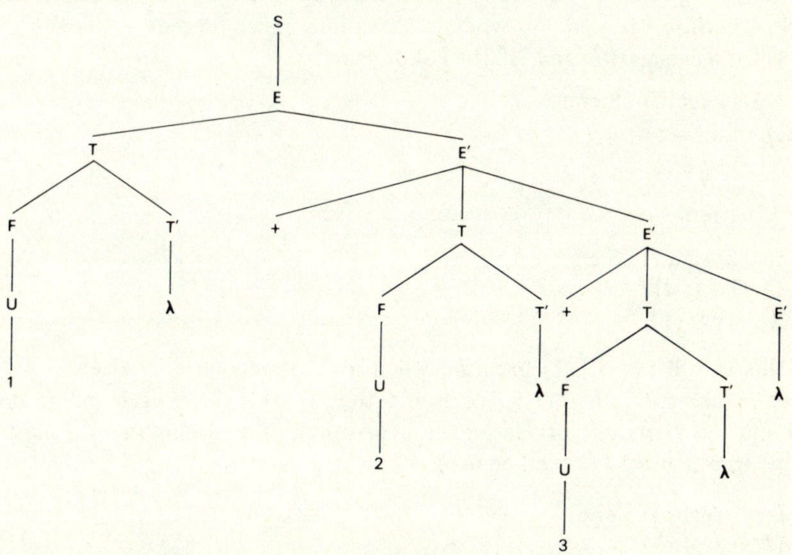

Fig. 4.8

which looks as if it imposes *right* associativity on "+". Some might even say that "+" is not directly associating its arguments at all on the tree.

One way round this problem is to leave it to the semantic part of the compiler (which 'knows' which operators associate which way) to sort out. This is the approach taken by Foster [1] in his Syntax Improving Device (SID). Here functions representing semantic actions can be interspersed with the normal objects on the right hand side of productions. Foster shows that, when a grammar is transformed (in particular to remove left recursion), the semantic rules can be 'carried around' following the syntactic entities they are attached to so that correct semantics results, even from a distorted tree.

Another way of looking at this problem is to rewrite equations (9), which give the general solution to a direct left recursive problem, using a notation borrowed from our second convention (extended BNF) for writing grammars, as:

A —⟩ Y [X] *

Thus for grammar G we get:

E —⟩ T [+ T] *

and a similar rule for multiplication. This gives an **iterative** flavour to the rules rather than the 'normal' recursive one, and this is reflected by the fact that a parser could make use of a **while** loop to parse this sort of construct rather than recursion. We shall see this in action in some detail in sections 6.5 and 12.3.

We shall also see what to do if all else fails and we cannot make our grammar LL(1) by any of the above techniques. Sometimes *ad hoc* methods may be used. The following example, similar to one given by Griffiths [6], is based on the block structure of Algol 60 where declarations must precede statements. "d" stands for a declaration and "s" for a statement:

B —⟩ begin D ; S end
D —⟩ d | D ; d
S —⟩ s | S ; s

After removing the left recursion one gets:

B —⟩ begin D ; S end
D —⟩ d [; d] *
S —⟩ s [; s] *

but this is still not LL(1) because, when a ";" is encountered after a "d", the parser is not sure whether to go round the "[; d] *" loop again or go on to "; S end". No amount of factorisation or substitution seems to work, but the following which is LL(1) can be used:

B —⟩ begin D S end
D —⟩ d ; [d ;] *
S —⟩ s [; s] *

Note that the ";" has migrated to the other end of the "d" and will not be involved in the director sets for productions for D.

If a shot in the dark such as the above doesn't work, all hope is not yet lost because we can resort to dirty tactics. An example of this and its solution are given in sections 6.5 and 10.6 where a conflict arises because in S-algol a sequence of declarations and clauses can end in an expression or in a void clause, one variety of which is an assignment. There is no LL(1) way of distinguishing the left hand side of an assignment, which must be a name (a rather restricted sort of expression) from the more general type of expression with which we are allowed to end a sequence. The solution is to leave the context-sensitive part of the parser to patch this up.

4.7 SUMMARY

In this chapter we have reiterated our need for a deterministic method of parsing a program from the top down. We have investigated a method for checking whether a given grammar admits of such a parser where the lookahead is 1 terminal symbol. Such a parser is called LL(1). This involves calculating director sets of terminals for each alternative production, which in turn requires calculating which terminals can come first in a string of $(N \cup T)^*$ and which can follow certain non-terminals.

We have also given a number of rules for transforming grammars which may help to make them LL(1) parsable. These include removal of left recursion, factorisation and substitution. We have pointed out that such rules are not foolproof and that other *ad hoc* methods, based on common sense, may need to be applied. Finally we have shown that, in a real life situation, we *may* have to cheat to achieve results.

REFERENCES

[1] Foster, J. M. (1968), A syntax improving device, *Computer Journal,* **11**, **1**, 31-34.

[2] Lewis, P. M. II and Stearns, R. E. (1968), Syntax directed transduction, *JACM,* **15**, **3**, 465-488.

[3] Knuth, D. E. (1971), Top down syntax analysis, *Acta Informatica,* **1**, 79-110.

[4] Backhouse, R. (1979), *Syntax of Programming Languages,* Prentice-Hall.

[5] Rosencrantz, D. J. and Stearns, R. E. (1969), Properties of deterministic top down grammars, *ACM Symposium on the Theory of Computing,* Marina del Rey, California.

[6] Griffiths, M. (1976), LL(1) grammars and analysers, *Compiler Construction – an Advanced Course,* (Lecture Notes in Computer Science 21, Eds. Goos, G. and Hartmanis, J.), Springer Verlag.

[7] Aho, A. V. and Ullman, J. H. (1972), *The Theory of Parsing, Translation and Compiling,* Prentice–Hall.

[8] Finkbeiner, D. T. II. (1978), *Introduction to Matrices and Linear Transformations, 3rd edition,* Freeman.

CHAPTER 5

Compiler Construction

5.1 THE ROLE OF S-ALGOL

In these next chapters we will outline a method of constructing recursive descent compilers. This is intended as a practical guide to compiler construction using the theoretical results developed in Chapters 1 to 4. It is our aim that the reader will be able to build his own compiler after assimilating the information.

We will not describe every technique or method which claims to be recursive descent. Rather we will concentrate on one particular method in order to give a detailed account of how to write such a compiler. Whenever it is instructive, we will highlight the consequences of different design decisions and sometimes explore alternative methods of progress. However, for the main part, we will stick to a detailed description of one technique and how it can be implemented. Of course any particular part of the general method may be varied to suit a particular language or implementation.

The compiler we will use to illustrate the technique is for the programming language S-algol. S-algol is typical of most modern day languages and has typical problems in compilation, such as static type checking, block structure, recursive procedures and an infinite number of data types. Furthermore, it has most of the common control structures like **for**, **case**, **if** . . . **then** . . . . **else** . . . , **while** etc., and has simple and aggregate data objects including dynamic arrays and pointer structures. Finally S-algol requires both a stack and a heap for implementation at run time. The language is therefore well suited to illustrate the problems encountered in building a recursive descent compiler.

Since S-algol is a powerful high level block structured language it is also suitable for writing compilers. Indeed the S-algol compiler is written in S-algol and we will use the language here. The problem of how to get started with a compiler written in the language it is compiling will be described in Chapter 13.

5.2 THE ONE PASS NATURE OF RECURSIVE DESCENT COMPILERS

The structure of compilers such as Algol W [1] and Whetstone Algol 60 [2] typify the method of compiler construction used before recursive descent became popular as a compiling technique. Such a compiler was constructed in three phases.

1. lexical analysis
2. syntax analysis
3. code generation

The lexical analysis phase converts the characters of the source text into the basic symbols of the language. The syntax analysis takes these basic symbols, parses them and produces an equivalent form of the program called the syntax tree. Finally the code generation takes the syntax tree and converts it into machine code for the target computer. This is shown diagrammatically in Fig. 5.1.

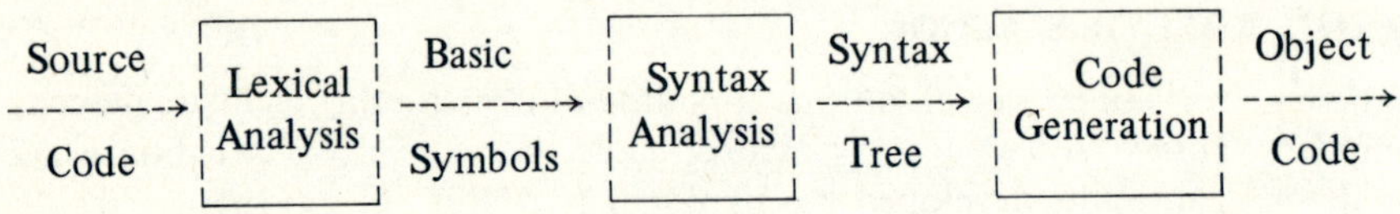

Fig. 5.1

The three phases can be organised in one or more passes and in the days of computers with small main stores it was more common to have the phases organised as separate passes. To arrange the phases otherwise pre-supposes an operating system which will support co-operating sequential processes of some sort, and even then there has to be enough store available for the whole compiler, to avoid unnecessary swapping of the phases. Either method of organisation very sensibly separates the machine dependent stages of code generation and lexical analysis from the machine independent stage of syntax analysis.

The description of compiler organisation given above is necessarily simplified as it can be shown that some grammars, such as those of Algol 60 and Algol 68, require more than one pass to parse them and that the code generation phase can easily be a multi-pass operation.

The major disadvantage of a compiler organised in passes is that the information transmitted from one pass to the next is encoded by some means and often written out to backing store to save space. This is slow and requires extra programming at each stage of the compiler to encode and decode the information. However it does mean that less store is required to run the compiler since only one pass need be resident in store at any one time.

With some methods of compiling, including recursive descent, the sentences of the language can be parsed in one pass. That means there is no need to keep a syntax tree for use by further passes of the parser or the code generator. The syntax tree for any construct may be thrown away immediately the parsing of that construct is complete. Indeed often there is not even a need for an explicit syntax tree.

In a recursive descent compiler every syntactic construct (i.e. non-terminal in the language to be compiled) has a procedure defined in the compiler that will parse and generate code for that construct. This forms a set of mutually recursive procedures to parse the language. The recursive nature of the grammar is modelled dynamically by the recursive evaluation of the compiler program itself. For example the **while** clause in S–algol is described in BNF by

while ⟨clause⟩ **do** ⟨clause⟩

The procedure which compiles the **while** clause will be called from the procedure which compiles clauses and will then call upon that procedure recursively to compile the sub-clauses in the **while** clause. It will also use the lexical analyser to recognise the symbols **while** and **do**. Since the compiler begins at the start symbol and descends the productions of the grammar, the compiling technique is called recursive descent.

Every procedure which parses a non-terminal in the language has the section of the syntax tree for that non-terminal defined implicitly by the variables it uses and the procedures it calls. Thus in the recursive evaluation of the compiler program, the section of the syntax tree of interest at any time is contained in the data area of the active procedures. On entering such a procedure a new section of the syntax tree is created implicitly in the data area for that procedure activation. On leaving the procedure the data area and therefore that section of the syntax tree disappears. Of course, this technique is ideally suited to a compiler written in a high level block structured language.

To eliminate completely the need for an explicit syntax tree, the code generation for each section of the tree is placed in the procedure to parse the construct, instead of being collected together in a separate pass. It is a short step to do the same for lexical analysis and make the whole process one pass. Of course the process can still be implemented as a set of co-operating sequential processes, but it seems unnecessary to involve the overhead of process switching when it is not imperative.

The one pass nature of the grammar and the fact that we have eliminated the intermediate encodings between the passes should make the compiler faster. Since the entire compiler has to be resident in store at the same time, it may require more store to execute, but this is not generally a serious problem on modern day computers. Indeed, even most micro-computers today have enough store to support many high level languages. The real significance of recursive descent compilers of this sort is that they are small in terms of total code, written in a high level language, and the code to compile each non-terminal is collected in one place. This results in better written, more portable and more easily understood compilers.

5.3 STEPWISE REFINEMENT

The technique of problem solving we shall employ in describing compilers is sometimes called stepwise refinement [3] since the problem is solved by a series of steps. At each step, all the sections of the program are considered for refinement and re-written if necessary. The process starts with an abstract description of the problem and the refinement is performed in steps until a final program which requires no further refinement is obtained. In this manner very large and complex problems may be mastered by considering a series of well defined sub-tasks.

A note on terminology is required here. Since the refinement of the abstract problem involves adding abstractions which are later refined and since these abstractions are implemented in a program by procedures, we will use the terms procedure and abstraction interchangeably.

The first step in the refinement process is to define the problem. In our case we wish to write a program (compiler) that will take another program (the source program) as input, check that it is legal and if it is, write out an equivalent form of the program (the object program). This can be summarised by the three steps

1. read in the source
2. check the syntax
3. generate the code

We can readily see how early compilers obtained their structure in terms of passes. However there is little need for the refinement process to develop in this manner. It is indeed the order in which information will flow through a compiler, but this is not necessarily the only method of constructing the compiler program. We will start with the syntax analysis and refine that. Whenever a section of the lexical analysis or code generation is required we may refine that as necessary.

We have already started some way along the design process since we have assumed that at least the programming language is well defined and suitable for compilation by recursive descent. If it is not, some of the techniques presented in the earlier chapters of this book may be applicable to make it so. The target computer may also be known but it may not, as we would probably wish the compiler to be adaptable to producing code for various machines. Within bounds, the details of the target machine may be left until a later level of refinement. However some of the details of the underlying machine will already have been decided with the language design. For example, most languages are designed to execute on Von Neumann type machines. The most obvious consequence of this is the store concept giving rise to the ideas of assignment, pointers and sequencing in high level languages. In languages without these concepts the underlying machine may be very different indeed. For details of one such alternative the reader is referred to Turner [4].

The main aim of the technique of stepwise refinement is to help us to develop the complete program without, at any time, being overawed by the complexity of the task at hand.

5.4 THE STRUCTURE OF A RECURSIVE DESCENT COMPILER

The structuring technique which we will use to build a recursive descent compiler was first outlined by Ammann [5] where he developed a compiler for the language Pascal. He was not the first to build a recursive descent compiler and earlier examples are the compilers for Algol 68 [6] and the Burroughs Algol 60 compiler [7]. In the cases of Algol 68 and Algol 60, the languages have to be altered to allow compilation in one pass whereas Pascal was specifically designed for one-pass compilation. The structure of each compiler varies slightly according to the naunces of the language being compiled, and the following is the structure used to build the S-algol compiler. Since S-algol is not quite LL(1), or indeed LL(k) for any fixed k, we will also use it to demonstrate how to overcome the problem of parsing a grammar that is not strictly LL(1).

The compiler is designed as a series of layers rather than passes or phases. Once the first layer is established, usually by writing the syntax analysis from a formal description of the language, the other layers are added rather like extra coats of paint. The stepwise refinement therefore consists of a series of steps each adding one layer. This is the view of the refinement process at the gross level. Within each layer we will use stepwise refinement again and again to simplify the tasks of the layers. Eventually we will end up with code for that layer. Of course, that code may be spread far and wide in the compiler itself.

The layers in the S-algol compiler consist of performing the following:

1. write a pure syntax analyser
2. write a lexical analyser
3. add the context free error diagnosis and recovery
4. add the type checking and type handler
5. add the environment handler and scope checker
6. add the context sensitive error reporting
7. add the data and code address calculation
8. write the code generation

Whilst the layering describes the structure of the compiler, it does not tell the whole story about building such a compiler. For that we must inspect each layer and design the interfaces between them. Indeed it will become obvious that some of the layers will not fit neatly on the framework of the syntax analysis procedures. Such layers will constitute separate sections of the compiler and will be used only in the abstract in the parsing procedures. Furthermore, we have to decide how information collected about the source program is to be recorded and accessed. Let us spend a little more time refining the layers described above and outline some of the design decisions which must be taken at each stage.

5.5 THE LAYERS OF THE COMPILER

5.5.1 Syntax Analysis

The syntax analysis forms the first layer of a recursive descent compiler. As has been suggested in Chapter 4, the syntax analyser may be written down from the formal definition of the syntax. Normally this description is written in extended BNF and each non-terminal in the grammar has a procedure defined in the compiler to parse it. Even at this early stage the syntax analysis is not isolated as a layer. The syntax analyser must also take notice of terminal symbols in the language and therefore we have to consider the interface between the syntax analysis and the lexical analysis. Lexical analysis is, by and large, a separate phase of the compiler and at this stage we need only define the abstractions which the syntax analyser will use when calling the lexical analyser to perform some function for it; for example, 'find the next basic symbol in the input stream'. Further refinement of the lexical analyser can take place later. The details of the syntax analysis layer are to be found in Chapter 6.

5.5.2 Lexical Analysis

The lexical analyser reads in the characters of the source program and forms them into the basic symbols of the language. This section of the compiler must necessarily know about the concrete syntax of the language, the concrete syntax being the actual characters that make up the basic symbols. For example, the lexical analyser must know how to form literals such as 1, 23.5 or "hello", special symbols such as "!", form composite symbols like "⟨=", and recognise identifiers and reserved words when necessary. These basic symbols must be represented inside the compiler by some means and left in a convenient place for use by the rest of the compiler.

Since the lexical analysis abstractions are usually implemented as procedures for use by the rest of the compiler, the abstract details of the lexical kind are now settled. Examples of this are a procedure to provide the next symbol in the input stream and the variable to store that symbol. Chapter 7 deals with the problems of lexical analysis.

5.5.3 Context Free Error Diagnosis and Recovery

It is possible for a parser, when parsing an LL(1) grammar, to discover an error immediately it occurs. This can be achieved very cheaply in terms of coding. However recovery from that error, in order that the compiler may continue, is arbitrarily complex depending on the grammar of the language.

A general strategy has to be devised to deal with error recovery. With most languages in use today it is impossible to devise a foolproof algorithm for error recovery. Therefore we have to decide how important error recovery is and how much code to invest in order to perform the required function. We should also consider the form of error reporting at this stage. Chapter 8 contains further details of error diagnosis and recovery.

5.5.4 Type Checking

This section refers not only to the checking of types of expressions but more generally to all the composition rules in the language. By associating a type with every unique syntatic form, the composition rules for blocks, statements, declarations, expressions etc., may be dealt with uniformly.

The data structures to represent the various types must be chosen and defined along with the procedures to check the compatibility of two types. Two types are compatible only if the rules of the language allow them to be used together. For example, most languages will allow integers to be added to integers and some will allow reals and integers to be added together. In this context real numbers and integers are type compatible. If the language has an infinite number of types, these procedures and data structures will be defined recursively.

It is essential to have a formal definition of the type and composition rules at this stage. This type checking layer is discussed in Chapter 9.

5.5.5 Environment and Scope Checking

The environment and scope checker handles all the details concerned with using identifiers. A data structure must be designed to record all the necessary information for an identifier. For a language with block or procedure structure, the data structure will be placed in a larger structure which models one level of scope. Finally an even larger structure is used to model all the levels of scope in use. This data structure is usually called the **symbol table.**

When designing each level of this large structure consideration must be given to how compact the data structure is and how quickly it may be accessed. For this reason hashing techniques or binary trees are often used. The abstractions that are used by the rest of the compiler centre around accessing and creating these data structures. Chapter 10 describes the symbol table details.

5.5.6 Context Sensitive Error Reporting

This layer modifies the last two layers to deal with context sensitive errors. A context free error is where a wrong symbol is used in a program. For example:

while a < b **if** a := b

The symbol **if** is used where we would expect a **do.** A context sensitive error is more subtle in that the program will parse correctly but will be meaningless. For example the expression

1 + **true**

These context sensitive errors may be type errors, duplicate names etc. It is usually sensible to make the method of error reporting similar to the one designed earlier for syntax errors.

5.5.7 Abstract Machine Definition

At this point in a refinement process an abstract machine must be defined in detail if this has not already been done. The abstract machine for any programming language is the machine which the implementor would design to implement the language, given freedom of choice. It may be realised by a real machine, by an interpreter, by micro code or a mixture of these. As mentioned above, the general nature of the abstract machine has already been kept in mind in the design of the language even if only implicitly. For example, a language with assignment requires a store in the abstract machine and some languages require stacks and heaps for their implementation.

The first level of refinement of the abstract machine is to decide on a storage layout. Every name in a program will require a storage location and therefore we must consider such questions as whether the item is a stack or a heap item and how the address is to be calculated at run time. The addresses, if known, are stored in the symbol table along with all the other information about identifiers. These addresses will be used later by the code generation. This layer therefore provides the link between the use of names in a program and the generation of code to find their values at run time. Further consideration is given to abstract machine design in Chapter 11.

5.5.8 Code Generation

This is the final layer in the compiler. At this stage a target machine must be fully defined. In order to generate code for a given machine the compiler must simulate the evaluation of the program in execution. For example, to calculate stack addresses it may be necessary to simulate the action of the stack and keep track of the stack pointers. How good the code is at the end of the day depends on how sophisticated this simulation is.

The code generator also has to decide the form of the compiler output. It may be a file to be input to an assembler or a loader, or it could be directly executable by a computer or an interpreter without further ado. If the latter method is chosen we have a 'load and go system'.

The code generation section is necessarily implementation dependent and to achieve portability it is usually wise to separate the code generation from the rest of the compiler. This may be done by ensuring that every abstract machine instruction has a procedure defined to simulate its execution and to output the necessary code. When the syntax analysis procedures wish to generate code the appropriate procedure in the code generation is called. Chapter 12 deals with the details of the code generation layer.

In order to transport the compiler to another machine it should only be necessary to alter these code generation procedures. However, in some cases, for example when changing character codes, it may also be necessary to alter the lexical analysis. Some devices may not have the full character set and alternatives may have to be decided upon. For instance, the character "{" is not present in the EBCDIC character set and it may be necessary to alter the lexical analysis to recognise "/(" or some other composite symbol.

5.6 SUMMARY

In this chapter we have outlined the general structure of one particular type of recursive descent compiler. The language S-algol has been introduced as a vehicle to demonstrate the problems of writing a recursive descent compiler since it is typical of modern day programming languages. Because S-algol is a block structured high level language with recursive procedures and data structures, it will also be used to write the compiler program.

The compiler will be constructed using the technique of stepwise refinement. The steps of the refinement have been described briefly and the interfaces between the steps and the problems of each step discussed. It is emphasised that the method described is not unique and that other techniques, notably table driven methods, may be used to construct recursive descent compilers.

The advantages of this type of compiler is that it is easier to write, therefore more likely to be correct, more portable and easier to understand. From a software engineering viewpoint it is desirable because it is easier to maintain.

REFERENCES

[1] Bauer, H., Becker, S. and Graham, S. (1968), Algol W implementation, *Technical Report No CS98,* Stanford University.

[2] Randell, B. and Russell, L. J. (1964), *Algol 60 Implementation,* Academic Press.

[3] Wirth, N. (April 1971), Program development by stepwise refinement, *CACM,* **14**, **4**, 221-227.

[4] Turner, D. A. (1979), *SASL Language Manual,* University of St. Andrews Department of Computational Science Report CS/79/3.

[5] Amman, U. (1973), The development of a compiler, *Proc. Int. Symposium on Computing,* 93-99, North Holland.

[6] Currie, I. F., Bond, S. G. and Morison, J. D. (1971), Algol 68R, its implementation and use, *Proceedings IFIP Ljubljana,* **3**, 43-46.

[7] Creech, B. A. (1969), Architecture of the B6500, *Proceedings COINS.*

CHAPTER 6

Syntax Analysis

6.1 THE FIRST LAYER

The syntax analysis forms the heart of a recursive descent compiler and is the first layer in the stepwise refinement of the compiler program. We will assume at this stage that the grammar has already been prepared for one pass compilation as far as possible using some of the techniques of factorising, substitution and removing left recursion as described in Chapter 4. When this is done the syntax analysis layer can be written down from a formal specification of the language, in extended BNF for example.

As mentioned in Chapter 5, the syntax analyser is made up of a set of mutually recursive procedures, one for each non-terminal symbol in the grammar. Strictly, there should be a procedure to parse each terminal symbol as well, but it is more sensible for the syntax analyser to deal only with basic symbols and let the lexical analyser handle the micro syntax of these basic symbols. Thus the details of advancing the input stream etc. can be confined to one place (the lexical analyser) rather than spread throughout the compiler. This is desirable since we may have to re-write the lexical analyser to transport the compiler to another machine.

The syntax analyser still has to take note of the terminal symbols and so we must design the interface between the lexical analyser and the syntax analyser. That is, the abstract form of the lexical analyser must be defined before the syntax analyser can be written.

6.2 THE LEXICAL ANALYSIS ABSTRACTIONS

The lexical analysis abstractions, implemented as procedures, are used by the syntax analyser to compile terminal symbols in the language. The syntax analyser only deals with the basic symbols of the language and not the individual characters that make up a symbol. Therefore the first procedure we require is one to identify basic symbols. Since the syntax analyser always asks for the next basic symbol in the input stream, we will call this first abstraction next.symbol. In an LL(1) grammar, the parser will ask for one symbol at a time and once the symbol has been recognised there is never any need to backtrack on the input to re-discover what the symbol was. Thus the lexical analyser does not need to remember the input symbols. Next.symbol is defined as follows:-

```
procedure next.symbol
! Place the next basic symbol in the global
! string variable called symbol.
! This will advance the input stream.
```

The terminal symbols can now be compiled by the procedure next.symbol and the basic symbol found in the string variable called symbol when necessary. For the moment we have used the character string to represent itself inside the compiler. Thus the reserved word **let** would be represented by the string "let". The implications of this decision are discussed later. Strictly speaking, procedure next.symbol is all that is required to write the syntax analyser. However we will make the job a lot simpler by defining two other procedures before we start. These are

```
procedure mustbe(cstring s)
! if s is the symbol in variable symbol then call next.symbol
! to compile the next basic symbol. Otherwise report an error.

procedure have(cstring s -> bool)
! if s is the symbol in variable symbol then call next.symbol
! to compile the next basic symbol and return true.
! Otherwise return false.
```

These procedures work on the principle that once a symbol has been recognised in recursive descent compiling, it is no longer of interest and can be discarded because backtracking is unnecessary. The procedure mustbe is useful in cases where there is no option in the choice of symbols. It is defined here since this situation occurs frequently in recursive descent parsers. The important point about the procedure is that not only does it check that we have the desired symbol, but also, if we have, it moves on to the next basic symbol automatically. Combining the two functions shortens the amount of code to be written and therefore should make the code easier to write and understand. The second abstraction, procedure have, is used when we have more than one choice in a production. The procedure will reject incorrect choices and move on to the next basic symbol automatically when the choice is correct. It is designed to be used as the boolean expression in an **if . . . then . . . else** or **while** clause. Again this will shorten the code with the same attendant benefits.

Another decision that we will make at this stage is one to allow us to parse identifiers and literals in a consistent manner. The syntax analyser does not wish to parse each identifier or literal separately and therefore, when the lexical analyser encounters such a symbol, it places "identifier" or "literal", whichever is appropriate, in the global variable called symbol. Naturally, the lexical analyser will have to place the actual identifier or literal in another global location, but since the syntax analyser is not interested in the actual values of these symbols we can leave the details to a later level of refinement.

6.3 BNF AND CODING

The full syntax of S-algol is given in Appendix A. For simplicity the syntax is defined by two separate sets of rules. The sets of rules are short and transparent and define the legal class of programs as briefly as possible. The two sets of rules are

1. a context free grammar written in extended BNF
2. a context sensitive set of rules to govern the possible types of expression in the language. These are called the type matching rules

For an S-algol program to be syntactically correct it must obey both the BNF and the type matching rules. However, to write the syntax analyser we only require the context free syntax and therefore we can leave the type matching rules until Chapter 9.

A study of the S-algol syntax will reveal that the grammar is not LL(1) or even LL(k). This problem only occurs in one place and we will highlight it later. We have chosen this syntax deliberately to demonstrate the power of recursive descent as a parsing technique. The parser will be easier to write if the grammar is LL(1), as is S-algol in most places, but the language designer may feel that this constrains the language too much. Each time the language designer allows the syntax to stray from the LL(1) style, the power the language gains must be weighed against the difficulty of writing the parser. When all other details are equal the designer should chose an LL(1) form rather than any other.

We are almost ready to write the syntax analyser but first we must discuss a number of tricks of the trade. For example, the analyser will be written from a specification of the language in extended BNF. Therefore productions of the form

⟨   ⟩ : := a⟨A⟩

translate directly into the code

mustbe("a") ; A

using the lexical analysis abstractions defined in section 6.2. A production of the form

⟨   ⟩ : := a⟨A⟩ | b⟨B⟩

translates into

if have("a") **then** A **else** { mustbe("b") ; B }

and more generally

```
⟨      ⟩ : := a⟨A⟩ | b⟨B⟩ | c⟨C⟩ | d⟨D⟩
```

translates into

```
case symbol of
"a"     : { next.symbol ; A }
"b"     : { next.symbol ; B }
"c"     : { next.symbol ; C }
default : { mustbe("d") ; D }
```

The repetition metasymbol "*" can also be coded.

```
⟨      ⟩ : := ⟨A⟩ [b⟨A⟩] *
```

translates into

```
repeat A while have("b")
```

This is a rather special case of * but it is one we will use in parsing expressions.

A more difficult situation to code is where each option in a production starts with a non-terminal symbol. In this case we must follow all but one of the non-terminals until all the legal starting symbols are found. For example,

```
⟨A⟩ : := ⟨B⟩ | ⟨C⟩
⟨B⟩ : := d⟨D⟩ | e⟨E⟩
```

translates to

```
case symbol of
"d"     : { next.symbol ; D }
"e"     : { next.symbol ; E }
default : C
```

This eliminates some procedures, in this case procedure B, from the compiler. Since the grammar is one pass this is always possible, but care should be taken especially when the productions that are removed are used elsewhere in the grammar.

Another solution to this problem is to make use of the director sets described in Chapter 4. For example, the productions

```
⟨A⟩ : := ⟨B⟩ | ⟨C⟩
⟨B⟩ : := d⟨D⟩ | e⟨E⟩
```

where "d" and "e" are directors for the productions of B translates to

```
case symbol of
"d", "e" : B
default  : C
```

This solution will always be less efficient since procedure B will have to distinguish again between the symbols "d" and "e". However it may be more convenient to write it in this way.

Adding to the above the ability to model the recursive nature of the grammar in the recursive calling of the procedures of the compiler program means we have enough tools to write the syntax analyser.

6.4 THE SYNTAX ANALYSER

Sections of the syntax of S-algol given in Appendix A will be reproduced where they are required. In the compiler, the procedure that parses a non-terminal has a name corresponding to the name of the production. For example an S-algol program is defined by

⟨program⟩ : := ⟨sequence⟩?

To parse this production we have

```
procedure program
begin
    next.symbol
    sequence
    mustbe("?")
end
```

Procedure program uses procedure next.symbol to find the first symbol in the program, procedure sequence to compile the non-terminal production ⟨sequence⟩, and procedure mustbe to compile the terminal symbol "?". The main section of the compiler is merely a call of the procedure program. To continue the syntax analysis

```
⟨sequence⟩ : := ⟨declaration⟩ [;⟨sequence⟩] |
                ⟨clause⟩ [;⟨sequence⟩]
```

Here we meet our first problem. Both of the alternatives of production ⟨sequence⟩ start with a non-terminal symbol. The first alternative starts with ⟨declaration⟩ and the other with ⟨clause⟩. We cannot call the procedures to compile the non-terminals in turn since this may lead to backtracking. Therefore we must use the rule described in the previous section; that is, follow one of the alternatives to find its start symbols thereby eliminating it. Since ⟨clause⟩ is used elsewhere in the language and ⟨declaration⟩ is not, we follow ⟨declaration⟩. A declaration can have start symbols of **let**, **procedure**, **structure** or **forward**. Notice also that the definition is recursive in that the last reference is to itself. This is called tail recursion and may be replaced by the generally more efficient iteration as suggested in section 6.3. We can therefore write

```
procedure sequence
repeat {
      case symbol of
      "let"          : let.decl
      "procedure"    : procedure.decl
      "structure"    : structure.decl
      "forward"      : forward.decl
      default        : clause }
while have(";")
```

This procedure compiles sequences of clauses made up of declarations and clauses separated by semi-colons. It will have to be refined later because if a semi-colon is missing, incorrect programs parsed by this procedure may stop compiling sooner than is desired for error recovery purposes. Of course there is now no procedure to compile declarations. The alternative to this is the code

```
procedure sequence
repeat {
      case symbol of
      "let", "procedure",
      "forward", "structure" : declaration
      default   : clause }
while have(";")
```

which follows the grammar better but is less efficient since the various start symbols have to be recognised again in procedure declaration. We continue to ⟨clause⟩ which is defined by

```
⟨clause⟩ : := if⟨clause⟩do⟨clause⟩|
              if⟨clause⟩then⟨clause⟩else⟨clause⟩|
              repeat⟨clause⟩while⟨clause⟩[do⟨clause⟩] |
              while⟨clause⟩do⟨clause⟩|
              for⟨identifier⟩=⟨clause⟩to⟨clause⟩
                    [by⟨clause⟩] do⟨clause⟩|
              case⟨clause⟩of⟨case.list⟩default:⟨clause⟩|
              ⟨name⟩:=⟨clause⟩|
              ⟨write⟩ | abort |
              ⟨expression⟩
```

Here all but three options start with a terminal symbol. For the moment we will compile ":=" as an infix operator and include this kind of clause along with expressions. We will see later that this choice is not made by accident, but for the present it allows us to code procedure clause.

```
procedure clause
case symbol of
"if"      : if.clause
"repeat"  : repeat.clause
"while"   : while.clause
"for"     : for.clause
"case"    : case.clause
"abort"   : abort.clause
"write"   : write.clause
default   : expression
```

We will take the process one stage further and write code for the **if** clause and the **write** clause before returning to declarations and expressions. All the other procedures may be coded in a similar manner.

The **if** ⟨clause⟩ has two variants

if ⟨clause⟩ **do** ⟨clause⟩

and

if ⟨clause⟩ **then** ⟨clause⟩ **else** ⟨clause⟩

We have

```
procedure if.clause
begin
    next.symbol
    clause
    if have("do") then clause else
    begin
        mustbe("then")
        clause
        mustbe("else")
        clause
    end
end
```

Notice that when we get into the **if** clause we immediately throw away the symbol "if" by calling next.symbol. It has served its purpose in getting us here and is no longer useful. This is done in every procedure where the production starts with a terminal symbol. Note also how procedure have is used to make the choice between the symbols "do" and "then".

We will now develop the **write** clause.

⟨write⟩ ::= **write**⟨write.list⟩

⟨write.list⟩ ::= ⟨clause⟩ [:⟨clause⟩] [,⟨write.list⟩]

which yields

```
procedure write.clause
begin
      next.symbol
      repeat { clause
                  if have(":") do clause }
      while have(",")
end
```

This shows an interesting variation on the looping construct described in section 6.3. We have also combined the two productions into one procedure.

Finally we will look at a declaration since it will be used later to illustrate further points. The parsing is performed in exactly the same manner.

```
⟨let.decl⟩ ::= let⟨identifier⟩⟨init.op⟩⟨clause⟩
⟨init.op⟩ ::= := | =
```

gives

```
procedure let.decl
begin
      next.symbol
      mustbe("identifier")
      if ~have("=") do mustbe(":=")
      clause
end
```

The problem of which particular identifier is being declared will be dealt with later in Chapter 10 as will the fact that we wish to perform different actions on encountering ":=" rather than "=". Nevertheless this procedure will parse the declaration and adequately fills the role of the first layer of the compiler.

The other declarations are more difficult to parse in the sense that they require more code. It will become tedious if we go through the exercise of writing code to parse them all. Instead we shall leave that as an exercise for the reader and concentrate on the problem of parsing expressions which deserves a section to itself.

6.5 EXPRESSIONS AND BLOCK EXPRESSIONS

So far it has been relatively easy to write the syntax analyser. This has been helped by the fact that until now the grammar has been LL(1). It is at this point that the grammar of S-algol is no longer LL(1). In fact we shall see that it is not LL(k) for any fixed k. However, it is still suitable for parsing by recursive descent. The full syntax of expressions is

```
⟨expression⟩ ::= ⟨exp1⟩ [or⟨exp1⟩] *
⟨exp1⟩ ::=       ⟨exp2⟩ [and⟨exp2⟩] *
⟨exp2⟩ ::=       [~] ⟨exp3⟩ [⟨relop⟩⟨exp3⟩]
⟨exp3⟩ ::=       ⟨exp4⟩ [⟨addop⟩⟨exp4⟩] *
⟨exp4⟩ ::=       [⟨addop⟩] ⟨exp5⟩[⟨multop⟩⟨exp5⟩] *
⟨exp5⟩ ::=       ⟨name⟩[(⟨clause⟩⟨bar⟩⟨clause⟩)] |
                 ⟨literal⟩ |
                 { [⟨sequence⟩] } |
                 begin [⟨sequence⟩] end |
                 vector⟨bounds⟩of⟨clause⟩ |
                 @⟨clause⟩of⟨type1⟩⟨bra⟩⟨clause.list⟩⟨ket⟩ |
                 (⟨clause⟩)
⟨name⟩ ::=       ⟨identifier⟩ |⟨expression⟩(⟨clause.list⟩)[(⟨clause.list⟩)] *
⟨bounds⟩ ::=     ⟨clause⟩::⟨clause⟩[,⟨bounds⟩]
⟨clause.list⟩ ::= ⟨clause⟩[,⟨clause⟩] *
```

The problem is caused in ⟨clause⟩ where

```
⟨clause⟩ ::= .
             .
             .
             ⟨name⟩ := ⟨clause⟩ |
             ⟨expression⟩
```

Since a name as well as an expression can be arbitrarily complex we cannot tell in any fixed number of symbols which of the above two productions we are parsing. The reason for such a production in a grammar is a matter of language design philosophy. In the above syntax it allows clauses to be expressions where sensible. It does not define where such occurrences are sensible since it is a context free syntax. Later we will use the type matching rules to define the legal uses of

⟨clause⟩ ::= ⟨expression⟩

The main point about such a rule is that it allows **if**, **case**, and block expressions. Whether this is desirable is a debate which is certainly not within the scope of this book.

Some languages, for instance Pascal, do not allow **if**, **case** and block expressions in order to preserve the LL(1) nature of the grammar. If it is done solely for this reason it is unnecessarily restrictive since we shall show that we can still use recursive descent to compile languages like S-algol which have **if**, **case** and block expressions.

When this type of problem arises in recursive descent parsing, the solution is to delay making the choice for as long as possible. It was suggested earlier that ":=" should be regarded as an infix operator which, like the other infix operators, has a left and a right expression. This suggests the code to parse expressions.

```
procedure expression
repeat exp1 while have("or")

procedure exp1
repeat exp2 while have("and")

procedure exp2
begin
    let not = have("~")
    exp3
    case symbol of
    "is", "isnt", "=", "≠", "≥", ">", "≤", "<" : {next.symbol ; exp3 }
    default : { }
end

procedure exp3
repeat exp4 while have("+") or have("−")

procedure exp4
begin
    let addop = have("+") or have("−")
    repeat exp5 while have("*") or have("/") or have("div") or
                      have("rem") or have("++")
end

procedure exp5
begin
    case symbol of
    "identifier" : next.symbol
    "literal"    : next.symbol
    "begin","{": block
    "vector"     : begin
                      next.symbol
                      repeat {clause ; mustbe("::") ; clause}
                      while have(",")
                      mustbe("of")
                      clause
                   end
    "@"          : begin
                      next.symbol
                      clause
                      mustbe("of")
                      type1
                      mustbe("[")
                      repeat clause while have(",")
                      mustbe("]")
                   end
```

```
        "("          : {next.symbol ;clause ;mustbe(")")}
        default      : {}
        if have("(") do compile.bracket
        if have(":=") do {next.symbol ; clause}
end

procedure block
begin
        let last = if symbol = "{" then "}" else "end"
        next.symbol
        if ~have(last) do {sequence ; mustbe(last)}
end
```

At this point we run into another problem. In the procedure compile.bracket when the left expression is a string we wish the code

```
next.symbol
repeat {clause
        mustbe("|")
        clause
        mustbe(")")}
while have("(")
```

to parse it which allows expressions of the form

A(i|j) (k|m)

However if the left expression is a vector, structure or procedure we require

```
repeat {next.symbol
        repeat clause while have(",")
        mustbe(")")}
while have("(")
```

The difficulty is that we do not know which code sequence will be appropriate because the syntax is context sensitive at this point. Fortunately it can be overcome using recursive descent. One way of resolving the problem is to select a different type of bracket for strings. If this is not desirable, we can leave the code informally defined at this stage. We know that it can be compiled if we have some context sensitive information on the left expression. In this case the type of the left expression will do. The problem can therefore be resolved at a later level of refinement when the application of the context sensitive parts of the rules are considered.

The same applies to the assignment clause. We have been excessively generous in compiling it as

⟨expression⟩ := ⟨clause⟩

However this can again be restricted by some further context-sensitive information and the code refined at a later level. We will return to both these points.

The problem of compiling assignment clauses disappears if we use right assignment instead of the more common left assignment. For example

a —⟩ b(i)

means b(i) becomes the value of a. Here there is less difficulty in compilation because we can apply the stricter rules to the name being assigned to since we have already encountered the "—⟩" symbol. Therefore we know it is an assignment and not part of something else. Indeed it is hard to justify using left assignment because it is more difficult to compile and less obvious in meaning.

There is at least one drawback to the recursive descent approach in compiling expressions. It can be easily seen that the amount of recursion required to parse even simple expressions is going to be large. For this reason it may be quicker to explore other techniques for parsing expressions. One such technique is operator precedence parsing which is often used in conjunction with recursive descent when parsing expressions (see section 3.8). However it is beyond the scope of this book to explore the depths of operator precedence parsing.

6.6 SUMMARY

We have taken the first step in writing our compiler. The syntax analyser forms the first layer, and it is this layer that we will refine until the compiler is complete. Many people, we are sure, will be surprised with the ease with which this layer was written. There are two reasons for the simplicity. First, considerable work has already been done on the grammar to make writing the parser an easy task. For example the grammar is LL(1) in most places although there is considerable freedom here because recursive descent is used to compile some constructs which are not even LL(k) for any fixed k. Indeed we deliberately did not choose an LL(1) grammar, but one to highlight the diverse syntactic problems which can be handled by recursive descent parsers. Second, the choice of abstractions for the lexical analysis was not made at random, but with a certain amount of skill built up from writing and studying compiler programs over a number of years. Putting this skill together with a well defined syntax does indeed yield a simple method of generating parsing programs.

We have left a number of sections of the parser incomplete. In some cases this was done because it would be tedious and not very instructive to write more code. In other cases, notably in the parsing of expressions we left some problems to be resolved by later levels of refinement. These we will return to.

CHAPTER 7

Lexical Analysis

7.1 THE FUNCTION OF A LEXICAL ANALYSER

It is not absolutely necessary to write the lexical analyser at this stage in the development of the compiler, but since it has already been used in the abstract and has to be written at some time, it is perhaps better out of the way. A working lexical analyser will, of course, allow testing of the parser in its skeletal form.

The lexical analyser forms the characters in the input stream into basic symbols (sometimes called lexemes or terminals) of the language when requested by the syntax analyser. It does this in two logical parts, by scanning the input stream and then screening the symbols formed by the scanner. Scanning involves forming all the basic textual units of the language such as identifiers, literals of various types, single and multiple character symbols, plus all the punctuation characters. Screening involves discarding some of these textual elements to leave only the basic symbols of the language for the syntax analyser. This will normally involve removing from the input such symbols as spaces, tabs, newlines and comments. The screening part of the lexical analyser will also recognise which of the identifiers are reserved words if such objects exist in the language.

Finally, it is quite common for the lexical analyser to organise the printing of the program text with suitable annotation if this is required.

7.2 SCANNING

Recognising the terminal symbols of most programming languages is usually a relatively simple task. The syntax of the most difficult part, that of identifiers and literals, is usually in the form of a regular expression or Chomsky type 3 language as described in section 3.2. Regular expressions may be parsed as special cases of most parsing techniques used for a full programming language, and this is therefore a simple problem to solve. The remainder of the lexical analysis, that of forming single and multiple character symbols can also be recognised using a regular expression parser.

Even though it is a simple task to write a lexical analyser, it is often worth a considerable amount of careful design because of its overall effect on the efficiency of the compiler. Typically, lexical analysers represent about 5-10% of the source code but may use up to 50% of the execution time of the compiler. This is due to the massive reduction in bulk of the input which the lexical analyser effects. A large number of characters can be reduced to a single basic symbol and although the cost to process one character is low, the overall total cost can be high. For this reason we must be conscious of efficiency when designing and coding the lexical analyser.

We could use recursive descent to parse the terminal symbols. However the compression of the input characters into basic symbols is rather like a bottom up parsing technique. That is, at this level we look at the input in order to decide what lexemes to produce; we do not ask for a particular lexeme and complain if we do not get it. That task is left to the top down parser. Often the lexical analyser is coded from a **transition state diagram** of the syntax using **case** and **while** clauses. For example forming an identifier from the BNF rules

```
⟨identifier⟩ ::= ⟨letter⟩ [⟨id⟩] *
     ⟨id⟩    ::= ⟨letter⟩ | ⟨digit⟩ | .
```

can be achieved by the code

```
let identifier := "" ; let more := true
if letter(peek) do
repeat {
      let s = peek
      case true of
      letter(s), digit(s), s = "." : identifier := identifier ++ read
                            default : more := false }
while more
```

with the result remaining in the variable called identifier. This example directly reflects that the syntax at this level (often called the micro syntax) can be parsed by a regular expression parser.

We can also use a reduced recursive descent technique. Recursive descent is rather too powerful to parse terminal symbols, because the only type of recursion in the syntax involves tail recursion. Tail recursion is where the last action of a procedure is to call itself. Since we are conscious of efficiency, we can replace the tail recursion by iteration. By a strange coincidence this gives us a technique similar to the bottom up method.

We will again use stepwise refinement to build the lexical analyser. The scanning process will be written first. Instead of the screening process acting on the output of the scanner, it will be built into the scanner by layering in just the same way as we are building the rest of the compiler. Although there may be many layers there will still be only one pass on the source text.

7.3 S-ALGOL SCANNING

The contract for the scanning process is to form the characters it reads into the basic textual units of the language. In the case of S-algol these units can be identifiers, literals of type integer, real, boolean or string, composite symbols such as "::" and single character symbols such as "=". Any symbol which is not a literal, an identifier or a composite symbol can be regarded by the scanner as a single character symbol whether or not it is legal. The screening process will remove some of these single character symbols such as punctuation, and will also change some of the identifiers into other basic symbols such as reserved words.

In Chapter 6 when designing the lexical analysis abstractions, we used the character string of the symbol to represent that basic symbol inside the compiler. Thus the symbol **else** is represented by the string "else" in the compiler. This is not a common practice and often the basic symbols are coded into integers and passed around the compiler as integer values. Normally this is done for efficiency or simply because the language the compiler is written in does not have a data type string with string operations. In such a compiler the writer has to remember the integer coding of each basic symbol. Furthermore there must be a reverse process to obtain the basic symbol from the integer value in order to write error reports. Such compilers are often difficult to read, alter and maintain. We have already stated that one of the design aims of recursive descent compiling is to rid the compiler of such intermediate forms. Thus, since we have a language that will support strings properly, we will use character strings to represent the basic symbols.

We will make one concession to efficiency here without affecting the clarity of the compiler. Instead of using the string literal to represent the basic symbol in the compiler, we will define an S-algol string constant for that basic symbol. For example the else symbol has the constant declaration

```
let else.sy = "else"
```

in the compiler. This ensures that there is only one copy of the literal value in the compiler even if the compiler does not. All the constant names which represent the basic symbols will end in ".sy" and will be of fairly obvious meaning to help the clarity of the compiler. Anywhere in the compiler where the basic symbol is used, the constant name rather than the string literal is used. There is no loss of clarity in printing error messages since printing the string constant do.sy will yield the string "do". Thus the procedure to compile the **if** clause which is given in section 6.4 should really be

```
procedure if.clause
begin
      next.symbol
      clause
```

```
    if have(do.sy) then clause else
    begin
        mustbe(then.sy)
        clause
        mustbe(else.sy)
        clause
    end
end
```

Changing all the other syntax analysis procedures accordingly along with using the lexical analysis abstractions in the syntax analyser constitutes the lexical analysis layer of the stepwise refinement but we will not rewrite the syntax analyser here as we will have plenty of opportunity to study the results in later chapters.

Let us return to the scanning process and examine the micro syntax of the basic symbols before writing code. The lexical analyser is the procedures next.symbol, have and mustbe to the rest of the compiler. The procedure next.symbol reads the input text and leaves the basic symbol in the string variable called symbol. As we examine each basic symbol category we will invent further conventions in order that the lexical analyser may perform its function.

An identifier in S-algol is defined by

⟨identifier⟩ ::= ⟨letter⟩ [⟨ident⟩] *
  ⟨ident⟩ ::= ⟨letter⟩ | ⟨digit⟩ | .

Some of the identifiers will be reserved words but we will ignore this problem at the moment because the screening process will find them. The string variable symbol is set to the value identifier.sy when an identifier is found and we will leave the actual value of the identifier in another string variable called the.name. Notice that there is no restriction on the length of identifiers. There is no limit to the length of an identifier in the syntax and it is not the job of the lexical analyser to introduce such artificial limits. If such a limit exists it should be included in the definition of the language and not imposed by the implementation. In compiling a language such as Fortran where the identifiers are of fixed maximum length, it is usual for the compiler to recognise the whole identifier and then truncate it to the fixed maximum length.

Literals may be of various types. When a literal is found the string variable symbol is given the value literal.sy and the actual value of the literal is placed in one of the variables int.literal, real.literal, string.literal or bool.literal for literals of type int, real, string or bool respectively. The screening process can be left to recognise the boolean literals **true** and **false** from the identifiers, since these are reserved words.

The composite symbols in S-algol are

:: := <= >= ~= -> ++

The string variable symbol is set to the value of the composite symbol if one is recognised. We must look for these before we decide that we have a single character symbol and set the value of the variable symbol accordingly.

Each one of the above lexical categories, except for integer and real literals, can be distinguished by its first character. In writing the code for the lexical analyser, we will use the S-algol function peek to look at the next character in the input stream without moving the input on, and the procedure next.ch to read the next character and move the input on. The need for the procedure next.ch will become obvious when we discuss the problem of program printing.

We will look for a composite symbol when we have recognised its first symbol. Procedure try must attempt to form the composite symbol by looking at the next character in the input stream and the next character in the target symbol. If the two characters are the same, we have a composite symbol. In S-algol the composite symbols are all of length two and so we can write

```
procedure try(cstring s)
if s(2|1) = peak do { let discard = next.ch ; symbol := s }
```

That is, if we have a composite then we must move on the input stream one character but otherwise do nothing. The coding device

```
let discard = next.ch
```

simply moves on the input stream. This procedure is sometimes thought of as part of the screening process but we prefer to regard it as part of the scanner.

We will now write procedure next.symbol.

```
procedure next.symbol
begin
     if digit(peek) then number else
     if letter(peek) then try.name else
     case peek of
     colon.sy     : begin
                          symbol := next.ch
                          if peek = colon.sy then
                          begin
                               let discard = next.ch
                               symbol := dcolon.sy
                          end else try(assign.sy)
                    end
     lt.sy        : { symbol := next.ch ; try(le.sy)}
     gt.sy        : { symbol := next.ch ; try(ge.sy) }
     not.sy       : { symbol := next.ch ; try(neq.sy) }
     minus.sy     : { symbol := next.ch ; try(arrow.sy) }
```

```
    plus.sy     : { symbol := next.ch ; try(dplus.sy) }
    dquote.sy   : begin
                      let discard = next.ch
                      symbol := literal.sy
                      string.literal := read.string
                  end
    default     : symbol := next.ch
end
```

A careful study of this procedure will reveal most of the secrets of the lexical analyser. The procedure looks for a digit, in which case we have an integer or real literal, if a digit is not found the procedure looks for a letter, in which case we have an identifier. The procedure then looks for all the composite symbols and string literals and finally if it has not found one of the above we have a single character symbol.

Finally procedure read.string will read the rest of the string literal and the enclosing double quote and can be written as

```
procedure read.string(-> string)
begin
    let s := ""
    while peek ≠ dquote.sy do s := s ++ next.ch
    let discard = next.ch
    s
end
```

This first attempt at procedure read.string is rather simplistic. It does not allow for special characters inside the string literals. Special characters are characters that we wish to represent inside the string literal without writing them down. For example if we wish a backspace character in a string literal we may not always wish to type the backspace key because this may spoil the program listing. Other such characters are tabs, newpage and newline. We may also wish the double quote character inside a string literal. These problems must be solved by the language designer.

In S-algol, the single quote character is taken as an escape character when used inside a string literal. Thus to represent a double quote inside a string literal we use '". Of course this complicates the problem of representing a single quote since if we write "'" this is an incomplete S-algol string literal rather than the character '. The representation of the rest of the special characters inside a string literal are

'n	newline
'p	newpage
'b	backspace
't	tab

An escape character inside a string may represent itself as long as it cannot be made into a special character. Otherwise it must use the escape character. We can now rewrite procedure read.string.

```
procedure read.string(-> string)
begin
    let s := ""
    while peek ≠ dquote.sy do s := s ++ next.char
    let discard = next.ch
    s
end

procedure next.char(-> string)
begin
    let ch = next.ch
    if ch = squote.sy then
        case peek of
        "n"          : { let discard = next.ch ; nl.sy }
        "t"          : { let discard = next.ch ; tab.sy }
        "b"          : { let discard = next.ch ; bs.sy }
        "p"          : { let discard = next.ch ; np.sy }
        dquote.sy    : { let discard = next.ch ; dquote.sy }
        squote.sy    : { let discard = next.ch ; squote.sy }
        default      : ch
    else ch
end
```

We continue with procedure try.name.

```
procedure try.name
begin
    symbol := identifier.sy
    let s := next.ch
    while ok do s := s ++ next.ch
    the.name := s
end

procedure ok(-> bool)
letter(peek) or digit(peek) or peek = dot.sy
```

It should be fairly obvious that this code will form the identifiers according to the syntax of S-algol given above.

The only unresolved part of the scanning process is now procedure number which recognises integer and real literals. Although the writing of this procedure forms a nice demonstration of a piece of structured programming, it would be quite tedious to develop it here. We feel that a procedure to parse integer and real literals has been done so well and so often before in the literature that there is little value in repeating the exercise. If the reader wishes, it will form a nice little programming problem and, if difficulties arise, other pieces of literature, especially Wirth [1], can be referenced. For completeness the procedure number is given in Appendix C. We will assume that it has been written and pass on to the screening process.

7.4 SCREENING

As described earlier, the screening process discards some of the textual units of the program. In S-algol this means eliding spaces, tabs, newlines and comments. The second function of the screener is to convert certain symbols into others. In particular this means recognising reserved words and literals such as **true** and **false** and separating them from the identifiers. The screening function is written as a layer of the scanning process rather than as a separate pass on the input. Therefore the two functions of the screener may be applied at different stages in the recognition of the text. The elision of punctuation may be performed before the scanning starts and the identification of the reserved words and so on performed after the identifiers have been formed.

Punctuation may appear between any two symbols. Therefore the first action the procedure next.symbol must take is to remove the punctuation. If this procedure calls procedure layout to remove this punction then the procedure layout may be coded thus.

```
procedure layout
begin
      let more := true
      repeat
            case peek of
            space.sy,tab.sy,nl.sy : { let discard = next.ch }
            comment.sy            : while next.ch ≠ nl.sy do { }
            default               : more := false
      while more
end
```

Procedure layout throws away all combinations of spaces, newlines and tabs. A comment in an S-algol program is the characters from the symbol "!" up to the end of the input line. This is also thrown away. When we encounter a character which is not one of the above, we leave procedure layout because its task is complete.

The second part of the screening process is to separate the reserved words and boolean literals from the identifiers. This may be done by rewriting procedure try.name.

```
procedure try.name
begin
      let s := next.ch
      while ok do s := s ++ next.ch
      symbol := case s of
                  true.sy   : { boolean.literal := s ; literal.sy }
                  false.sy  : { boolean.literal := s ; literal.sy }
                  default   : if reserved.word(s) then s else
                              begin
                                    the.name := s
                                    identifier.sy
                              end
end
```

Thus once the identifier has been formed we check that it is not a boolean literal or a reserved word before assigning a value to the variable symbol.

The recognition of reserved words is done by procedure reserved.word which returns the value true if the input string is a reserved word and otherwise the value false. This may be done in many ways from simply scanning a list of reserved words through searching a binary tree balanced according to the frequency of usage of the reserved words, to a perfect hashing function. If a simple list is used, the average length of the search of a list of length n will be $n/2$. This will most certainly be too expensive for a large number of reserved words. Using a binary tree, balanced according to the frequency of usage of occurrence of the reserved words, will be much faster especially for the most commonly accessed words [2]. However it may take some time to gather enough statistics on the use of the reserved words to form a well balanced tree. An ordinary binary tree constructed alphabetically may also be used. This guarantees that in a balanced tree the longest search through a tree of n reserved words is proportional to $\log n$.

A compromise between the linear scan method and a balanced binary tree is a technique called a **binary chop**. In the binary chop method we take a vector of reserved words ordered in some way, probably alphabetically, and apply the following algorithm. The section of the vector in which the target reserved word might lie is bounded by the variables top and bottom. We choose the mid-point of the vector and compare it with the string we are searching for. If they are equal we have found the reserved word and have finished. Otherwise, if the required string comes before the mid-point in the chosen collating order, we repeat the process with the bottom half of the vector and, if the required string comes after the mid-point, we use the top half. We repeat this halving of the vector until the string is found or we can no longer half the vector. Again the number of accesses for a vector size n is at most proportional to $\log n$. The algorithm may be coded as

```
procedure binary.chop(*cstring words ; cstring s -> bool)
begin
    let bottom := lwb(words) ; let top := upb(words)
    let found := false
    while bottom <= top and ~found do
    begin
        let middle = (bottom + top) div 2
        case true of
        words(middle) > s : top := middle - 1
        words(middle) < s : bottom := middle + 1
        default           : found := true
    end
    found
end
```

The procedure returns the value true if the string is found in the vector of words and false otherwise.

A **hashing function** may also be used to identify the reserved words. A hashing function in this case is a procedure which takes the characters that make up the identifier and produces an integer value. Any hashing function for reserved words should give a unique integer value for each reserved word. A perfect hashing function is one where all the integer values of the hash are consecutive. However the construction of such a perfect function is not an easy task [3]. The unique integer of the hash can then be used as an index into a table of reserved words. Even when the hash value is legal, i.e. within the bounds of the table, the table entry and the original string must still be compared in case there is another identifier with this hash value. We will return to this subject in Chapter 10 when we discuss methods of constructing and accessing the symbol table.

7.5 LEXICAL ERRORS

The main difficulty in dealing with lexical errors is that there is usually very little redundancy in the micro syntax of the lexical items. The next character in the input stream is either part of the symbol being formed or it is not. Therefore an error, if there is one, will only show up as part of the next symbol to be formed.

There are a number of characters which are not legal in S-algol if they are formed into symbols. For example the character "#" is not an S-algol symbol. The character is legal as part of a string literal but not on its own. The screening process could find such symbols and report errors but we feel that it is just as simple to pass the symbol to the syntax analyser allowing it to find the error and handle it in the uniform manner described in Chapter 8. Otherwise every single character symbol has to be screened.

Another source of possible error is in the forming of literals. Integer and real literals if converted to integer and real values inside the compiler may not be within the range of the host or target machine. This type of error should be detected but care must be taken to ensure that the compiler does not 'blow up' during any conversion. In some compilers this 'blow up' happens on real or integer overflow.

The most difficult error of all to deal with is a missing double quote at the end of a string literal. Any method of solving this will almost certainly be unsatisfactory. If we decide that the double quote is missing after so many symbols, then we indirectly impose an artifical limit on the size of string literals. If we do not impose a limit, then the rest of the program may be read in as part of the string literal. Neither method gives a satisfactory solution.

7.6 LISTING THE SOURCE PROGRAM

The last duty of the lexical analyser is to organise the listing of the source text. Whether this is a desirable feature of a compiler depends upon the language designer's philosphy. In some well known operating systems e.g. UNIX [4], the compilers do not produce source listings. This is because there are other facilities in UNIX for listing a file and the underlying philosophy is never to duplicate effort. However most compilers are written in such a way as to be independent of both operating systems and machines and so we should cater for all tastes. Also the compiler knows more about a program than any utility and may use this information to annotate the listing accordingly. The listing and the annotation should be made optional to the user for the whole or part of the program.

The annotation facilities can be considered at several levels. The annotation of the whole program may include facilities such as underlining the reserved words and producing a cross reference listing of the identifiers. Annotation of a page of output may include facilities to produce page numbers and titles on the page and an ability to control the number of lines printed on a page. Finally the annotation of a line of output may give line numbers and block counts. A block count is an indication of how deeply nested a program is. Every time a block is entered the count is increased by one and then decreased on block exit. This allows missing **begins** or **ends** to be found easily. A first attempt at producing a program listing could be this code for procedure next.ch.

```
procedure next.ch (-> string)
begin
      let ch = read
      write ch
      ch
end
```

To implement the annotation features described above means developing procedure next.ch to include them. To implement some of the facilities such as block counts may require the whole line of input to be collected together before it is printed. This is usually also necessary for printing error messages in the correct place.

We will not write the code for this section of the compiler in this book as it is very subjective as to what a 'good' program listing looks like. However we will issue a word of warning before we go on. The task of implementing a program listing facility with the above annotation facilities can be expensive in terms of code and the run time of the compiler. It is very easy indeed to double the size and the run time of the lexical analyser in producing such a listing.

7.7 MUSTBE AND HAVE

We can now write the two outstanding lexical abstractions mustbe and have. These are defined by

```
procedure have(cstring s -> bool)
! if s is the symbol in variable symbol then call next.symbol
! to compile the next basic symbol and return true.
! Otherwise return false.
if symbol = s then { next.symbol ; true } else false

procedure mustbe(cstring s)
! if s is the symbol in symbol then call next.symbol
! to compile the next basic symbol. Otherwise report an error.
if symbol = s then next.symbol else ! error
```

Which brings us very neatly to the syntactic error diagnosis and recovery of Chapter 8.

7.8 SUMMARY

We have now written the lexical analyser and designed the outstanding conventions that the rest of the compiler requires in order that it may use it correctly. We did not need to write the lexical analyser at this stage in the development of the compiler, but we took the opportunity of getting it out of the way. We did not rewrite the syntax analyser since most of the lexical layer is already there. The only change we would have made would be to change the string literals which represented the basic symbols into string constant names. We indicated how this would be done for procedure if.clause and assumed that it was done throughout. We will see the results of this layer in later chapters.

The lexical analyser is split into two logical sections, scanning and screening. The scanning process forms all the characters in the input stream into the textual units of the language. These textual units may be identifiers, literals, single and multiple character symbols and punctuation. The screening process removes some of these textual units, for example punctuation, and converts some identifiers into reserved words or literals leaving only the basic symbols for the rest of the compiler. The two processes of scanning and screening are not independent and the screening process is built as a layer on top of the scanning process. This ensures that there need only be one pass made on the input text.

The problems of lexical error detection are both dealt with and passed on. Illegal single character symbols are passed to the syntax analyser so that a syntax error message may be issued in the uniform manner which will be discussed later. The detection of illegal literals is dealt with by the lexical analyser. However no strategy is proposed for recovery after such an error.

Finally the problems of producing and annotating a source listing are discussed. The lexical analyser is now complete. The abstractions mustbe, have and next.symbol have been written and the conventions for passing on information to the rest of the compiler are defined.

REFERENCES

[1] Wirth, N., (1976), *Algorithms + Data Structures = Programs,* Prentice-Hall.

[2] Kari-Jouko Raiha and Zweben, Z., (September 1979), An optimal insertion algorithm for height balanced binary search trees, *CACM,* 22, 9, 508-512.

[3] Cichelli, R. (January 1980), Minimal perfect hash functions made simple, *CACM,* 23, 1, 17-19.

[4] Ritchie, D. M. and Thompson, K. (July 1974), The UNIX time sharing system, *CACM,* 17, 7, 365-375.

CHAPTER 8

Syntax Error Diagnosis and Recovery

8.1 WHAT CAN WE DO ABOUT ERRORS?

It is an unfortunate fact of life for the compiler writer that some users will submit programs that are syntactically incorrect. The compiler must react to an erroneous program by detecting the errors and furthermore it must be able to deal with any of a large number of possible kinds of error. This chapter considers how the compiler may react to such errors and how the code for the syntax analyser may be refined to handle them.

Fortunately for us, LL grammars and especially LL(1) grammars have good error detection properties. The program is scanned top to bottom, left to right. For every input symbol the compiler has a goal symbol which may be one of a number of symbols. If the input symbol is not one of the goal symbols an error has been detected. In an LL(1) grammar where we look only one symbol ahead, we can discover whether or not the input symbol is legal before moving on.

What should the compiler do when an error is detected? Naturally, the user should be informed that an error has occurred; we will return to the subject of error reports in section 8.4. The question really is 'what attempt should the compiler make to remedy the situation?'.

The first solution is to give up. This is not such a stupid suggestion as it first seems. When an error is encountered the compiler issues an error report and then stops. The compiler is therefore easy to code and in some environments, such as a good time sharing system where re-compilation is fast and inexpensive, this approach may indeed be a feasible solution.

A scheme that detects only the first error and gives up should be regarded as the minimum response a compiler can give. In practice it is usually never acceptable since it may make the debugging of a large program a very trying exercise. More importantly, the compiler designer has to design the compiler to be machine independent and cannot depend on the compiler living in a good environment. In a batch environment the above type of operation is definitely unacceptable. If we do not adopt this approach, however, we are forced to consider error recovery.

An error recovery scheme ranges from the very simple (e.g. we could carry on with lexical analysis alone in order to detect further lexical errors) through the intermediate where we try to repair the error, to the very expensive where we try to correct the error. An error repair is where we attempt to minimise the effect of the error without trying to correct it so that we may carry on with the syntax analysis. An enormous amount has been written on the subject of syntax error recovery and could easily fill a book by itself. We do not wish to spend any great effort adding to this literature and would therefore refer the reader to Backhouse [1] or Aho and Ullman [2] if more than we give is required on the subject.

The underlying philosophy of error recovery, be it repair or correction, is to change an incorrect program to the 'nearest' syntactically correct one. How much the designer is willing to invest in an error recovery scheme depends on how worthwhile he considers error recovery to be. If it is not considered worthwhile we return to a 'detection only' scheme.

An error recovery scheme can never be foolproof since that would involve reading the mind of the programmer. It is also unwise to attempt to make the recovery scheme foolproof since the law of diminishing returns applies. The nearer we get to making the scheme foolproof, the more we need to invest in code to catch a few relatively unusual types of error. A compromise is to design a simple scheme that is low in cost in terms of time and code and will still recover from the majority of errors.

The compiler designer must attempt to find out the most common sources of error among the user population. We would suggest the following as common types of error

1. the insertion of extra symbols
2. the omission of symbols
3. the replacement of symbols
4. the transposition of two symbols

Any error recovery scheme that can recover from the above types of errors has a high chance of being successful overall.

Careful design of the language can also help in error recovery. The careful design involves building redundancy into the syntax in order that the compiler may use the extra symbols as landmarks for recovery – for example the Algol 68 habit of reversing a keyword in certain places to mark the end of the sphere of influence of the keyword. If the S-algol **while** clause was designed as

while ⟨clause⟩ **do** ⟨clause⟩ **od**

then the extra keyword **od** could be used in error recovery as it delimits the whole **while** clause. Such techniques are often considered too expensive because they alter the appearance of the language and penalise the programmer who does not make syntactic errors because they make the language more verbose.

We will consider two techniques for error recovery. Both schemes are relatively simple and can be coded inexpensively. Furthermore they can both be extended. The first scheme was designed by Ammann for use in his Pascal compiler [3] and the second was invented by Turner [4] for use in a compiler for the applicative language SASL [5]. Both Pascal and SASL have grammars which are LL(1) and both compilers use recursive descent as the parsing technique.

8.2 THE PASCAL ERROR RECOVERY SCHEME

The Pascal error recovery scheme was designed by Ammann [3] who built one of the first Pascal compilers. The technique was so successful that most other Pascal compilers have copied it. The method is more of a mechanism on which error recovery can be built than a strategy for recovery. This allows different implementers to tune the strategy for particular applications without having to redesign the whole recovery method.

The basis of the scheme is to divide the legal Pascal symbols into two disjoint sets, the set of relevant symbols and the set of irrelevant symbols. Here the technique makes good use of the Pascal concept of a set. The two sets, although disjoint, are dynamic in nature and will change depending on the production being parsed. Every procedure that parses a non-terminal in the grammar is given as a parameter the set of relevant symbols. If an error occurs and depending on the recovery strategy, the parsing procedure may skip all the input symbols up to the first relevant one. The syntax analysis can now continue but without any further reading from the input stream until a point is reached where the new symbol is accepted as correct. This will allow the recursion to unwind if necessary. It is the duty of the parsing procedure to augment the set of relevant symbols when it thinks a symbol might be skipped which it does not wish to be. The parsing procedure must also pass on the set of relevant symbols to any other parsing procedure that it calls.

For example, in compiling the **while** clause, before the procedure tries to compile the boolean clause following the **while** symbol, it would add the symbol **do** to the set of relevant symbols. If an error is detected in compiling the boolean clause, the error recovery will not skip past the **do** symbol. The syntax analysis can now continue without reading any further symbols until it returns to the procedure compiling the **while** clause. It may then resume normal service from the recognition of the **do** symbol.

The technique is basically both simple and sound. It attempts to balance the input stream with the branch of the syntax tree which it is on. The method does not force skipping but allows the compiler designer to decide where this may be done. Also the method does not define when a symbol becomes relevant but again leaves the decision up to the compiler writer. For this reason the method is very flexible with the recovery strategy built into the set of relevant symbols and the application of the skipping.

Ammann's technique is particularly well suited to the syntax of Pascal. However like any other recovery scheme it may, depending on the input, recover at the wrong point. This is more likely with a language that has a highly recursive grammar which includes such syntactic categories as block expressions. Even then it will not perform too badly, because at worst it will only skip further than is absolutely necessary.

8.3 THE S-ALGOL ERROR RECOVERY SCHEME

The S-algol error recovery scheme is borrowed directly from Turner [4] who invented it whilst developing a compiler for the language SASL [5]. The technique can easily be built into our compiler. An error is detected when a call of the procedure mustbe encounters a symbol in the input that is not the goal symbol. Therefore we may make the first refinement to procedure mustbe

```
procedure mustbe(cstring s)
! if s is the symbol in symbol then call next.symbol
! to compile the next basic symbol. Otherwise report an error.
if symbol = s then next.symbol else syntax(s)

procedure syntax(cstring s)
error.message("** Syntax Error ** ",s," found where ",symbol," expected")
```

Procedure error.message will print the error report in the appropriate place as discussed in section 8.4.

If we were to stop here, the error detection would be very low cost indeed. However it turns out that with only a little more thought we can dramatically improve the technique. The problem with the above is that it does not attempt to recover. Therefore it is most likely that it will generate an unpredictable number of spurious error messages after the correct one. Notice however that if an error does occur, the error message is issued and the compiler continues as if the symbol were present. For example in compiling

```
while a < b a := b
```

the compiler will detect that the symbol **do** is missing and repair the error by inserting it. This allows the compiler to continue.

Turner approaches the general problem of recovery from the opposite direction to the Pascal method. Instead of skipping the input for a relevant symbol and then continuing the syntax analysis without moving the input until the symbols balance, Turner continues the syntax analysis until the next goal symbol. This occurs on the next call of procedure mustbe. At this stage the compiler may have already recovered, as will be the case when only one symbol is missing, or it is now forced to recover by skipping the input until the goal symbol and the input symbol match. The syntax tree and the input are now balanced as well as they can be.

An example of this recovery can be seen in compiling

if a < b c **then** a := 2 **else** b := 3

Since the operator between "b" and "c" is missing, the compiler will find "c" when looking for **then**. It will attempt to continue the syntax analysis and eventually try to recognise the symbol **else**. At this point the input stream will be far behind where it should be and so the compiler skips the intervening symbols until the **else** symbol is found in the input.

It is emphasised that this method, although similar in aims to the Pascal technique, is not the same and will perform quite differently. Turner's method provides a recovery strategy without using any tables or forcing the designer to concern himself with error recovery at each stage of the syntax analysis. Furthermore the method does not disrupt the flow of control in the compiler, allowing context sensitive actions such as type matching to continue across the error. The overall simplicity of the method and its extremely low cost are its main attractions.

To implement Turner's method we rewrite procedures mustbe and syntax.

```
let recovering := false

procedure mustbe(cstring s)
! if s is the symbol in symbol then call next.symbol
! to compile the next basic symbol. Otherwise report an error.
if recovering then
begin
     while symbol ≠ s do next.symbol
     recovering := false
end else
if symbol = s then next.symbol else syntax(s)

procedure syntax(cstring s)
if ~recovering do
begin
     error.message("** Syntax Error **",
                    s," found where ",symbol," expected")
     recovering := true
end
```

The boolean variable recovering, initially **false**, is set **true** when an error has been detected and we are trying to recover from it. If we are recovering from an error and procedure mustbe is called with a goal symbol, then the input is skipped until the goal symbol is found in the input. If we are not recovering and the procedure mustbe is called, then either the symbol in the input is the goal symbol or we have an error, in which case we call procedure syntax which will report the error and put the compiler into recovery mode. To eliminate a large number of useless error messages, procedure syntax refuses to issue an error message if the compiler is already recovering.

It can be readily seen that Turner's method is extremely low cost. How well then does it perform? The method will recover from all first order errors such as a missing symbol, an extra symbol and a replaced symbol. However, if two nearby symbols are incorrect, especially where the symbol we are recovering on is in error, then an unduly large proportion of the input may be skipped. This may still be not too bad because at least the user will not be inundated with redundant error messages. The worst case is where the second symbol in error which we are recovering on does not occur again in the input stream. For this reason the **while** clause in procedure mustbe should be written

```
while ~eof and symbol ≠ s do next.symbol
```

Fortunately misadventures of this kind rarely occur in practice. However, one place where it *may* occur is when an **end** symbol is missing and the block it delimits gets out of synchronization. In this case the recovery reduces to lexical checking of the input.

If at any stage the above recovery scheme is felt to be inadequate, the compiler writer can resort to Ammann's trick of incorporating local checking and skipping to augment the strategy. It is not often necessary to augment the error recovery but we indicated in section 6.4 that procedure sequence may terminate sooner than is desirable for error recovery, when a program is in error. In particular it stops parsing clauses and declarations if a semi-colon is not found as a separator. If the compiler is already recovering from a syntax error, it should try to force recovery at this point. This will be done if we rewrite procedure sequence as

```
procedure sequence
begin
      let more := true

      repeat {
            case symbol of
            let.sy           : let.decl
            procedure.sy  : proc.decl
            structure.sy   : structure.decl
            forward.sy     : forward.decl
            default          : clause

            if ~have(semi.sy) do
                  if recovering then
                  begin
                        while symbol ≠ semi.sy and ~eof do next.symbol
                        recovering := false
                  end else more := false }
      while more
end
```

8.4 ERROR REPORTING

The most important point about an error report is that the message is clearly understandable and that there is a clear indication to what the message refers. We do not consider it useful that the compiler issue a message such as

error number 34

which the user can look up in a manual. The compiler should communicate to the user as much relevant information as possible. LL(1) grammars have good error detection properties which makes it relatively easy to pinpoint the errors and there is therefore no need for this type of error report in a recursive descent compiler.

There are many solutions to the problem. We will suggest one and leave the reader to think of variations. The program is listed in lines. Each time a line is printed the compiler will also print any error messages for errors which have been discovered on the line along with the symbol "^" under the offending symbol. Here is a sample of output from the S-algol compiler

```
3 -- let b = 2
4 -- let a = 1
5 -- while a < 2 { let a = 3 ; write b }
                 ^
***** Syntax Error ***** { found where do expected
6 -- ?

Compilation Fails
Number of Error Messages = 1
```

We consider the above to be a clear indication of the error. There should be one message and one "^" symbol for every error encountered. However it is too easy to confuse the user by inundating him with error messages. Therefore the wise compiler designer would limit the number of error messages issued, since it may reasonably be assumed that after so many errors something has gone drastically wrong with the error recovery. This may be done by only issuing the "^" symbol and not the error message itself after so many errors. The controlling of the number of error messages is part of the annotation of the program listing and the user may wish to control the number of error messages per line or in total. If this is the case then the facility should be made available.

To implement the above scheme we need to write procedure error.message in such a way that it records the position of the error and the messages for one line. Procedure next.ch is then refined to print any error messages after a line of source has been printed.

8.5 SUMMARY

Error detection is an essential part of the design of any compiler. Top down deterministic parsing techniques such as recursive descent have good error detection capabilities and we have used this fact to diagnose errors and to build an error recovery scheme.

Since error recovery can never be foolproof we have adopted a software engineering approach to the problem. Two methods of error recovery, due to Ammann and Turner, are given as examples of inexpensive but very effective error recovery mechanisms. Both methods attempt to balance the parser and the input string after an error has occurred, but each takes a different approach to the problem. We have taken Turner's method and used it in our compiler.

Finally we discussed the problems involved in issuing error reports. The syntax error diagnosis and recovery layer of refinement is very thin indeed. This is because we incorporated the error reporting and recovery into the lexical analysis abstractions which were already in use by the syntax analyser. The layer consists of the above plus any *ad hoc* tuning that may be felt necessary to augment the error recovery. An example of such tuning is given by rewriting procedure sequence in the syntax analysis. Fortunately it is seldom necessary to augment the syntax error recovery scheme.

REFERENCES

[1] Backhouse, R. (1979), *Syntax of Programming Languages,* Prentice-Hall.

[2] Aho, A V. and Ullman, J. H. (1977), *Principles of Compiler Design,* Addison-Wesley.

[3] Ammann, U. (1973), The development of a compiler, *Proc. Int. Symposium on Computing,* 93-99, North-Holland.

[4] Turner, D. A. (August 1977), Error diagnosis and recovery in one-pass compilers, *Information Processing Letters,* **6**, **4**, 113-115.

[5] Turner, D. A. (1979), *SASL Language Manual,* University of St. Andrews, Department of Computational Science, Report **CS/79/3**.

CHAPTER 9

Type Matching

9.1 CONTEXT SENSITIVE ANALYSIS

The next stage in the stepwise refinement of the compiler is to design and write the layer which performs the context sensitive analysis. We have developed the compiler as far as possible by analysing the context free syntax, and now we must try to make sense of the analysed program. The context sensitive analysis is developed in two parts and this, the first part, is concerned with checking the types of the clauses of the program. The second part of the context sensitive analysis is concerned with the legal use of names and will be dealt with in Chapter 10.

In a recursive descent compiler the syntax analysis is performed as the recursive evaluation of the compiler program progresses. The type of a syntactic element can only be checked after the element has been parsed and so each procedure must check the type of any syntactic element that it causes to be parsed. Therefore any parsing procedure must produce, as a result, the type of the syntactic element it has just parsed in order that the type may be checked by the calling procedure. Thus the syntax analysis is performed as the recursion progresses and the type checking carried out on the return journey. A convenient way to do this is to make every procedure in the syntax analysis into a function which returns a codified representation of the type of the clause it has just parsed. The calling procedure may then check that an appropriate type representation has been returned.

Before we can refine the syntax analysis procedures we must build ourselves some tools. We need to define how the data types will be represented inside the compiler and need to invent abstractions which will check for the legal use of these types. First of all, however, we shall return to the language specification to obtain a formal definition of the type rules.

9.2 TYPE MATCHING RULES

We have already seen in Chapter 6 that by manipulating the syntax of the language we can ease the problem of writing the parser. We also suggested that the language be formally specified in two parts, a context free syntax written in extended BNF and a set of type rules to qualify the BNF. Here we present the notation for the formal specification of the type rules and indicate how the two sets of rules interact.

For each BNF production in the language there is an equivalent type matching rule which further qualifies the manner in which the syntactic construct may be used. In a production where any of the terminal or non-terminal symbols has a data type associated with its legal use, the type rule has that data type name enclosed in the meta symbols "{" and "}" instead of the terminal or the non-terminal symbol's name itself. The type rule also indicates the result type of the production by use of the meta symbol "=⟩".

e.g. the **or** expression

BNF ⟨expression⟩ **or** ⟨expression⟩
TR { bool }**or** { bool } =⟩ { bool }

The BNF indicates that an expression may be formed by taking two sub-expressions and applying the operator **or** to them. The type rule (TR) further qualifies this by showing that both subexpressions must be of type bool and that the result is also of type bool. Anything else is illegal.

e.g. 1 **or true** is not permitted by the TR

Furthermore the **if** clause is defined by

BNF **if** ⟨clause⟩ **then** ⟨clause⟩ **else** ⟨clause⟩
TR **if** { bool } **then** { T } **else** { T } =⟩ { T }

These rules indicate the form of the **if** clause and show that the first clause must be of type bool. The two alternatives can be of any type but must be the same, producing a result of that type.

Thus **if** a < b **then true else** 4 is not permitted
whereas **if** a < b **then** 4 **else** 6 is valid and of type **int**

If we regard clauses which do not produce a data object to be of type void they can also be included in the type rules.

e.g. the **for** clause

BNF **for**⟨identifier⟩=⟨clause⟩**to**⟨clause⟩ [**by**⟨clause⟩] **do**⟨clause⟩

has a type rule

TR **for**⟨identifier⟩={ int }**to**{ int }[**by**{ int }]**do**{ void } =⟩ { void }

It is our opinion that the two sets of rules taken together make the syntactic rules easier to understand than if there were only one set of rules. As a by-product, defining the language in this way eases the compiler writer's difficulties because the compiler can now be defined more easily in layers, as we are doing, by mapping the types of entities onto the values returned by the recognition procedures.

The type matching rules can be made as comprehensive as required. We have already indicated that the rules can be used to specify more than just the legal construction of data objects. By including the type void to represent clauses which do not produce a result (e.g. Algol 60 statements) we can specify all the program construction rules for such clauses. In S-algol we have to stretch this further to include types for procedures, structure classes and structure fields, all of which can be named but not assigned like data objects. Each language translator will have similar decisions to implement.

The full type matching rules for S-algol are given in Appendix B but for clarity we will reproduce them where necessary for use in examples.

9.3 THE REPRESENTATION OF THE DATA TYPES

Each data type in the language being compiled must have a unique representation inside the compiler. This is necessary because a parsing procedure returns this representation of the type of the syntactic element it has just parsed. It is these representations that will be compared when the types are checked.

The number and structure of the representations of the data types depend on the language being compiled. The situation is analogous to the problem of representing the basic symbols for the syntax analyser. When two types do not match, the compiler will have to issue an error report which indicates the two types involved and the reason for their incompatibility. Therefore as with the basic symbols, the type representations should include the name of the type as a string. We will now show how to represent the S-algol data types and allow the reader to adapt these to other languages.

First we will look at the legal S-algol data types. There is an infinite number of data types in S-algol defined recursively by the following rules.

1. The scalar data types are int, real, bool, string and file.
2. For any data type T, *T is the data type of a vector with elements of type T.
3. The data type pntr comprises a structure with any number of fields, with any data type allowed in each field.

In addition to the above data types there is a number of other objects in S-algol where it is convenient to give them a type, in order that the compiler may check their use for consistency. The user needs to know about these types in order to follow the complete type matching rules.

4. The type of a procedure with parameters T1, ... , Tn and result type Tm is (T1, ... , Tn —> Tm).

5. Clauses which yield no value are of type void.
6. The class of a user defined structure with fields of type T1, ... Tn is of type **(T1,......, Tn)-structure and its field names are of type Ti-field.**

We will deal with each of these categories in turn defining structure classes in the compiler to represent the data types. The scalar data types will be represented inside the compiler by a structure class defined by

```
structure scalar(cstring   t.name)
```

Each of the scalar data types will have a constant pointer to a structure of this class. For clarity the name of the constant pointer will be the type name in capitals. Thus

```
let real.sy = "real"
let REAL = scalar(real.sy)
```

defines the representation of the reserved word **real** and the data type real inside the compiler. Any time we wish to represent the type real we will use the constant name REAL. In this way there is only one structure incarnation for each scalar type. The string constant will be used for error messages and there is an equivalent pair of declarations for each scalar data type. We could have defined a different structure class for each scalar data type but this is unecessary because all the structure classes would have the same shape, namely one field that holds a string constant.

The structure class called scalar is sufficient to represent the types int, real, bool, string and file. It can also be used for the types void and pntr since these act in the same manner as scalars. A vector is represented by

```
structure VECTOR(cpntr elements)
```

Thus a vector of integers would be represented by

```
VECTOR(INT)
```

and a two dimensional vector of reals by

```
VECTOR(VECTOR(REAL))
```

Notice that we do not give the vector representations constant names. This is because there is an infinite number of types of vector, and so we leave the representations to be constructed as required. Notice also that the bounds of the vector are not part of the type in S-algol and are therefore not represented. A compiler for a different language might have included these.

A procedure representation will require to retain the types of the parameters and the result for complete type checking of a call of the procedure. We therefore represent a procedure type by

```
structure proc(cpntr args,result)
```

The parameters will be formed into a linked list of types using the structure class

```
structure cons(pntr hd,tl)
```

A structure class itself is represented by

```
structure STRUCTURE(pntr fields)
```

The fields are again a linked list of types. Finally a structure field is represented by

```
structure field(cpntr field.type)
```

We do not have constant names to represent procedure, structure class or structure field types because again there is an infinite number of them.

9.4 CHECKING THE EQUALITY OF TWO TYPES

Now that we have defined a representation of every data type in the language, we must build an abstraction to check the equality of two types. In a recursive descent compiler where the type checking is performed on the unwinding of the recursion, the compiler always has a goal type. For example in compiling the expression x **or** y the compiler will parse the clause x, check that its type is boolean, then compile the clause y and check that it is also boolean. At any time during the parsing the compiler has a goal type (boolean in this example) and an actual type. Therefore the compiler requires an abstraction which will take the representations of two data types and produce a boolean result depending on whether or not the types are equal. We will call this abstraction procedure eq and it must check equality for every data type. Since there is an infinite number of possible data types in S-algol defined recursively the procedure eq will be recursive to model this. It may be written as follows:

```
procedure eq(cpntr a,b -> bool)
a = b or
a is VECTOR and b is VECTOR and eq(a(elements),b(elements)) or
a is STRUCTURE and b is STRUCTURE and eq(a(fields),b(fields)) or
a is proc and b is proc and eq(a(args),b(args)) and
                            eq(a(result),b(result)) or
a is field and b is field and eq(a(field.type),b(field.type)) or
a is cons and b is cons and eq(a(hd),b(hd)) and eq(a(tl),b(tl))
```

Procedure eq has a body which is a rather large boolean expression which will check that the data type representations of two S-algol data types are equal. For scalar data types it is sufficient to test the two constant pointers for equality. For vectors, both the pointers must point to vector structures and have the same type of elements. Notice that the recursive calling of procedure eq deals with the case where a vector has more than one dimension. For procedures, the two representations must both represent procedures and must have a one to one correspondence in parameter and result types. Two structure classes must have the same fields and two fields must have the same field types before they are equal. Included in the procedure eq is a check that two linked lists have elements representing the same type. This allows the linked list of types for procedure arguments and structure class fields to be compared. The procedure will therefore accommodate any combination of the above data types.

It should be noted that procedure eq will only check that two type representations are the same. It will not check that either type is a legal type for the language being compiled. For example, the procedure would give the result **true** if it compared the representations of two vectors of procedures. Vectors of procedures are not allowed under the type construction rules of S-algol. Therefore the compiler must check elsewhere that illegal data objects are not being formed.

9.5 TYPE ERRORS

When the compiler discovers that the program it is compiling does not conform to the type rules of the language it must issue an error report. Again the situation is analogous to the syntax analysis layer where the compiler has a goal symbol and an actual symbol. Here the compiler has a goal type and an actual type. Therefore we will adopt the same approach as we did with the syntax analysis and build ourselves an abstraction similar to procedure mustbe in the syntax analysis which will take two types, check that they are equal and issue an error report if they are not. If we call the abstraction procedure match, it may be written as

```
procedure match(cpntr a,b)
if ~eq(a,b) do bad.types(a,b)

procedure bad.types(cpntr a,b)
error.message("** Type Error ** Type ",display(b),
              " found where Type ",display(a)," expected ")
```

If by convention, in the compiler, the first type represents the goal type and the second type the actual type, then the user will have little difficulty in understanding the error message. Notice that we have used the same procedure to print the error message as the syntax analysis does, thus unifying the error reporting mechanism. Procedure display takes a representation of a data type and produces the string name of that type. This is a simple task for scalar types but the procedure must again be recursive, like procedure eq, in order that it may evaluate all the possible data type combinations. The following will suffice.

```
procecure display(cpntr t -> string)
case true of
t is scalar        : t(t.name)
t is VECTOR        : star.sy ++ display(t(elements))
```

```
t is STRUCTURE  : "structure(" ++ display(t(fields)) ++")"
t is proc       : "procedure(" ++ display(t(args)) ++
                  "->" ++ display(t(result)) ++")"
t is field      : "field" ++"(" ++ display(t(field.type)) ++")"
t is cons       : display(t(hd)) ++ comma.sy ++ display(t(tl))
default         : ""
```

Procedure display will take care of the recursive nature of the type representations. Notice that we have again included a method of unravelling a linked list of types.

We will find later that there are a few occasions when not one but a number of types are legal. For example, if we compile the expression

a + b

then when we check the type of the first clause it may be int or real. In this case it is not sensible to issue the above error report, and we invent another abstraction called procedure bad.type to issue a clearer error message.

```
procedure bad.type(cpntr t)
error.message("** Type Error ** Type",display(t),
              "is not compatible here","","")
```

The two empty strings are to balance the number of parameters for procedure error.message.

The above settles the problem of reporting context sensitive type errors. What about recovery? Fortunately this problem is not as great as it was for syntax analysis. For every production in the syntax there is a type rule which means that in most cases we know the resultant type of the production. For example the **for** clause is always of type void and the **or** expression is always of type bool. Therefore we can report a type error and force recovery by always returning the correct type to the calling procedure. Thus the calling procedure will not see any type error and recovery will be complete. However in an incorrect program it is not always possible to form the types correctly and we must allow for this in the compiler. For instance what type should we force on

if a < b **then** 1 **else true**

When the compiler cannot form the type of a production correctly because it is in error, then we wish to report that error only once. Therefore we will introduce type ANY which the compiler can use in such cases. Type ANY is defined in the compiler by

let ANY = scalar("undefined")

By ensuring that type ANY will match any other type in the compiler we also ensure that no more error messages will be generated by this error. Type ANY will only be used until the syntax analyser has recovered at which point the legal type rules can be enforced by the parsing procedure.

To ensure that type ANY matches any other type we simply refine procedure eq to

```
procedure eq(cpntr a,b -> bool)
a = b or a = ANY or b = ANY or
a is VECTOR and b is VECTOR and eq(a(elements),b(elements)) or
a is STRUCTURE and b is STRUCTURE and eq(a(fields),b(fields)) or
a is proc and b is proc and eq(a(args),b(args)) and
                          eq(a(result),b(result)) or
a is field and b is field and eq(a(field.type),b(field.type)) or
a is cons and b is cons and eq(a(hd),b(hd)) and eq(a(tl),b(tl))
```

We have developed a very simple and inexpensive technique for matching types, reporting errors and recovering from type errors and will now demonstrate how the abstractions and the concepts involved are used in refining the syntax analyser.

9.6 THE TYPE CHECKING LAYER

Every procedure in the syntax analysis concerned with data types and type checking (and that includes nearly all of them in S-algol) must be re-written in this layer. We have already seen the declarations required in the compiler to represent the data types. We will assume that they have been made. The task of every procedure in the syntax analysis at this level is to check the type of everything that it causes to be parsed and to return the appropriate resultant type to the calling procedure.

We will develop this refinement in some detail in order to give the reader sufficient insight to perform it for his own language. The reader is advised to study this section well because it displays the essence of writing a recursive descent compiler by stepwise refinement. It should be compared with the version of the compiler in section 6.4. Let us start with procedure program.

```
BNF   <program> ::= <sequence> ?
TR    { VOID } ? => { VOID }
```

That is, the only valid programs are void sequences followed by "?"s. We may therefore write

```
procedure program
begin
      next.symbol
      match(VOID,sequence)
      mustbe(question.sy)
end
```

Procedure program does not need to return a type because it is only called from the main program and the type of the compiled sequence has already been checked. The call of procedure match takes the goal type void and the result of compiling a sequence. We move on to compiling sequences.

```
BNF  ⟨sequence⟩::= ⟨declaration⟩[;⟨sequence⟩] |
                   ⟨clause⟩[;⟨sequence⟩]

TR   ⟨declaration⟩ =⟩ { VOID }
     { VOID } ;{ T } =⟩ { T }
```

Thus a declaration is always of type void. The second rule indicates that a sequence is legally constructed only if every declaration and every clause followed by a semi-colon is of type void. If they are followed by a semi-colon and a further clause or declaration, of type T (where T can be void) then the whole sequence is of type T. Since declarations are always of type void the construction rule really applies to sequences of clauses but has to be made complete for the formal definition. The following will do for procedure sequence

```
procedure sequence(-> pntr)
begin
    let type := VOID
    let more := true

    repeat {
        match(VOID,type)
        case symbol of
        let.sy          : let.decl
        procedure.sy    : proc.decl
        structure.sy    : structure.decl
        forward.sy      : forward.decl
        default         : type := clause

        if ~have(semi.sy) do
            if recovering then
            begin
                while symbol ≠ semi.sy and ~eof do next.symbol
                recovering := false
            end else more := false }
    while more
    type
end
```

This constitutes the first major re-write. Each time round the loop (including the first time) the type is checked to be void. Since the declarations are all void and since the declaration procedures are only called from procedure sequence, they need not return a type. The declaration procedures will not alter the value of the variable called type. The result type is therefore either void or the type of the last compiled clause.

We continue to procedure clause

```
procedure clause(-> pntr)
case symbol of
if.sy          : if.clause
repeat.sy      : repeat.clause
while.sy       : while.clause
for.sy         : for.clause
case.sy        : case.clause
abort.sy       : abort.clause
write.sy       : write.clause
default        : expression
```

Little has changed here expect that the procedures on the right hand side of the case expression all return a type which is the result type of the clause being compiled.

Let us now take some of these clauses and consider them in turn. The **if** clause has two forms:

BNF **if**⟨clause⟩**do**⟨clause⟩
TR **if** { BOOL }**do** { VOID } =⟩ { VOID }

and

BNF **if**⟨clause⟩**then**⟨clause⟩**else**⟨clause⟩
TR **if** { BOOL }**then** { T }**else** { T } =⟩ { T }

which can be translated to

```
procedure if.clause(-> pntr)
begin
     next.symbol
     match(BOOL,clause)
     if have(do.sy) then { match(VOID,clause) ; VOID }  else
     begin
          mustbe(then.sy)
          let t = clause
          mustbe(else.sy)
          match(t,clause)
          t
     end
end
```

The first clause must be of type bool. In the **if . . . then . . . else** parsing, the two types must be the same giving the result type and in the **if . . . do** parsing, the type must be void. Notice how the type rule is enforced for the calling procedure by the **if . . . do** parsing section returning the type void whether a match was made or not. This is done whenever possible in the compiler for context sensitive error recovery. For example the **while** clause

```
BNF     while⟨clause⟩do⟨clause⟩
TR      while { BOOL }do { VOID } =⟩ { VOID }
```

would be coded as

```
procedure while.clause(–⟩ pntr)
begin
     next.symbol
     match(BOOL,clause)
     mustbe(do.sy)
     match(VOID,clause)
     VOID
end
```

It should be obvious that most of the S-algol clauses can be easily coded using the above technique. Some of the procedures present a few different ideas but nothing radically new. We will therefore turn our attention to expressions which require a little more persuasion to conform to our type matching technique than has been required up to now. We can also resolve the problems left by Chapter 6.

Let us start with the first two rules

```
BNF     ⟨expression⟩ ::= ⟨exp1⟩ [ or⟨exp1⟩] *
TR      { BOOL }or{ BOOL } =⟩ { BOOL }
```

A little explanation should help here. The type rule indicates that two expressions separated by the reserved word **or** must be of type bool with the result being type bool. Any other type combination is illegal in this context. However the BNF allows an expression on its own in which case the type will be decided by procedure exp1 and not procedure expression. Also the type rule may be applied any number of times allowing any number of boolean expressions separated by the reserved word **or**. We may code this as

```
procedure expression(–⟩ pntr)
begin
     let t = exp1

     case symbol of
     or.sy     : begin
                          match(BOOL,t)
                          while have(or.sy) do match(BOOL,exp1)
                          BOOL
                 end
     default   : t
end
```

Notice that if the **or** symbol is not present, then the type returned from procedure exp1 is the result type. Otherwise the result type is bool. We have re-arranged the code for this procedure so that the type of the first expression is checked before we parse the **or** symbol. In this way we keep the syntax and type error messages in phase and in the correct place on the printed line. We must remember to do this whenever necessary in the compiler.

Procedure exp1 is written from the rules

BNF ⟨exp1⟩ ::= ⟨exp2⟩ [**and** ⟨exp2⟩] *
TR { BOOL }**and**{ BOOL } =⟩ { BOOL }

which gives the code

```
procedure exp1(-> pntr)
begin
     let t = exp2

     case symbol of
     and.sy        : begin
                          match(BOOL,t)
                          while have(and.sy) do match(BOOL,exp2)
                          BOOL
                     end
     default       : t
end
```

which requires little explanation because it has the same form as procedure expression.

The next expression in the definition is more difficult mainly because it parses more symbols and deals with more data types. The procedure must also deal with our first unary operator. The defining rules are

BNF ⟨exp2⟩ ::= [~] ⟨exp3⟩ [⟨relop⟩⟨exp3⟩]

The relevant type rules are

~ { BOOL } =⟩ { BOOL }
{ PNTR } **is** { STRUCTURE } =⟩ { BOOL }
{ PNTR } **isnt** { STRUCTURE } =⟩ { BOOL }
{ T }={ T } =⟩ { BOOL }
{ T }≠{ T } =⟩ { BOOL }
{ TT }⟨relop⟩ {TT } =⟩ { BOOL }

where TT is one of the types int, real or string and T is any type. That is, equality and inequality are defined between any two S-algol data objects but the other relational operators are only defined on types int, real and string. We can code the procedure as

```
procedure exp2(-> pntr)
begin
    let not = have(not.sy)
    let t := exp3
    if not do { match(BOOL,t) ; t := BOOL }
    case symbol of
    is.sy,isnt.sy  : begin
                         match(PNTR,t)
                         next.symbol
                         mustbe(identifier.sy)
                         BOOL
                     end
    eq.sy,neq.sy : begin
                         next.symbol
                         match(t,exp3)
                         BOOL
                     end
    le.sy,lt.sy,
    ge.sy,gt.sy    : begin
                         t := rel.type(t)
                         next.symbol
                         match(t,exp3)
                         BOOL
                     end
    default        : t
end
```

There are two new problems here. First of all in compiling the relational operators **is** and **isnt**, we have not checked the type of the identifier. This will be done by the second stage of the context sensitive analysis and we shall leave it until Chapter 10 where we consider the use of identifiers. Secondly we must write procedure rel.type to check for a legal type for the selected relational operators. The following will serve

```
procedure rel.type(pntr t -> pntr)
case true of
t is STRING,
t is INT,
t is REAL : t
default     : { bad.type(t) ; ANY }
```

We now see how to code the situation where more than one but not all types are legal. Notice that when there is an error in a relational operator, the compiler issues an error message through procedure bad.type and not procedure bad.types (see section 9.5) before forcing recovery by returning type ANY.

We will leave out procedures exp3 and exp4 since we have probably given enough detail already. The procedures contain a few extra problems but again nothing essentially new.

Therefore we arrive at the parsing of the basic units of the expression. We cannot type check anything involving names yet but we will try the rest. For brevity we will not include any form of the vector expression because it is straightforward and we will leave it to the reader to code.

```
BNF
     ⟨exp5⟩ ::=  ⟨name⟩[(⟨clause⟩⟨bar⟩⟨clause⟩)] * |
                 ⟨literal⟩ |
                 {[⟨sequence⟩] } |
                 begin [⟨sequence⟩] end |
                 vector⟨bounds⟩of⟨clause⟩ |
                 @⟨clause⟩of⟨type1⟩⟨bra⟩⟨clause.list⟩⟨ket⟩ |
                 (⟨clause⟩)
TR
                 ⟨name⟩({ INT } | { INT }) =⟩ { STRING }
                 {literal } =⟩ { literal.type }
                 begin { T } end =⟩ { T }
                 vector { INT }::{ INT }, . . . . . of { T } =⟩ { *T }
                 @{ INT }of⟨type1⟩[{ T-clause.list }] =⟩ { *T }
                 ({ T }) =⟩ { T }
```

This gives rise to the code

```
procedure exp5
begin
     let t :=
     case symbol of
     identifier.sy      : { next.symbol ; ANY } ! for the moment return ANY
     literal.sy         : { let t = literal.type ; next.symbol ; t }
     begin.sy,lcb.sy    : block ! lcb stands for left curly bracket
     vector.sy,at.sy    : vector.exp
     lp.sy              : begin
                                   next.symbol
                                   let t = clause
                                   mustbe(rp.sy)
                                   t
                              end
default                 : { syntax("Expression") ; ANY }

if have(lp.sy) do if t = STRING then t := substring else
                  if t = PNTR or t is vector then t := exp.list(t)
                                                 else syntax(lp.sy)
if have(assign.sy) do
```

```
    begin
        next.symbol
        match(t,clause)
        t := VOID
    end
    t
end
```

This is not quite complete. The identifiers have not been type checked yet. Also an identifier may be the name of a structure creation or a procedure call both of which cases will be dealt with in Chapter 10. Procedure block would be

```
procedure block(—⟩ pntr)
begin
    let last = if symbol = begin.sy then end.sy else rcb.sy
    next.symbol
    if have(last) then VOID else
    begin
        let t = sequence
        mustbe(last)
        t
    end
end
```

to cover the type rules

begin end =⟩ { VOID }
begin { T }**end** =⟩ { T }

with similar rules for braces. The left parenthesis rule covers

({ T }) =⟩ { T }

and finally if it is none of these, we issue a syntax error report and return type ANY.

We have procedure substring to implement the type rule

⟨name⟩({ INT }⟨bar⟩{ INT }) =⟩ { STRING }

```
procedure substring(—⟩ pntr)
begin
    repeat {
            match(INT,clause)
            mustbe(bar.sy)
            match(INT,clause)
            mustbe(rp.sy) }
    while have(lp.sy)
    STRING
end
```

Finally procedure exp.list will require to find the types of structure fields when compiling field accesses and we will therefore save it up for Chapter 10 where declarations are considered more fully.

This completes a rather lengthy discussion of the stepwise refinement for the type matching layer. As can be seen the code has expanded and we will therefore only use sections of it in future refinements to keep this book to a reasonable length.

9.7 SUMMARY

The type checking layer constitutes the first major re-write in the stepwise refinement of our compiler. We have introduced a method of defining the type rules that works as a set of qualifying rules on the BNF specification of the context free syntax. It is our view that defining the language in this way has a twofold advantage. First, separating the two sets of rules makes the program forming rules easier to understand for the user and second, it makes it easier for the compiler writer to build the compiler in layers as we are doing.

Before we could write the code for this refinement we had to build representations of the data types being compiled and procedure eq was invented to check the equality of two data type representations. Using procedure eq and the representations we built an abstraction to match two data types and issue an error report if they were not compatible. It was also found necessary to have another method of error reporting when the compiler had more than one possible legal type.

The strategy for context sensitive error recovery was then devised. Using the type rules, every procedure in the syntax analysis was redesigned in order to check the type of any syntactic element it caused to be parsed, and to return the type of the object it had just parsed to the calling procedure. Thus each procedure becomes a function which performs the syntax analysis as the recursion progresses and the type checking as the recursion unwinds. When a syntax error was found and the type could not be formed correctly, the type ANY was used to eliminate spurious error messages and force recovery.

Finally, since it is the first major re-write of the syntax analysis, we spent a lot of effort describing how the ideas in this chapter are used in practice.

CHAPTER 10

Name and Scope Checking

10.1 THE NEED FOR A SYMBOL TABLE

In the second part of the context sensitive analysis we are concerned with the use of names in a program. The compiler needs to collect information on a name when it is declared and utilise that information when the name is subsequently referenced in order to check that it has been used legally. For the moment, in our compiler, all we need to record is the name itself and its type, but we will see later that we must extend this information to help in the generation of code. The link between declaration and use is made by recording the information in a data structure called the symbol table.

The symbol table is also used to help detect errors in a program. When a name is declared, a check must be made to ensure that it does not already exist in the same scope environment. Also when a name is used, the symbol table is consulted to ensure that it has been declared. If either of the above errors is detected then the abstractions which manipulate the symbol table must issue an error report. Obvious variations would be appropriate if we were compiling another language. For instance in Fortran the first use of a variable may also be its defining occurrence.

The symbol table is central to the operation of the compiler and must therefore be used efficiently. The main intrinsic aims of using the symbol table are to insert entries, access entries and model the scope rules of the language. The technological problems in using the symbol table centre around how to organise it in order that the intrinsic aims may be implemented efficiently in terms of time and space.

10.2 SYMBOL TABLE ORGANISATION

The problem of the symbol table organisation is essentially the same as the one we had in Chapter 7 when we considered the accessing of reserved words. The difference is that there are a fixed number of reserved words and that they are known in advance. This allows sensible predictions to be made on how the table should be laid out and accessed. Unfortunately the compiler writer has little chance of predicting which names a programmer will invent and therefore has to chose a general method of organisation that will perform well in most cases. Whichever method is used it is possible to invent a pathological set of names where the method will perform badly. As with the reserved word problem the three main methods of organisation are linear lists, binary trees and hash tables. We will study each in turn.

A symbol table which is organised as a linear list may be implemented by a vector or a linked list. If a vector is used, then the table will be of fixed size, enforcing an artificial limit on the number of names, but will carry no redundant information for each entry. If a linked list is used then the list may grow dynamically with the number of names in the program, but each entry must contain the overhead of the link. With both methods the insertion of an entry to the head of the linked list or the first free element of the vector is fast. The modelling of scope is also fast because we only have to remember where the scope levels start in the vector or list on entering a new level, and on scope exit we re-use the space in the vector or throw away part of the list for the **garbage collector** to deal with.

The main advantage of a linear technique is that it is simple to organise and code. The main drawback of the method is that it is very slow to access entries. The list must be scanned sequentially and in the correct scope order, since the same name may appear legally at different levels of scope. If there are n entries in the list there will be on average $n/2$ comparisons in an access but it will be much worse than this if names defined in outer blocks are used frequently.

Although the linear list method is simple to organise it almost never performs well enough in practice because of this excessive access time. Attempts have been made to speed up the access time but this usually comes at the expense of something else. For example, re-ordering the list if it is implemented as a vector and accessing the entries using a binary chop. This speeds up access but complicates the modelling of scope and slows down the insertion time. The scoping problem can be overcome by using a different vector for every level of scope but the insertion problem remains.

A symbol table organised as a binary tree gives the performance of the binary chop method without penalising insertion or scope modelling too badly. To each entry in the symbol table we add two fields, left and right, which are used to link the entries into a binary tree. We will assume that the tree is ordered alphabetically. The tree is organised such that any entry has the property that all the names which may be accessed through the left field are less than (i.e. come before in dictionary order) the name in the current node, and all the names that can be accessed through the right field are greater.

If the binary tree is balanced and has n entries then the average number of comparisons for insertion or access is $\log n$. This will almost certainly be faster than the sequential search. The problem of modelling scope is overcome by having a separate tree for every level of scope. This solution is reasonable since the table is not of fixed size but dynamically allocated. Therefore the only redundant space in the trees is in the left and right fields of every entry.

One disadvantage to the binary tree method is that the tree may become very unbalanced and therefore reduce to a linked list. This may be overcome by balancing the tree from time to time although this can be time consuming. However the problem is not too serious since it only arises if the programmer declares his names in alphabetical order. This is unlikely to happen unless the program has been produced automatically by some computational process e.g. a macro-generator.

The last technique for organising a symbol table that we will discuss is a hash table. The position of an entry in the hash table is determined by manipulating the characters in the name to give the **hash key** to the table. To calculate the hash key, the hash function may take into account the length of the string, the position of the characters in the string and the characters themselves. The hash key is then used to index the symbol table to find the required entry. In designing the hash function the trade-offs are between the speed of calculation of the key, the range of hash keys that the hash function gives and therefore the size of the hash table, and the distribution of the names over the table.

To insert a name into the hash table we calculate the hash key and index the table. If there is an entry already in the table at this position we have a **collision**. To overcome this problem we may use a second hash function to calculate a new key or we may link all the entries for one hash key together. Thus we may have to chain down a linked list to insert the entry. To access an entry in the symbol table the mechanism is the same as for insertion.

If too many names turn out to have the same hash key then we have a situation called **clustering**. Obviously we wish to avoid clustering because the mechanism may degenerate into searching a linked list. The choice of hash function controls the distribution of names over the table but it should be remembered that, even if the hash function performs well in testing, it may not in practice because the distribution of names in the test may not conform to real life situations. For this reason the hashing algorithm should be tested on non-random as well as random data and monitored in use.

An often neglected problem with hash tables is that it is awkward to model the notion of scope present in many so called Algol-like languages. The hash table could be duplicated for every level of scope but this is unwise because of its fixed size. Another method is to link all the entries for one level of scope together in a linked list in the table. However this will make insertion and scope exit expensive since we will have to construct and unravel the linked list.

Hash tables usually provide very fast insertion and access facilities. However they work better with languages which do not have Algol type scope rules e.g. Fortran and assemblers. How well a hash table will perform in practice depends on the hashing function, the set of programmer-provided names and the frequency of scope changes.

We must choose one of the above methods to implement our symbol table. Since we are primarily interested in the layering of the compiler and not the performance of the symbol table, we will use the binary tree method with a new tree for each scope level. This will illustrate the problems well and give fair performance.

10.3 MODELLING SCOPE

The symbol table for each level of scope is organised as a binary tree. When a new level of scope is entered a new binary tree is created and it is thrown away when we leave that level of scope. If the levels if scope are modelled as a linked list, then entering a scope level entails making a new node in the list. Leaving a level of scope entails throwing away the last node made in the list. By using the structure class called cons we can write the abstractions for entering and leaving a level of scope. They are:

```
let env.list := nil
procedure enter.scope ; env.list := cons(nil,env.list)
procedure exit.scope  ; env.list := env.list(tl)
```

The variable called env.list points to the start of the linked list of binary trees. On entering a level of scope a new node is constructed with a new binary tree as its head and the rest of the environment list as its tail. On leaving a level of scope we merely remove the current binary tree from the list. At any time in between, the local binary tree is addressed by env.list(hd).

We may now rewrite procedure block to model the scope levels.

```
procedure block(-> pntr)
begin
     let last = if symbol = begin.sy then end.sy else rcb.sy
     next.symbol
     if have(last) then VOID else
     begin
          enter.scope
          let t = sequence
          exit.scope
          mustbe(last)
          t
     end
end
```

The insertion of the two procedure calls ensures that all the names declared in the sequence are declared at the correct level and removed when we leave that level. This very simple mechanism must be used wherever the scope level changes.

10.4 DECLARATIONS

At this stage in the development of our compiler, the entries in the symbol table will contain the name of each object and its type. We therefore require a structure class to contain this information. It may be defined by

```
structure link(cstring name ; pntr type,left,right)
```

We will now consider the construction of the binary trees that model each level of scope. We must build an abstraction that will take a name and the type of an object and enter it in the tree. This is procedure declare

```
procedure declare(cstring s ; cpntr t)
env.list(hd) := enter(env.list(hd),link(s,t,nil,nil))
```

Procedure declare forms a new entry and calls procedure enter to place it in the tree. Since the binary tree may be empty we must update the head of the tree. No attempt is made to balance the tree in this version. However it could be made to do so at considerable expense. Procedure enter may be written as

```
procedure enter(cpntr head,new -> pntr)
case true of
head = nil                   : new
new(name) < head(name)  : begin
                                  head(left) := enter(head(left),new)
                                  head
                              end
new(name) > head(name)  : begin
                                  head(right) := enter(head(right),new)
                                  head
                              end
default : { error.message("The name",new(name),
                         "has","already been","declared") ; head }
```

The procedure enter takes an entry and places it on the binary tree unless the name is already there, in which case it reports an error. The parameter head is the head of the binary tree currently being scanned and new is the new entry.

We can now re-code the procedure to compile the **let** declaration to use these abstractions.

```
procedure let.decl
begin
    next.symbol
    let n = the.name
    mustbe(identifier.sy)
    let eq = have(eq.sy)
    if ~eq do mustbe(assign.sy)
```

```
        t := clause
        if t = VOID or t is field do { bad.type(t) ; t := ANY }
        declare(n,if eq then const(t) else var(t))
    end
```

This procedure is considerably different from what we last saw in section 6.4. We have introduced the type information and the checking for legal types. We have also introduced a new idea. When the name is declared we have made the type into a field of another structure which indicates whether the name is constant or variable. This is determined by whether the name is introduced using ":=" or "=". The definitions of the structure classes are

```
    structure const(cpntr const.type)
    structure var(cpntr var.type)
```

We will see shortly how this information is used.

There is one final point about the procedure to parse a **let** declaration: if the name is a duplicate then the error message will appear after the initialising clause which can be arbitrarily long. If this is not considered good enough then a check for duplication can be made earlier remembering to suppress the second error report that will be issued when the object is entered in the tree.

10.5 ACCESSING THE BINARY TREE

In accessing the symbol table, the syntax analysis procedures will provide a name and expect its type in return. Therefore we must provide an abstraction for this.

```
    procedure lookup(cstring s -> pntr)
    begin
        let entry = search.table(s)
        if entry = nil then
        begin
            error.message("Undeclared name **",s,"** has ","been ","used")
            declare(s, ANY)
            ANY
        end else entry(type)
    end
```

Procedure lookup searches the name table and if it finds a valid entry it returns the type of that object. If the search does not yield an entry then we have an undeclared name and an error report is issued. In this case the type ANY is returned to suppress further type errors. Notice that we have also declared the name so that the user only receives one error message for every undeclared name. To search the table we use

```
procedure search.table(cstring s -> pntr)
begin
      let tree := env.list ; let entry := nil
      while tree ≠ nil and entry = nil do
      begin
            entry := search.tree(s,tree(hd))
            tree := tree(tl)
      end
      entry
end
```

This procedure takes each binary tree in the environment list in turn and uses procedure search.tree to look for the name in the tree. The process stops when the entry is found or when we get to the end of the table. Notice that the binary trees are searched in scope order. We may write procedure search.tree as

```
procedure search.tree(cstring s ; cpntr head -> pntr)
begin
      let entry := head

      while entry ≠ nil and s ≠ entry(name) do
      entry := if s < entry(name) then entry(left) else entry(right)
      entry
end
```

Procedure search.tree searches the binary tree for a particular level of scope. The process stops when an entry is found or the tree has been completely scanned. Otherwise we descend the tree going left or right depending on the value of the name and the entry in the tree.

We have not quite finished with procedure lookup. When we entered the links in the tree we recorded whether the names were constants or variables. However this is only important if the names are used as L values i.e. on the left hand side on an assignment symbol. If the names are used as R values then it is of no importance whether they are variables or constants since we are not trying to assign to them but only require their value. We will need to rewrite procedure lookup to return the correct type if the name is used as an R value and its type plus the constant/variable information if the name is used as an L value. The procedure will be told how the name is used and we rewrite it as

```
procedure lookup(cstring s ; cbool r.value -> pntr)
begin
      let entry = search.table(s)
      if entry = nil then
      begin
            error.message("Undeclared name **",s,"** has ","been ","used")
```

```
            declare(s, ANY)
            ANY
        end else
        begin
            let this = entry(type)
            if r.value then
                case true of
                this is var : this(var.type)
                this is const : this(const.type)
                default : this
            else this
        end
    end
```

10.6 REFINEMENT OF THE SYNTAX ANALYSER

We are again in a position to refine the syntax analyser. This time we will refine any procedures which refer to the compilation of names in order to complete the type checking. The first place we encountered a name was in procedure exp2 (see section 9.6) and that part may be rewritten as

```
case symbol of
is.sy,isnt.sy : begin
                    match(PNTR,t)
                    next.symbol
                    t := lookup(the.name, R.value)
                    if t isnt STRUCTURE do bad.type(t)
                    mustbe(identifier.sy)
                    BOOL
                end
```

where R.value and L.value are defined by

```
let R.value = true ; let L.value = false
```

The procedure exp2 when compiling the sections for **is** and **isnt** now looks for the type of the name just found by the lexical analyser and checks that the type represents a structure class. The name may only be used as an R value in the situation.

The major use of the symbol table comes in procedure exp5. In the section that compiles identifiers we must complete the parsing and return the type. This will give the first part of procedure exp5 as

```
identifier.sy : begin
                    let n = the.name
                    next.symbol
```

```
        let t = lookup(n,symbol = assign.sy)
        if t is proc then proc.call(t) else
         if t is STRUCTURE then structure.creation(t) else t
    end
```

There are two items to notice here. Firstly, the identifier may be used as an L value or an R value and therefore the syntax analyser looks at the next symbol to see if it is the assignment symbol before indicating this to the procedure lookup. Secondly, if the type of the name is a procedure, then we have a procedure call which is parsed by the procedure proc.call. This procedure must return the correct type for the call. It may be coded as

```
procedure proc.call(cpntr t -> pntr)
begin
    let params := t(args)
    if params ≠ nil do
    begin
        mustbe(lp.sy)
        repeat { let param = params(hd)
                 if param is proc or param is STRUCTURE then
                 begin
                     match(param,lookup(the.name, R.value)
                     next.symbol
                 end else match(param,clause)
                 params := params(tl) }
        while have(comma.sy) and params ≠ nil
        mustbe(rp.sy)
    end
    t(result)
end
```

It can be seen in this procedure why we need to record the complete type information for procedure names. The procedure proc.call takes the linked list of parameter types, if there are any parameters, and checks them one by one against the clauses compiled. The apparent complication in matching the parameter types is because procedures and structure classes may be passed as parameters in which cases the clause will be an identifier only. The parsing of the parameters ceases when we run out of target parameters or commas. The procedure finally returns the result type of of the compiled procedure.

There is a procedure similar to proc.call to compile structure creations.

We can now return to the problem of parsing the assignment clause. In Chapter 6 we made the decision to parse it as

⟨expression⟩ ::= ⟨clause⟩

and correct this overgenerosity using the type rules. We now have to apply these type rules and restrict the left hand side to assignable objects. We laid the foundations of this earlier by recording in the symbol table an indication of whether an object is variable or not. We can therefore parse the assignment part of procedure exp5 by

```
if have(assign.sy) do
begin
    t := if t is var then t(var.type)
                     else { bad.type(t) ; ANY }
    next.symbol
    match(t,clause)
    t := VOID
end
```

The simplicity of this indicates the strength of the earlier design. However it still leaves one problem in the parsing of expressions. The problem arises in parsing clause lists that constitute vector or structure accessing. Since structure and vector accessing can be mixed freely in S-algol we can compile both in the same section of code. The resultant type of indexing will never be variable but we may wish to assign to a vector element or a structure field. We must therefore take care of this in procedure exp.list which can be written as

```
procedure exp.list(cpntr t -> pntr)
begin
    let base := t ; let new.type := nil
    mustbe(lp.sy)

    repeat new.type := subscript(base,clause)
    while have(comma.sy) do base := new.type

    mustbe(rp.sy)
    if symbol = assign.sy then var(new.type) else new.type
end

procedure subscript(cpntr base,index -> pntr)
if eq(PNTR,base) and index is field then index(fieldt) else
if base is vector and eq(INT,index) then base(elements) else
begin
    bad.types(base,index)
    ANY
end
```

These procedures compile any combination of structure field and vector element accesses as defined by the syntax. Note how the type checking is enforced by procedure subscript and how the type is altered if the element can be assigned to.

10.7 SUMMARY

The compiler uses the symbol table as a link between the declaration of a name and its use. The information placed in the symbol table on the declaration of a name is used to check that subsequent uses of the name are valid. Whilst the symbol table is used in performing this function it will also be used to report errors when they are encountered.

Since the symbol table is central to the operation of the compiler it must be used efficiently. The intrinsic aims of the symbol table involve inserting entries, accessing entries and modelling scope. The technological problems of implementing the symbol table centre around implementing these intrinsic aims efficiently.

The methods of implementing the symbol table were discussed in detail. As with the reserved word problem in Chapter 7, the three methods are linear lists, binary trees and hash tables. For our compiler we chose a linked list of binary trees for the symbol table.

Abstractions to insert entries, access entries and model scope in the symbol table were then invented and coded and finally applied to the syntax analyser to complete the context sensitive analysis.

CHAPTER 11

Abstract Machine Design

11.1 COMPILER OUTPUT

We have completed both the syntactic and the context sensitive analysis phases of our compiler and are now ready to add the final layers of code generation. The code generated by the compiler is a program which is semantically equivalent to the source program but may vary depending on the target machine. There are a number of design aims that the compiler writer may wish to achieve in generating code. For example, the designer may wish the compiler to produce code which may be input to an assembler, another compiler or a loader or be directly executable on a real machine or even by an interpreter. No matter which of the above options or variants of these options is chosen, the compiler's task is essentially the same and only the output strings differ.

The designer may also wish the compiler to be portable or to produce efficient code. These are usually conflicting design aims; the more efficient the code becomes, the more specialised the code generation has to be thereby losing its generality of application and portability. The code generation will always be machine dependent and all the compiler writer can achieve is to limit the machine dependency while attaining an acceptable level of code efficiency. The portability of the compiler and the efficiency of the generated code therefore depend on the emphasis placed on these aims when designing the compiler.

To generate any code at all the compiler must simulate the execution of the program being compiled. The simulation may vary from a simple simulation of the stack levels in an Algol-like language to an elaborate static analysis of the program being compiled. The efficiency of the code depends on the sophistication of this simulation. The portability of the code produced also depends on the simulation but it should be realised that this is different from the portability of the compiler itself which will depend on how isolated from the rest of the compiler the code generation can be made. This can be achieved by inventing abstractions for the code generation and restricting the machine dependencies to these abstractions. Implementing the compiler on another machine should only entail rewriting the code generation abstractions and then compiling this new version of the compiler with the already existing working one. This idea is called bootstrapping and is discussed further in Chapter 13.

In the earlier chapters we deliberately restricted ourselves to one pass recursive descent compilers as outlined in Chapter 5. So far in the syntactic and the context sensitive analysis we have not met any design aim that would cause us to alter the one pass nature of the compiler. However, to achieve portability, it may be sensible to organise the compiler as two separate programs or passes. The first pass would perform the lexical, syntactic and context sensitive analysis and output a machine-independent form of the program. The second pass would then take this intermediate form and produce code for the target machine. This means that all the machine dependencies could be contained in the second pass which would be the only part of the compiler to be rewritten when moving to another machine.

Several well known and successful compilers are organised in this manner. For example, the Pascal P-code compiler [1] is a recursive descent compiler which produces as output an assembly language program for a hypothetical abstract machine, the P-code machine. The assembly code can then be assembled, loaded and executed by an interpreter. Alternatively the assembly code can be translated into real machine code by a second pass code generator. This achieves a fair level of portability but has the drawback that the full power of the target machine may be difficult to realise, especially if the P-code instructions are less powerful than the target machine instructions.

The problem of code generation could easily fill a book on its own. We do not have the space to involve ourselves in discussing solutions to the problem at great length. The reader is therefore referred to Aho and Ullman [9] for further coverage of this topic. In order to keep this section understandable and short, and since the variety of real machines is so great, we will design an abstract machine to run S–algol and invite the reader to adapt this abstract machine for his own use where necessary. We can then generate code for this abstract machine and complete our compiler.

While it is obviously easier to generate code for an ideal abstract machine than a real computer, the mechansim is the same and our compiler will be just as complete. We will not adopt the Pascal approach but rather meet all the problems head on by producing code which can be directly executed without the aid of an assembler or loader. This is equivalent to producing a directly executable core image for a real machine. To produce code for a real machine, the code generation section of the compiler could be altered so that, instead of issuing the abstract machine instructions, it could issue a sequence of instructions for the real computer. We will therefore gain little in illustrating the construction of the compiler by generating real machine code rather than abstract machine code.

For the rest of this chapter we will discuss the design of the S–algol abstract machine.

11.2 THE S-ALGOL ABSTRACT MACHINE

The architecture of any abstract machine should be determined by the power of the language it has to support. The recursive nature of the block structured languages, such as the Algols, lends itself to implementation by a stack as described by Hauck and Dent [2]. Most of the implementations of the Algols are based on variations of the beta machine of Randell and Russell [3]. However it should be noted that the beta machine is not sufficient to support languages such as Algol W, Pascal, Algol 68 or S-algol which, although predominately stack based, require a second area of dynamically allocated store usually known as the heap. Many variations of the beta machine exist (e.g. Pascal P-code [1] is such a machine) and wherever possible the S-algol machine has drawn on their experience. The overall design tenet was to design a simple machine to support S-algol. The resultant machine is the S-algol machine and its description falls naturally into the three categories of stack organisation, heap organisation and the instruction set.

11.3 THE STACK

The S-algol compiler produces S-code which is a form of **reverse polish** instruction code. The S-code is ideally executed on a stack machine. The stack is used to facilitate block and procedure entry and exit, to provide space for programmer-named objects and to provide space for expression evaluation. Expression evaluation is always performed on the re-usuable space at the top of the stack and, since the technique is well known, little more will be said about it here.

On block or procedure entry or exit, information is placed on or removed from the stack. This information which contains a **Mark Stack Control Word** (MSCW), space for local objects, parameters and working space for expression evaluation, is sometimes known as a **stack frame**. Since the length of each stack frame can be different, they must be linked together to allow correct exit from the block or procedure. Therefore, the MSCW contains a **dynamic link** which points to the base of the previously activated stack frame. Thus the dynamic links form a chain of the currently activated blocks or procedures, known as the **dynamic chain**.

By its very nature the stack records the dynamic evaluation of a program. Some method is required to reflect the static nature (i.e. the scope rules), since not all of the stack frames available on the stack need be in scope. The MSCW contains a second pointer, known as the **static link**, which points to the stack frame of the immediate static outer block or procedure. These static links form the **static chain** which can be used to find the stack frame base of any block or procedure that is in scope.

The position of a stack frame for a block or a procedure on the stack may vary depending on the dynamic evaluation of the program. Therefore, the compiler cannot calculate the absolute address of stack items other than those of the outermost block. However, if dynamic vectors are disallowed as stack items (it will be shown later that S-algol vectors cannot be implemented on the stack anyway), the address of a stack item relative to its stack frame base may be calculated at compile time.

For each item on the stack the compiler produces an address pair ⟨ll,dd⟩ where ll is the lexicographic level and dd is the displacement from the stack frame base.

This address pair is used at run time to calculate the absolute address of the stack item. Note that if the stack frame base of the item was to be found by chaining down the static chain, the clever compiler [4] would calculate, instead of ll, the difference in the current lexicographic level and that of the required item, because this is the number of times to link down the static chain.

The next refinement is to use a vector or even better fast registers to form a display [3]. The display duplicates the values in the static chain and thus the absolute address of any item on the stack is

display(ll) + dd

Finally, Wichmann [4] has shown that stack frames are only required for procedures, as blocks can be considered as part of the procedure and their stack item addresses calculated relative to the procedure stack frame base. This technique is called **procedure level addressing** and extends with a slight modification to languages with block expressions.

11.4 THE S-ALGOL STACK

S-algol was designed to be used to write programs in the style of structured programming. By studying programs written in such a manner, two observations relevant to this discussion can be made. Firstly, structured programs tend to consist of a large number of small procedures which are called many times. Secondly, the objects referred to in these procedures tend to be local or outer block globals. It is therefore reasonable to design an abstract machine which takes advantage of this to obtain an efficient implementation.

The display method of implementing the stack has two major drawbacks. Updating the display may be complex. If the environment changes drastically, the overhead in updating the display is increased. This situation occurs on returning from a procedure declared at a lower level than the calling one, and with procedures passed as parameters. Some compilers (e.g. Algol W [5]) panic because of this and simply dump the whole display on to the stack on procedure entry and restore it on exit. This is a gross misuse of storage and is not sensible unless a great deal of store is available and the dumping process is fast.

The other main difficulty of the display scheme is that it relies on there being enough spare registers on the target machine to reflect the depth of static nesting in any program. In most cases this usually leads to some arbitrary restriction on the depth of nesting. While this may be good enough for handwritten programs it is very rarely satisfactory for automatically produced programs.

The S-algol abstract machine requires two registers, called **stack base**, SB, and **stack front**, SF, which point to the global and local stack frame bases respectively. Only one register, SF, is absolutely necessary since the base of the stack may be fixed. On procedure entry SF is made to point to the new stack frame base and on exit it is restored from the dynamic link.

Thus, since the compiler will be made to issue separate instructions for locals and outer block globals, they can be quickly accessed by using the SF and SB registers. Other free variables are accessed via the static chain. The method is as fast as the display technique for accessing locals and outer block globals, and does not suffer from any artificial limit on the static depth.

A simple and efficient method of procedure entry and exit is now possible. Since a procedure can be passed as a parameter and is subject to the same scope rules as other items, it suggests that it could be implemented as a stack item. When a procedure is declared two items are placed on the stack as an initialisation. These are the procedure entry point address and its static link and are collectively called the **procedure closure.** Each procedure forms a segment of code. The only evidence of one segment having been part of another is the instruction to load the closure. The static link may be calculated when the load closure instruction is executed: it is merely the current stack frame base since this represents the environment in which the procedure was declared. This can simply be copied and need not be recalculated on each procedure call.

A procedure call consists of an instruction to load the closure, code to evaluate the parameters, and an instruction to enter the procedure. The mark stack control word contains

1. The procedure address
2. The static link
3. The dynamic link
4. The return address

The first two items form the procedure closure and the second two are calculated just before entry. The closure uniquely represents the procedure on the stack. To pass a procedure as a parameter requires the closure to be copied. Thus, the procedure parameter will look like a locally declared procedure when it is called.

Procedure exit is extremely simple since resetting the SF pointer is all that is required. No updating of the static chain is required as it is uncovered to the position on the point of entry automatically. Naturally, stack retraction must take place on procedure and block exit and extra care must be taken if they return values.

Whether this technique is more efficient than the display method depends upon:

1. The number of spare registers on the target machine.
2. The number of non-global free variable accesses
3. The number of procedure calls
4. The number of procedures passed as parameters

and is discussed further by Morrison [6].

11.5 THE HEAP

The design of the world of data objects in S-algol makes it impossible for the language to be implemented on a stack-only system. In particular, strings, vectors and structures need a second area of dynamically allocated store known as the heap.

In S-algol, vectors are first class data objects. They enjoy the same **civil rights** as any other data object including assignment, being fields of other vectors or structures and being passed to procedures. On a stack system with variable size vectors, as in S-algol, it is impossible to copy the vectors on assignment because the space required to hold the vector on the stack cannot be predicted. Therefore, a vector is represented by a pointer on the stack with the elements on the heap. The value of the vector is the pointer and assigning the vector means copying the pointer. Because pointers are of uniform stack size, the problem is overcome.

The S-algol structures suffer from the same problem as the vectors. Indeed the language is designed to make vectors and structures behave in a similar manner. Structures may be of any class and so of any size. For exactly the same reasons as with vectors, structures are implemented as pointers on the stack which point to the structure fields on the heap.

Since the programmer may alter the fields of a structure or the elements of a vector, he needs to know that vectors and structures are implemented as pointers. For example, a vector passed to a procedure which alters one of the elements has the element altered forever. Strings, on the other hand, are pure data objects and may not be altered internally by the programmer. However, strings also have the same size problems as vectors and structures. They are therefore implemented on the heap with a pointer to them on the stack. The pointer in this case is not seen by the programmer.

The abstract machine data structures on the heap must also contain some housekeeping information to allow them to be used correctly. They are listed for each item

1. Vectors must carry their bounds for run time bound checking and an indication if the elements are pointers for garbage collection purposes.
2. Structures must carry a **trademark** for run time structure class checking and some means of specifying which fields are pointers for structure creation and garbage collection.
3. Strings must carry their size for index checking.

How this is implemented efficiently on a given target machine is a problem for the ingenuity of the implementor.

The above discussion is rather specific to S-algol and other solutions, though similar, may have to be found to implement other languages.

11.6 HEAP ORGANISATION

The Algol family of languages present the user with a conceptually infinite store. The stack simulates this by reusing the store allocated to blocks no longer in use. The design philosphy of S-algol does not wish to alter this and since the difference between stack and heap objects is hidden from the user, the heap as well as the stack must be re-used. Of course, the pretence breaks down when the store is finally exhausted and can not be re-used. The technique of garbage collection is used with the heap to simulate an infinite store.

At any point in the execution of an S-algol program, the space on the heap may be

1. allocated and in use
2. allocated and not in use
3. free

Space is allocated on the heap until there is no more available. At this point it is possible to have space allocated which is no longer in use. When the free space is exhausted it is the job of the garbage collector to free the space which is allocated and no longer in use. This is performed in two stages by marking and collecting.

In the marking phase, the pointers on the stack are used to identify some heap items in use. The search is recursive since heap items may point to other heap items. Readers of Chapter 2 may see this as a closure operation. Thus all the space in use will be marked. Once the heap has been marked all the unmarked space is freed with the possibility of coalescing the free areas into larger blocks or compacting the used space to one end of the heap.

The main difficulty in this is to identify the pointers on the stack at any instant during the execution of a program. Some pointers are trivial to find because they are at a fixed location relative to the stack frame base. However, the position of some other pointers on the stack depends upon the dynamic flow of the program. Consider the example

structure vecs(***int** V1)
let A = vecs(@1 **of int** [1,2,3])

If a garbage collection strikes between the creation of the vector [1,2,3] and that of the structure, the pointer to the vector will be at an arbitrary position on the stack and therefore difficult to identify. A solution could be to chain all the pointers on the stack together but this will slow down the use of items with pointers. Of course, a tagged data architecture machine has no difficulty with this problem and is the best solution all round. However for implementation on traditional machine architecture S-algol proposes a new, simple and extremely obvious solution.

The S-algol system has a separate stack for all pointers. The compiler can always predict the type of an item and therefore on which stack it will live. The marking algorithm has no difficulty in finding the initial pointers because they are all on the pointer stack. Thus a potentially awkward situation is overcome.

The drawbacks to the two stack solution are as follows.

1. A third area of dynamically allocated store must be found in the total address space. This is often no problem at all.
2. The second stack must be administered like the first to map the static and dynamic flow of the program.

The solution to the second problem is to allocate two registers, **pointer stack front**, PSF, and **pointer stack base**, PSB, to point at the current pointer stack frame base and the global pointer stack frame base. The main stack already maps the dynamic and static flow of the program. By including in the mark stack control word a pointer across to the equivalent pointer stack frame base, all the intermediate pointer stack frames may be found by linking down the main stack static chain and then using the pointer to the pointer stack frame.

The mark stack control word now contains

1. the procedure address
2. the static link
3. the dynamic link
4. the pointer stack link
5. the return address.

This, of course, complicates procedure entry and exit. However, the problem of identifying these anonymous pointers is such a nasty one that the price paid is felt to be small.

11.7 THE ABSTRACT MACHINE CODE

The S-algol abstract machine uses four storage areas

1. the instruction code area
2. the main stack
3. the pointer stack
4. the heap.

It also has seven special purpose registers

1. stack front	SF
2. stack base	SB
3. pointer stack front	PSF
4. pointer stack base	PSB
5. stack top	SP
6. pointer stack top	PSP
7. code pointer	CP.

The S-code generated by the compiler for each syntactic construct is given in Appendix E and the S-code instructions are described in detail in Appendix D. A general discussion of the more unusual items of the S-code design are given here.

11.8 THE STACK INSTRUCTIONS

The S-code machine has the usual battery of stack instructions. There are arithmetic instructions, such as plus, which perform operations on the top of the stack and leave their result there. The relational operations such as less than operate on ints, reals and strings and leave a boolean result on the top of the stack. There are instructions to load literal values on to the stack and instructions to load other stack items on to the top of the stack prior to being used. This last group requires three forms since the stack objects may be local, global or intermediate depending on their scope. The type of the operand is used to indicate which stack is to be used.

There are a number of miscellaneous instructions such as 'erase the top of the stack', 'exchange the top two elements' and 'assign the top element to the address given in the second top'. Another stack instruction is retract which is used on block exit.

No code is required for block entry if we use procedure level addressing. However, on block exit the stack top registers may have to be changed to get rid of any locals on the stack. For instance the block

```
begin
   let a = 3
   let b = 4
   write 3 * 4
end
```

will have to remove the items called "a" and "b" from the stack on block exit. Furthermore, if the block returns a value this must be copied to the new stack top.

11.9 THE HEAP INSTRUCTIONS

The heap instructions fall into two categories

1. those which create heap objects and therefore may cause garbage collection
2. those which use the heap items

The string operations which create strings on the heap are concat.op which concatenates two strings forming a new one, substr.op which selects characters from a string to form another, and finally read.string.

Creating structures is more complicated.

e.g.

structure abc(**int** a ; **cstring** b ; ***real** c)
let A = abc(1,"ron", @1 **of real** [1,2,3])

The code generated for the structure creation is

load the trademark from the stack
evaluate the expressions for the fields
form.structure(*n*)

The trademark, which uniquely identifies the structure class and will be generated by the compiler, is loaded on to the top of the stack and is *n* elements from the stack frame base. The expressions are evaluated on the appropriate stack depending on their type. The trademark must carry some indication of which fields are pointers in order to take them off the correct stack when filling them in. This information is also required in the marking phase of the garbage collector.

There are two forms of vector creation. An example of the first

@1 **of int** [2,3,45]

generates the code

```
ll.sint(1)
ll.sint(2)
ll.sint(3)
ll.sint(45)
make.vector(n)
```

The expression types are int and therefore on the main stack. If the expressions are pointer values they will be found on the pointer stack. *n* gives the position of the lower bound on the main stack relative to the stack frame base. It is a simple matter to calculate the size of the vector, create it on the heap and fill in the elements. The second form of vector creation is illustrated by

vector 1::10,2::11, ... **of** "abc"

which generates

evaluate the bound pairs on the stack
evaluate "abc"
iliffe.s(n)

The base type of the vector is string. The name illiffe is after Iliffe [7] who first proposed such a structure. *n* is the number of bound pairs. This instruction is not trivial to implement as the creation of the vector entails the recursive creation of the constituent vectors.

There are a number of instructions to access the heap items, the most important being the subscripting operations which have to check an index against vector bounds, that a field is correct for a structure class or that a substring is legal for the size of string being accessed. The run time structure class checking of S-algol is performed by these instructions.

11.10 FLOW OF CONTROL INSTRUCTIONS

These instructions are necessary to map the rich set of high level language constructs in S-algol which alter the program flow of control. The first pair of these instructions is used to implement the non-strict version of **and** and **or**

E1 **or** E2 => jumptt(l) E2 l:

Non-strictness refers here to the fact that the expression is evaluated from left to right until the result is known. This may occur before all the sub-expressions are evaluated. Since **true or** anything gives **true**, and **false or** anything gives anything, jumptt branches if the top stack element is **true** and merely removes it otherwise. A similar sequence can be used for **and** but with jumpff replacing jumptt.

An unconditional jump and a jump if the top stack element is false is sufficient to implement the **if** and loop clauses.

if E1 **then** E2 **else** E3 => E1 jumpf(l) E2 jump(m) l: E3 m:

and

while E1 **do** E2 => l:E1 jumpf(m) E2 jump(l) m:

The **for** clause is controlled by two instructions, one to perform the test at the beginning of the loop and one to perform the step at the end. The code generated for the **for** clause is

for i = E1 **to** E2 **by** E3 **do** E4 =>
E1 E2 E3 l :fortest(m) E4 forstep(l) m:

The control constant, limit and increment are at the top of the main stack. The fortest instruction decides if the loop is finished and jumps if it is. This is used in conjunction with the forstep instruction at the end of the loop which adds the increment to the control constant and jumps back to the beginning of the loop. Notice that the limit, increment and initial value are only calculated once before the start of the loop. This would have been different if we had been implementing the Algol 60 **for** statement which re-evaluates the values on every iteration.

Finally, under flow of control instructions, the code sequences to perform procedure entry and exit are examined. The code to call a procedure is

```
mst.load
evaluate the parameters
apply.op(m)
```

The mst.load instruction, of which there are three forms depending on the scope of the procedure, loads the closure on to the top of the stack, fills in the dynamic link, the pointer stack link and the return address. After the parameter expressions have been evaluated on the stack, apply.op is used to call the procedure. The number m gives the position of the new value of SF relative to SP.

Apply operates like this

1. calculate new SF = SP − m
2. PSF = PSL
3. fill in the return address
4. move the contents of the stack location pointed at by SF to CP. This will perform the branch.
5. check that there is enough stack space to execute the procedure.

If there are no parameters the mst.load and apply instructions are combined into one instruction. The code for the procedure itself ends with the return instruction. The first two words of the procedure are the maximum amount of stack space, on each stack, that the procedure may require. The apply instruction checks that the space is available. On some machine architectures (see Multics [8]) this is not necessary. The return instruction is more complex and works like this.

1. move the result of the procedure, if any, at SP or PSP to the new stack top at SF or PSF and set SP and PSP to these values
2. move the dynamic link to SF
3. move the pointer stack link of the uncovered frame to PSF
4. move the return address to CP.

11.11 SUMMARY

It can be seen that the S-code machine retains the spirit of the beta machine for its stack environments. The display mechanism however is gone. It was necessary to add a heap to the machine to implement vectors, structures and strings. The problem of identifying the pointers on the stack at garbage collection time leads to the implementation of a second stack for the pointers only. This complicates the abstract machine but it is felt that it solves the original problem so well that the complexity is a good investment.

The implementation of S-algol on a machine with two stacks and a heap requires that the abstract machine code will be different from other abstract machine codes. However, a lot of the instructions are common to most reverse polish machines and it is only the architecture of the S-machine which makes the instructions different. There are also some new instructions which allow the more esoteric S-algol constructs to be implemented at a fairly high level.

It was one of the design aims of S-algol that the user need not know the difference between stack and heap objects. It was therefore necessary to re-use the heap just as the stack is re-used. This introduced the garbage collector which in turn led to the invention of the two stacks.

REFERENCES

[1] Nori, K. V. *et al.* (1974), *The Pascal P Compiler Implementation Notes,* Technical Report No. 10, Zurich.

[2] Hauck, E.A. and Dent, B.A. (1968), Burroughs B6500/6700 stack mechanism, *AFIPS SJCC,* 245-251.

[3] Randell, B. and Russell, L. J. (1964), *Algol 60 Implementation,* Academic Press.

[4] Wichmann, B. (1973), *Algol 60 Compilation and Assessment,* Academic Press.

[5] Bauer, H., Becker, S. and Graham, S. (1968), Algol W implementation, *Technical Report No. CS98,* Stanford University.

[6] Morrison, R. (1977), A method of implementing procedure entry and exit, *Software Practice and Experience,* 7, 537-539.

[7] Iliffe, J. K. (1968), *Basic Machine Principles,* Elsevier.

[8] Corbato, F. J. and Vyssotsky, V. A. (1965), Introduction and overview of the multics system, *AFIPS FJCC,* 27, 185-196.

[9] Aho, A. V. and Ullman, J. H. (1977), *Principles of Compiler Design,* Addison-Wesley.

CHAPTER 12

Code Generation

12.1 SIMULATED EVALUATION OF THE S-ALGOL MACHINE

In Chapter 11 we introduced the S-code machine which is the target computer for our compiler. We are now ready to use the definition of the S-code machine to add the final layer of code generation to the compiler. However the first part of the code generation layer is to decide how detailed the simulation of the abstract machine should be and how it may be modelled inside the compiler.

To compile a language that has block expressions into code for a machine with procedure level addressing, the compiler must simulate the action of the stack pointer in order to calculate the address of a declared object relative to the stack frame base. For example in

```
procedure abc
begin
    let a = 3
    let c := if a < 2 then
             begin
                   let b = 4
                   .
                   .
                   .
                   .
```

To calculate the position of "b" on the stack we must record the position of everything else declared before it on the stack. In the case of S-algol the position of the top of both the main stack and the pointer stack must be simulated. We introduce the integer variables sp and psp by

```
let sp := 0 ;  let psp := 0
```

to record the number of stack units that the top of each stack is displaced from its stack frame base. Since these values are relative to the stack frame bases they must be stored and re-stored every time a new procedure declaration is compiled. Thus a procedure always starts with the value zero for sp and psp.

We also require abstractions to simulate the actions of pop and push on both stacks. The following will do

```
let st.size = 1 ; let pst.size = 1
procedure pop.ms ; sp := sp − st.size
procedure push.ms ; sp := sp + st.size
procedure pop.ps ; psp := psp − pst.size
procedure push.ps ; psp := psp + pst.size
```

We use separate constants for the two stack sizes because in some implementations they may be of different sizes. The code for these abstractions should be obvious, but it is worth pointing out that at this compile time simulation level we do not care what the values on the stacks are as we only require to calculate their addresses.

The next part of the code generation is to simulate the execution of each abstract machine instruction inside the compiler. This is done by inventing an abstraction for every S-code instruction that will manipulate the stack pointers. We will also make these abstractions generate code for the instruction. When the syntax analyser wishes to generate code for a particular construct it uses the code generation abstractions. By restricting the simulation to these abstractions and gathering them together in the compiler we can localise the machine dependent parts and improve portability.

To illustrate the general form of the code generation abstractions we will give one example now and the others as required. The code generated from the **div** expression is defined by

E1 **div** E2 =⟩ E1 E2 div.op

The div.op instruction takes two integers from the main stack, performs a **div** operation on them and leaves the integer result on the main stack. The simulation inside the computer updates the stacks and generates code. For the **div** instruction it is

```
procedure div.op
begin
    generate.code(div.inst)
    pop.ms
end
```

This very simple procedure performs the simulation for the **div** instruction. First of all it generates the code to be output using the procedure generate.code which we will return to shortly. For every instruction there is a constant integer defined as the operation code of that instruction. In this case the constant is called div.inst and corresponding names will be used for the other operations. The net effect of the operation is to remove one element from the main stack.

To generate code for the S-code machine it is not sufficient just to simulate the action of the stack pointers. Because some of the instructions, those for flow of control, contain code addresses, the compiler must also simulate the action of the code pointer. We introduce the variable cp by

```
let cp := 0
```

to simulate the code pointer. Every time an instruction is generated the code pointer is incremented by one. Before we use this however we must resolve an organisational problem.

In a one pass compiler, the code is produced as the compilation progresses. In a program with procedures, the code for the procedure will appear in the middle of the enclosing segment, a segment being the main program or a procedure. The compiler must take some action to ensure that the procedure is only executed on a call and not on the occurrence of its declaration. Furthermore the one pass organisation causes problems for instructions with forward code references; that is, some instructions contain references which are not known when the instruction is generated. These two problems can be solved for S-algol by the same mechanism.

When code is generated by the compiler it is stored in a vector instead of being written out immediately. The jump instructions in S-code are only generated by high level language constructs. Since there is no goto clause in the language it is a simple task to separate forward and backward references. For backward references the parsing procedure must retain the position of the jump address (by recording the value of cp) and supplying it to the code generation procedure. In S-code all the jump addresses are self relative, that is relative to the position of the jump instruction itself, therefore the following procedure will simulate an unconditional backward jump to the position in the code given by old.cp.

```
procedure bjump(cint old.cp)
begin
     generate.code(bjump.inst)
     generate.code(cp − old.cp + 1)
end
```

There is no updating of the stacks required here, only the generation of the jump instruction and the jump address.

Forward references present a much more difficult problem. Because the jump cannot be calculated when the instruction is generated, the compiler must remember all the references to a forward label until the value of the label is known. For instance this occurs in a **case** clause where each internal case must end with a jump to a common continuation point after the default option. This is easily done in our system by chaining together all these references by a backward linked list in the code vector. Each link in the list points to the previous reference to the label. The list may be terminated by an illegal address such as −1. To simulate the action of the unconditional forward jump, the code generation procedure takes the list so far and places this reference at its head before returning the start of the new list.

```
procedure fjump(cint list -> int)
begin
    generate.code(fjump.inst)
    generate.code(list)
    cp - 1
end
```

That is, the procedure places the previous head of the list in the code vector using the procedure generate.code and returns the position of this reference. Thus the syntax analysis procedures only have to remember the last reference to a label, the rest of the list being held in the code vector.

When the value of a label is known the compiler must chain down the linked list and alter every reference to the correct self relative value. If the code is held in the vector called code.vector then the following procedure will resolve all the forward references to a label.

```
let end.list = -1

procedure setlab(cint list)
begin
    let this.link := list
    while this.link ≠ end.list do
    begin
        let next.link = code.vector(this.link)
        code.vector(this.link) := cp - this.link -1
        this.link := next.link
    end
end
```

When a segment is completely compiled there will be no unresolved references within the segment since all the references are generated by complete high level language constructs. Also, because there is no goto clause, there will be no external references in the segment. This means that the segment is complete and may be written out. If the segment is a procedure it will be replaced by its closure in the code vector. Thus the segments are all positioned in the program separately. In no case will one be embedded in another and we therefore need not generate jumps around them. The position of the segment in the code is recorded by its closure if the segment is a procedure, and by the program start address if the segment is the main program. Thus we have solved the problem of procedures only being executed by a call, and the forward reference problem by storing up the code for a segment in a vector until the segment is complete.

The code instructions are placed in the code vector using the procedure generate.code which may be written as:

```
procedure generate.code(cint n)
begin
      code.vector(cp) := n
      cp := cp + 1
end
```

Notice that it is this procedure which increments the value of the code pointer every time an instruction is generated.

The simulation we have proposed is the bare minimum required to generate code for S-algol. For portability the simulation is confined to the code generation abstractions. By rewriting these procedures code can be produced for different machines. Similarly the abstractions may be further refined to produce more efficient code. We will return to the simulation procedures but let us now turn to the first code generation layer.

12.2 DECLARATIONS AND THE USE OF THE SYMBOL TABLE

The first layer of code generation involves redesigning the symbol table and rewriting the abstractions that use the symbol table. For every item recorded in the table we must add the stack address of that item to the symbol table information. The stack addresses are in pairs ⟨ll,dd⟩ as described in Chapter 11 and therefore the structure which holds the symbol table information is now defined by:

```
structure link(cstring name ; cint ll,dd ; pntr type,left,right)
```

The stack address calculated from ll and dd will be a main stack address except for objects of type vector, pntr or string, in which case the pointer stack address is recorded. The procedure declare will enter this information in the symbol table. The displacement of an item from the stack frame base is the value of the simulated stack pointer at the point of declaration. We introduce the variable lex.level to record the current lexicographic level. The variable lex.level is incremented when a lexicographic level is entered and decremented on exit. The procedure declare uses lex.level to enter the stack addresses in the symbol table. We now have

```
procedure declare(cstring s ; cpntr t)
begin
      let dd.add = if pointer(base.type(t)) then psp else sp
      let t1 = link(s, lex.level,dd.add,t, nil, nil)
      env.list(hd) := enter(env.list(hd),t1)
end
```

This is not vastly different from before (see section 10.4). The stack address is entered depending on whether or not the item is a pointer. Since data objects may be variable or constant the procedure base.type is used to strip off this attribute. It may be written as:

```
procedure base.type(cpntr t -> pntr)
case true of
t is var    : t(var.type)
t is const  : t(const.type)
default     : t
```

Procedure pointer may be written as

```
procedure pointer(cpntr t -> bool)
case t of
STRING,PNTR : true
default     : eq(VECTOR(ANY),t)
```

which will return the value true if the data object resides on the pointer stack and false otherwise.

The link between the declaration and the use of a name is made through the symbol table. Every time a name is used in the program being compiled, procedure lookup is called to find the type of the name. The compiler also has to generate code to load the object on to the top of the appropriate stack. The simplest method of doing this is to refine procedure lookup so that it will generate this code as well as returning the type (see section 10.5). This will give

```
procedure lookup(cstring s ; cbool r.value -> pntr)
begin
    let p = search.table(s)
    if p = nil then
    begin
        error.message("Undeclared name ** ",s,"** has ","been ","used")
        declare(s)
        ANY
    end else
    begin
        let p1 = p(type)
        let p2 = base.type(p1)
        name.op(p(11),p(dd),pointer(p2),r.value)
        if r.value then p2 else p1
    end
end
```

The refinement here is to generate code by using the procedure name.op in the code generation. The compiler passes on to procedure name.op the stack address, an indication of which stack is to be used and whether the name is used as an R-value or an L-value. If the name is used as an L-value the code generation procedure will issue code to load the address of the object instead of its value on to the top of the stack. We will now write procedure name.op

```
procedure name.op(cint lex,disp ; cbool ptr,r.value)
case true of
lex = lex.level   : local(disp,ptr,t.value)
lex = 0           : global(disp,ptr,r.value)
default           : load(lex,disp,ptr,r.value)
```

This splits the instructions into those which access the local, global and intermediate environments. To generate code we must write the procedures local, global and load. We chose procedure local to illustrate the method:

```
procedure local(cint disp ; cbool ptr,r.value)
case true of
r.value and ptr  : { generate.code(plocal.inst) ; push.ps }
r.value and ~ptr: { generate.code(local.inst) ; push.ms }
~r.value and ptr: { generate.code(plocaladdr) ; push.ms }
default          : { generate.code(localaddr) ; push.ms }
```

Procedure global and load are similar to procedure local. Thus we have now refined the compiler to generate code for names when they are used in a program.

12.3 THE FINAL REFINEMENT OF THE SYNTAX ANALYSER

We are nearing the completion of our compiler. The final layer in the stepwise refinement is to rewrite the syntax analysis procedures to include the calls of the code generation abstractions. This is done for our compiler in accordance with the definition of the code strings given in Appendix E.

Starting at the beginning of our compiler we see that there is no need to generate code in procedure sequence nor in procedure clause. Therefore the versions of these procedures given in Chapter 9 are complete.

The **if** clause does generate code and therefore we have to rewrite the parsing procedure to take account of this (see section 9.6). The code strings are defined by:

if E1 **do** E2	E1 jumpf(L) E2 L:
if E1 **then** E2 **else** E3	E1 jumpf(L) E2 fjump(M) L: E3 M:

This allows the refinement of procedure if.clause as

```
procedure if.clause(-> pntr)
begin
    next.symbol
    match(BOOL,clause)
    let L = jumpf(end.list)
    if have(do.sy) then
    begin
        match(VOID,clause)
        setlab(L)
        VOID
    end else
    begin
        mustbe(then.sy)
        let t = clause
        let M = fjump(end.list)
        pop.stack(t)
        setlab(L)
        mustbe(else.sy)
        match(t,clause)
        setlab(M)
        t
    end
end
```

Most of the additions to this procedure are concerned with the generation of code and the maintenance of the label lists. All the jump instructions here contain forward references that cannot be resolved until the setlab instruction. Notice how the parsing procedure aids the code generation by remembering the chain of references. In this case the chains are always of length 1 and are defined by the constants L and M.

This procedure is unusual in that it also has to update the stacks. When compiling an **if** clause the jumpf instruction will remove the boolean clause from the top of the stack when the instruction is simulated. The code generation abstraction jumpf may be coded by:

```
procedure jumpf(cint list)
begin
    pop.ms
    generate.code(jumpf.inst)
    generate.code(list)
    cp - 1
end
```

The simulation must take the value of the boolean expression off the stack just as the real execution of the instruction will. However in compiling the **if**. . .**then**. . .**else** clause, both branches of the clause are compiled one after the other. When the program is executed only one branch will be executed. In the compilation, the simulation will simulate the evaluation of both branches and, if the type of the branches is not void, will leave two elements rather than one on the stack. The element should be removed from the stack before we compile the **else** section. This allows the space at the top of the stack to be re-used correctly. We therefore use procedure pop.stack to remove one of the elements for the simulation.

```
procedure pop.stack(cpntr t)
if t ≠ VOID do if pointer(t) then pop.ps else pop.ms
```

The only other procedure in the syntax analysis with this problem is the procedure to compile the case clause, and it can adopt the same solution.

We will now refine the procedure while.clause to illustrate the mechanics of using backward jumps. The code generated is defined by

```
while E1 do E2                    L: E1  jumpf(M)  E2  jump(L)  M:
```

which yields

```
procedure while.clause(-> pntr)
begin
    next.symbol
    let L = cp
    match(BOOL,clause)
    let M = jumpf(end.list)
    mustbe(do.sy)
    match(VOID,clause)
    bjump(L)
    setlab(M)
    VOID
end
```

The forward reference uses the same mechanism as before. The backward jump, bjump, is used to ensure the repetition. Notice again how the parsing procedure remembers the jump address. The code generation abstraction bjump is coded by

```
procedure bjump(cint label)
begin
    generate.code(bjump.inst)
    generate.code(cp - label + 1)
end
```

The expression cp − label + 1 calculates the self relative jump address.

The versions of **and** and **or** in S-algol are also implemented using the jump instructions. The code generated for the **or** expression is

E1 **or** E2   E1 jumptt(L) E2 L:

This implements the non-strict version of **or**. If the left hand side of the expression is true then the result is true and the right hand expression is not evaluated. If the left hand expression is false then the result is the value of the right hand expression. This allows us to implement the procedure expression as

```
procedure expression(-> pntr)
begin
      let t = exp1
      case symbol of
      or.sy : begin
                  match(BOOL,t)
                  let L := end.list
                  while have(or.sy) do
                  begin
                        L := jumptt(L)
                        match(BOOL,exp1)
                  end
                  setlab(L)
                  BOOL
            end
      default : t
end
```

The subtlety of this solution is that it caters for more than one **or** in the expression. When the code is executed the jumptt instruction only removes the stack top element if it is false. In the compiler simulation the element is removed every time to ensure that the stacks are updated correctly. The code generation procedure may be coded as

```
procedure jumptt(cint list)
begin
      pop.ms
      generate.code(jumptt.inst)
      generate.code(list)
      cp - 1
end
```

which requires little explanation.

The refinement of procedure exp1 will be exactly the same as for procedure expression and we will leave the exercise to the reader. For the relational operators the code generated is defined by

```
E1 ⟨relop⟩ E2          E1  E2  rel.op
 ~E                    E  not.op
```

Notice however that the expression ~E1 = E2 parses as (~E1) = E2 and the code generated is defined by

```
~E1 = E2               E1  not.op  E2  eq.op
```

This allows us to code the refinement of procedure exp2 as

```
procedure exp2(—> pntr)
begin
     let not = have(not.sy)
     let t := exp3
     if not do { not.op ; match(BOOL,t) ; t := BOOL }

     let s = symbol
     case symbol of
     is.sy,isnt.sy : begin
                          match(PNTR,t)
                          next.symbol
                          t := lookup(the.name, true)
                          if t isnt STRUCTURE do bad.type(t)
                          mustbe(identifier.sy)
                          if s = is.sy then is.op else isnt.op
                          BOOL
                     end
     eq.sy,neq.sy: begin
                          next.symbol
                          match(t,exp3)
                          if s = eq.sy then eq.op(t) else neq.op(t)
                          BOOL
                     end
     le.sy,lt.sy,
     ge.sy,gt.sy  : begin
                          t := rel.type(t)
                          next.symbol
                          match(t,exp3)
                          case s of
                          le.sy   : le.op(t)
                          lt.sy   : lt.op(t)
                          ge.sy   : ge.op(t)
                          default : gt.op(t)
                          BOOL
                     end
     default      : t
end
```

This refinement is fairly straight-forward. The only new coding idea is to store the input symbol for use later in selecting the correct code operation.

The procedures which compile the arithmetic operations are a more complicated version of this. However, since there is nothing essentially new in the refinement of procedures exp3 and exp4 we will leave them and move on the the more interesting problem of refining procedure exp5.

We will take each section of procedure exp5 in turn and apply the refinement to illustrate the application of the final layer of code generation. In the previous section we dealt with the problem of identifiers and generating code when an identifier is used. Since procedure lookup generates the code there is no need to refine procedure exp5 for identifiers. However we will refine procedure proc.call to generate code for a procedure call. The code is defined by

E(E1, ... En) E mark.stack E1 . . . . En apply.op

The code for E will be generated by procedure lookup before procedure proc.call is called. The rest of the code is generated here.

```
procedure proc.call(cpntr t -> pntr)
begin
      let params := t(args)
      mark.stack
      let level = sp ; let plevel = psp
      if params ≠ nil do
      begin
            mustbe(lp.sy)
            repeat { let param = params(hd)
                     if param is proc or param is STRUCTURE then
                     begin
                           match(param,lookup(the.name, true))
                           next.symbol
                     end else match(param,clause)
                     params := params(tl) }
            while have(comma.sy) and params ≠ nil
            mustbe(rp.sy)
      end
      let tl = t(result)
      apply.op(level,plevel,tl)
      tl
end
```

In the simulated evaluation, the mark stack instruction must leave space on the main stack for the contents of the mark stack control word. The procedure can be written as

```
procedure mark.stack
begin
      generate.code(mark.inst)
      for i = 1 to mscw.size do push.ms
end
```

Notice that we have abstracted the size of the mark stack control word to a name. This is so that any design change, such as a different method of scope organisation which alters this value, need only mean a change in one place in the compiler. The apply operation is more difficult because it must update the stacks after the call for the simulation. The stack pointers must be returned to their value before the call remembering to add an element for the result if it is not of type void. Notice how procedure proc.call helps by remembering the stack levels before the parameters are added. The procedure apply.op may be written as

```
procedure apply.op(cint level,plevel ; cpntr t)
begin
      generate.code(apply.in)
      generate.code(sp – level)
      psp := plevel
      for i = 1 to sp – level + mscw.size do pop.ms
      push.stack(t)
end
```

Procedure push.stack is the push operation defined by

```
procedure push.stack(cpntr t)
if t ≠ VOID do
if pointer(t) then push.ps else push.ms
```

The next section of procedure exp5 is to compile code for literals when they appear. In S-algol there are literals of type bool, int, real and string and the compiler must cater for all. The code generated is simply to load the literal value to the top of the stack. We can refine procedure exp5 to

```
literal.sy : begin
                  next.symbol
                  case literal.type of
                  INT      : load.int(int.literal)
                  REAL     : load.real(real.literal)
                  STRING: load.string(string.literal)
                  default  : load.bool(bool.literal)
                  literal.type
             end
```

The code generation abstraction load.int may be coded as

```
procedure load.int(cint n)
begin
    generate.code(ll.int)
    generate.code(n)
    push.ms
end
```

A little more ingenuity is required to place the other literal values in the integer code vector.

We will now refine procedure block so that any data objects placed on the stack during the evaluation of the block are removed on block exit. The code generated is defined by

```
begin E end                    E  retract.op
```

Of course, if the block is an expression block the retract instruction must copy the result to the new stack top. The procedure is now

```
procedure block(-> pntr)
begin
    let last = if symbol = begin.sy then end.sy else rcb.sy
    next.symbol
    if have(last) then VOID else
    begin
        enter.scope
        let level = sp ; let plevel = psp
        let t = sequence
        retract(level,plevel,t)
        exit.scope
        mustbe(last)
        t
    end
end
```

with

```
procedure retract(cint level,plevel ; cpntr t)
begin
    sp := level ; psp := plevel
    if t = VOID then generate.code(retract.v) else
        if pointer(t) then { generate.code(retract.p) ; push.ps }
                      else { generate.code(retract.m) ; push.ms }
    generate.code(level)
    generate.code(plevel)
end
```

The application of this final layer should now be transparent to the reader. We refine the syntax analysis procedures according to the definition of the code strings and write the code generation abstractions to generate the code, update the stacks and deal with the code pointer simulation.

12.4 SUMMARY

With the addition of the code generation we have now completed the stepwise refinement of our compiler. To generate code we simulated the evaluation of the program being compiled, using the two stack pointers and the code pointer. For every abstract machine instruction in the S-code we invented an abstraction in the code generator to perform the simulation by balancing the stacks and manipulating the code pointer. We also made these abstractions generate the code strings.

A measure of portability is achieved by restricting the simulation to the code generation procedures and a higher level of efficiency in the code can be achieved by refining the simulation.

The code is output from the compiler one segment at a time in order to avoid the problems of planting code to jump over procedure declarations and of resolving forward references.

The symbol table was extended to include the addresses of the declared objects and the procedures declare and lookup were refined to store and use this information respectively. Finally we applied the code generation layer using the definition of the code strings given in appendix E. In conjunction with this we coded the code generation abstractions.

CHAPTER 13

Bootstrapping and Portability

13.1 THE NEED TO PORT LANGUAGES

If programs are to be successfully used by a large community (and compilers are such programs) they should be available in all the operating environments used by that population. A modern university for instance is such a community and may contain a large variety of computers including micros, minis and larger mainframe machines. For ease of communication not only is it a good idea if such machines are able to speak to one another in a hardware sense by interconnecting them via networks, rings or direct links, but they must also be able to understand each other at a software level. If a research worker writes a program in a particular language and tests, debugs and develops it on his local departmental computer, he would often like to be able to transport (or **port**) the solution to his problem to the central service computer or to a colleague's machine in order, for instance, that long production runs may be made on a faster machine. A user may also wish to publicise the fruits of his labours to the wide world. In the particular case of a compiler the reason for transportation may be to compile larger programs or to compile object code which will run directly on the receiving computer. This last point is quite important because it points out a difference between porting a compiler and porting other kinds of program. In the case of a compiler, we often not only need to make it work on a different machine but we also need to alter it slightly to make it produce code for the new machine. In fact this not only applies to code generation; it may also apply to lexical analysis. It may be that, for reasons of economy perhaps, old fashioned input equipment is attached to a machine and we might wish to alter the input representation of the language to take account of this. Capital letters, for instance, may be the only ones available. Certain symbols, e.g. "{" and "≠" may not be available at all. However we will rather gloss over lexical analysis and concentrate on code generation difficulties.

It should be mentioned that it is sometimes desirable that a program be ported to a different operating system possibly on the same machine. We regard this as a difference in quantity rather than quality. A different operating system is a different operating environment and a compiler will probably have to generate different code for running under another system because, although most of the machine instructions will have the same meanings in the two systems, it is practically certain that supervisor calls will be different.

Let us approach the problem from another point of view. It will probably have occurred to the reader that the following difficulty arises. We have taken as our central example of a recursive descent compiler, one for the language S-algol *and* we have written that compiler itself in S-algol. How do we compile the compiler which we do not yet have? The connection between this problem of self-compilation and the previous one of transporting programs is that that the solution of the first is often a special case of the answer to the second. If we cannot compile the compiler on *our* machine, take it to another, which we assume already has a compiler, and compile it there. This of course begs the question of how the *first* compiler was compiled. We shall discuss that later in the chapter.

13.2 T-DIAGRAMS

Before getting involved with the details of how the portability of a compiler or any other program is achieved, let us introduce a diagrammatic notation invented by Bratman as far back as 1961 [1]. The idea, somewhat developed here, is that when any program runs three languages are involved: the language in which the program is written called the **implementation language** (IL); the language of the input data; and the language of the output results. For ordinary programs the input and output languages may have no complex structure. They may, for instance, only be lists of numbers. But when the program running is a compilation, then the input and output data are both programs themselves and we already have names for them, the source language (SL) and the object language (OL). Bratman represents this state of affairs by a **T-diagram**:

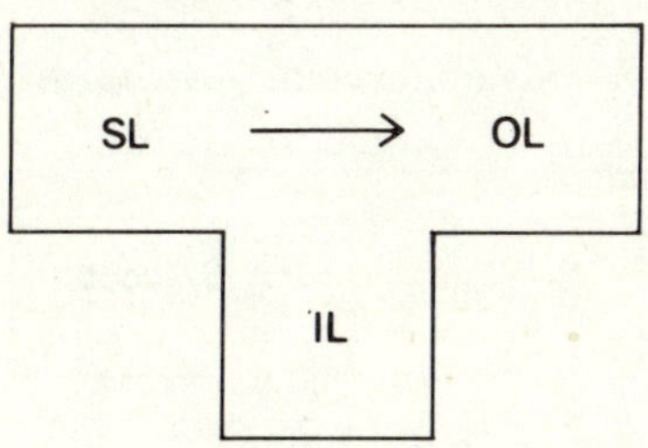

Fig. 13.1

Later users of T-diagrams (e.g. McKeeman *et al.* [2]) have added a strip along the top in some cases, in the form of a short name or comment telling us what is going on. Thus most of the subject of this book could be expressed by:

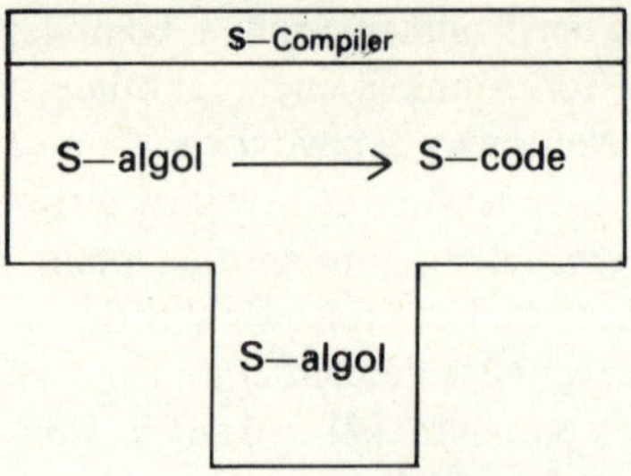

Fig. 13.2

which means that we have been investigating a compiler written in S-algol to translate S-algol into S-code.

Sometimes when we wish to indicate that a particular compiler is being *executed* either directly or indirectly (e.g. by interpretation), we can do so by adding a small cap to the bottom of the T-diagram. For instance, if we have a version of the S-algol compiler in machine code for machine A we might write:

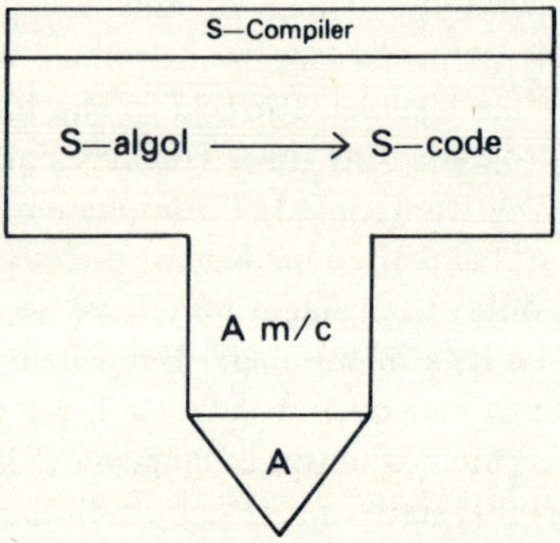

Fig. 13.3

or if we are interpreting S-code on machine A we might write:

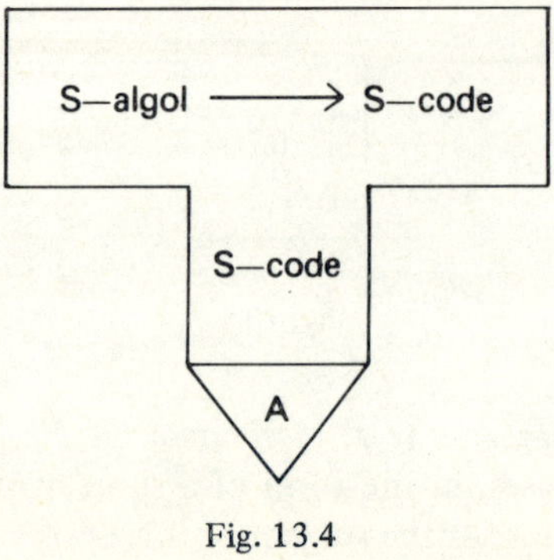

Fig. 13.4

13.3 CROSS COMPILATION

Imagine the case of a completely new computer A, delivered to a customer without any software, not even an assembler. It would at first seem that the only way to get a program to run on A is to hand code it in machine code and key it into A using the control panel or to enter it from some input medium (again in machine code) using a hardware loader if it exists. However this problem of hand coding disappears if we have access to another machine B which can already run suitable software.

Suppose we want to translate a program from language A_1 to language A_2 which in this case is probably A's machine language. The translation can be done on machine B using an existing compiler implemented in B's machine language B_1:

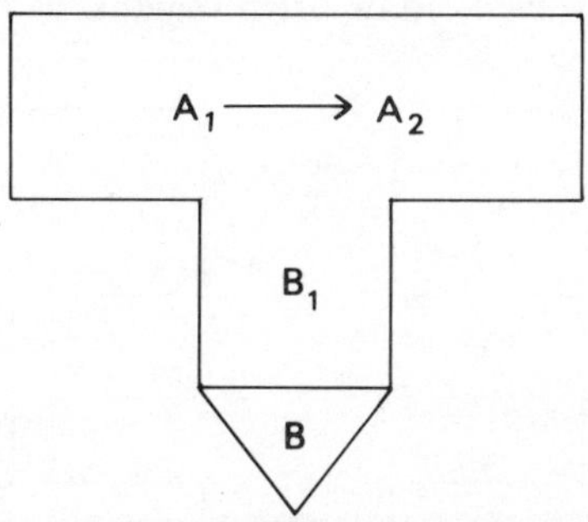

Fig. 13.5

This is called **cross-compilation** (or cross-assembly if A_1 is an assembly language) from machine B to machine A, and it allows A to get off the ground. Of course there is a problem of regression here. Originally, there must once have been a first machine without another to give it a helping hand. For such a case a different but related technique can be used (see section 13.5).

13.4 BOOTSTRAPPING BY PUSHING

If the program written in language A_1 in Fig. 13.5 is a translator (i.e. compiler or assembler) from language C_1 to language C_2:

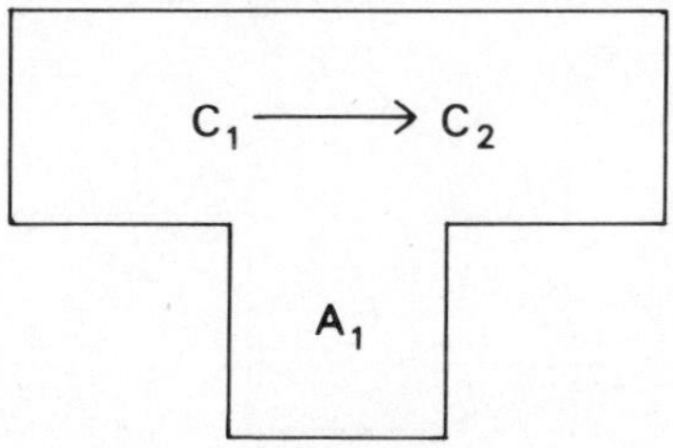

Fig. 13.6

then after the above process we will have another translator from C_1 to C_2 but written in a different language:

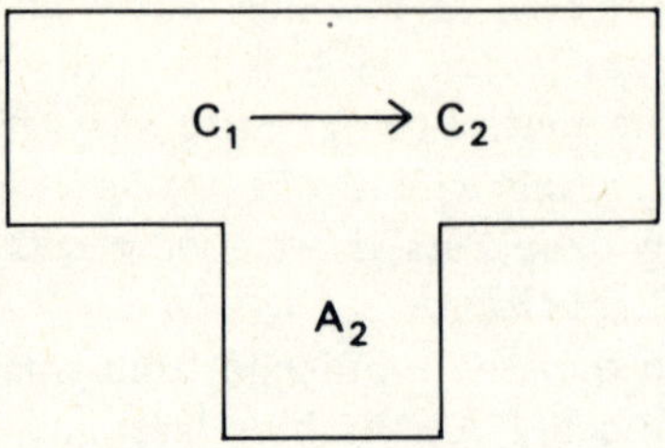

Fig. 13.7

The three T-diagrams involved can be fitted together as follows:

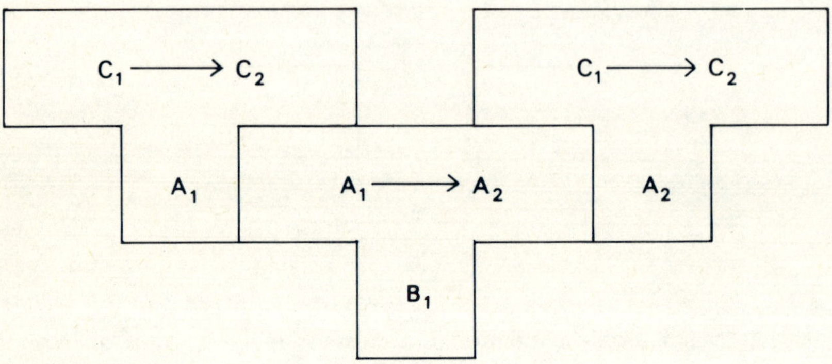

Fig. 13.8

Now consider a special case of this which often arises where $C_1 = A_1$ and $C_2 = A_2$. Then we have:

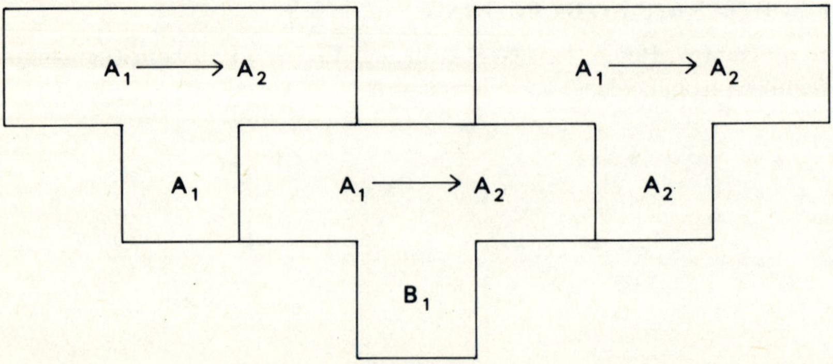

Fig. 13.9

Here we have assumed that a compiler $A_1 \rightarrow A_2$ is available on machine B, written in machine language B_1 or at least interpretable by B. We have to write a very similar one in language A_1 and we end up with a compiler which will run on the new machine. This is known as **bootstrapping by pushing.**

Consider a specific case. Suppose an interpreted version of S–algol is available on a PDP–11 computer:

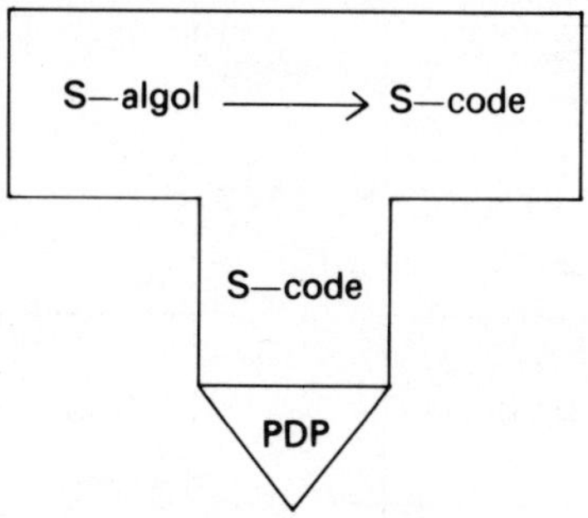

Fig. 13.10

For the moment we will not inquire too closely how that compiler got there. We will discuss that in further detail in the next section. Assume that its source code is also available:

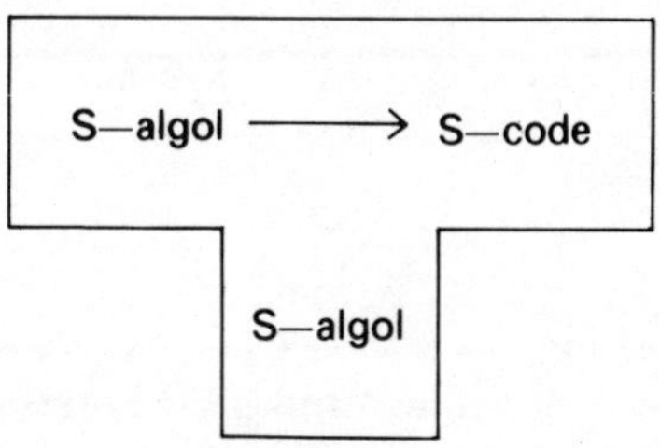

Fig. 13.11

Suppose we want to transport this to a different environment, say a VAX 11/780 computer running a different operating system; and that we want it to produce machine code for the VAX:

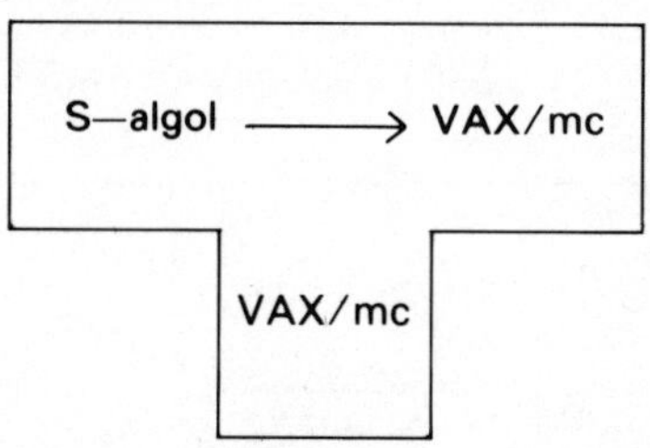

Fig. 13.12

The first thing to do is to change the code generator of Fig. 13.11 so as to produce VAX machine code:

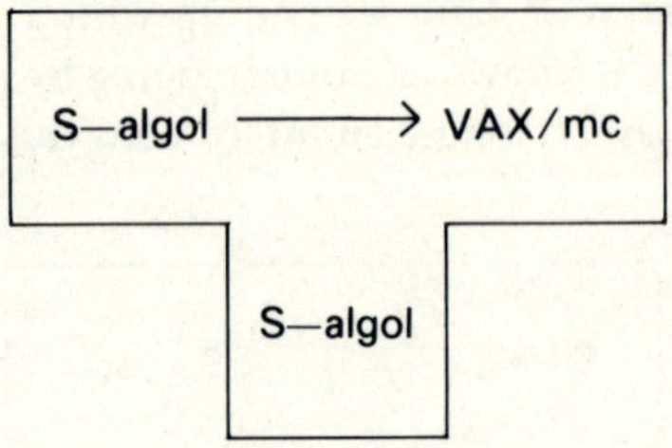

Fig. 13.13

Now compile this using Fig. 13.10:

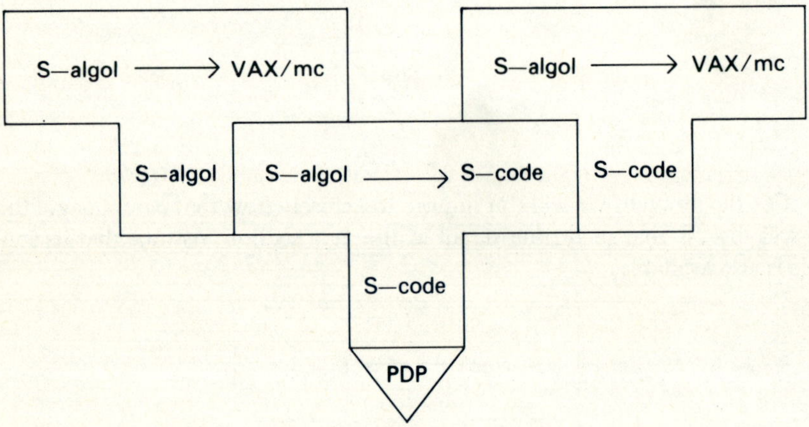

Fig. 13.14

This is an instance of Fig. 13.8 with $C_1 = A_1 =$ S-algol, $B_1 = A_2 =$ S-code and $C_2 =$ VAX machine code. If we interpret the resulting compiler and pass Fig. 13.13 through it (the compiler compiling itself) we have

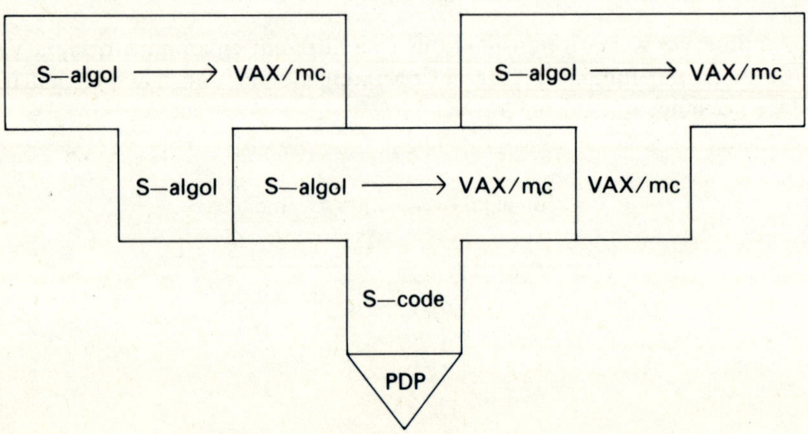

Fig. 13.15

which is an instance of Fig. 13.9 where A_1 = S-algol, A_2 = VAX machine code and B_1 = S-code. The resulting compiler can now run on the VAX and produces code for the VAX.

We have shown this bootstrap taking place on the donor machine, the PDP. In fact a different option is available which allows the whole process to take place on the VAX. The only extra task is to write an S-code interpreter for the VAX. Then the hats on the appropriate diagrams have to be changed to reflect this:

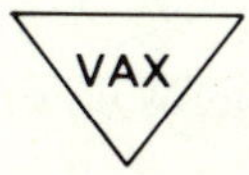

Fig. 13.16

This is, in fact, the option of which authors have direct experience. It has the possible advantage that all the work is done on the receiving machine where any debugging which has to be done can take place in the proper environment. However if the receiving machine is say a micro with little in the way of debugging tools available it may be of use to do the bootstrap on the donor machine.

13.5 BOOTSTRAPPING BY PULLING

We now come to the question of how the compiler in Fig. 13.10 was achieved. A simplistic answer is that we can take the source code of the compiler:

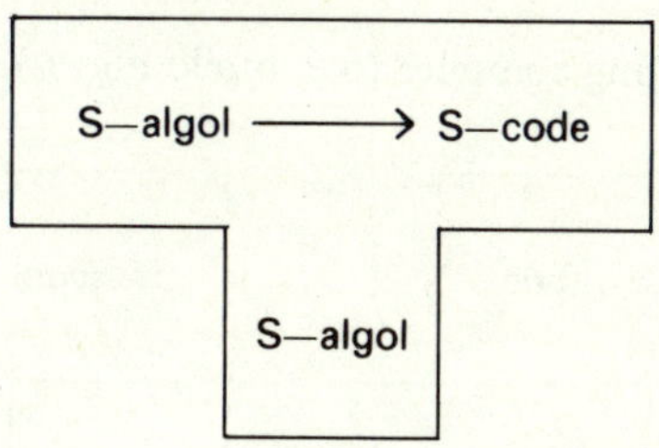

Fig. 13.17

and *hand translate* it. However this would be rather prone to errors as the compiler is a large program. If we can't translate it ourselves, can we get someone or something else to do it for us?

This leads us to consider a different kind of bootstrapping where, instead of changing machines, we change implementation languages. Hand translating a high level language into another one is much easier than doing the same task into a machine code, even for an idealised machine.

Consider a situation where we have another suitable programming language available to us, fully implemented. In the authors' case this was Algol W [3] running on an IBM/360:

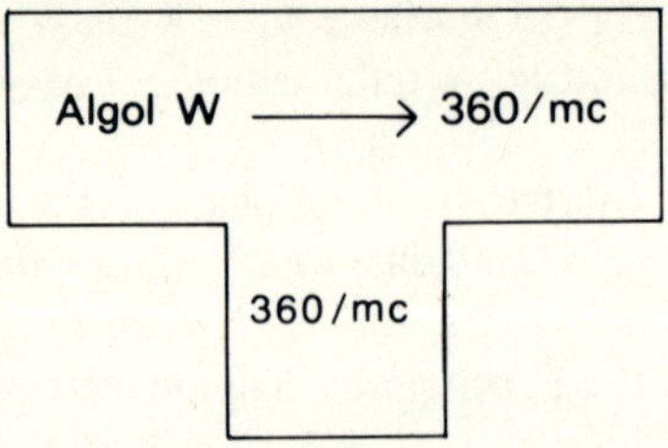

Fig. 13.18

If we rewrite Fig. 13.17 in Algol W we can carry out:

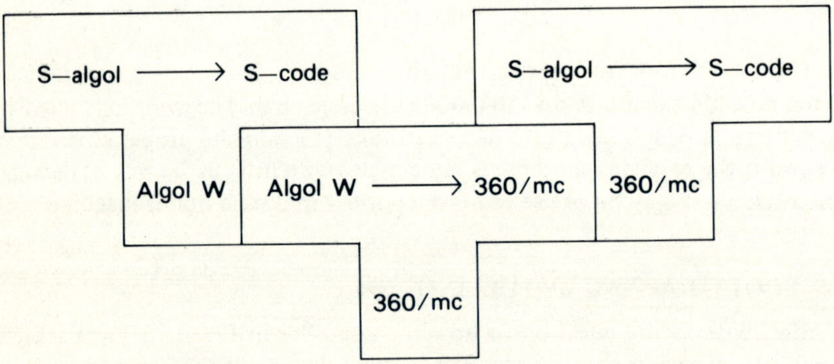

Fig. 13.19

and we can use the resulting compiler to compile Fig. 13.17 giving:

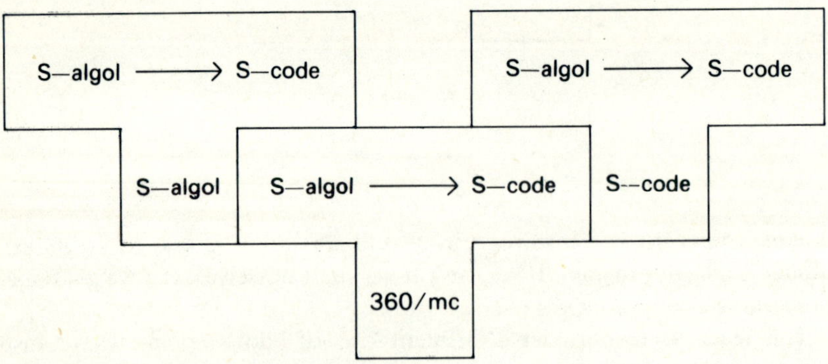

Fig. 13.20

which produces Fig. 13.10 as required.

This method where we use another language instead of another machine is called **bootstrapping by pulling**. The above example used a fully fledged programming language, Algol W, to do the pulling, but in other cases (e.g. Wilkes

[4]) a technique is used where this kind of bootstrap goes through several stages, each compiler being written in a language which is a subset of the one that the compiler has to cope with. In this way a sequence of languages is produced, each more comprehensive than the preceding one. The first language in this sequence is supposed to be so simple that it *can* be easily hand translated into a suitable machine code.

13.6 SUMMARY

In this chapter we have seen how to create compilers from thin air. Or, to use a metaphor which gives rise to the terminology, we have seen how compilers pull themselves up by their own bootstraps. We have shown that the idea of portability in general can be applied to compilers in particular and that this, with the added complication that we have to modify the compiler to produce code for a new machine, allows compilers to be moved from one operating environment to another. We have also seen how to arrive at a compiler by using another language or succession of languages to produce a more fully fledged language at each stage.

Further details of the ideas of portability and bootstrapping can be found in Brown [5], Poole [6] and Lecarme and Peyrolle-Thomas [7]. McKeeman *et al.* [2] use T-diagrams extensively and even apply them to the assembly and loading stages of a compiler.

REFERENCES

[1] Bratman, H. (March 1961), An alternative form of the UNCOL diagram, *CACM,* 4, 4, 142.

[2] McKeeman, W. M., Horning, J. J. and Wortman, D. B. (1970), *A Compiler Generator,* Prentice-Hall.

[3] Wirth, N. and Hoare, C. A. R. (June 1966), A contribution to the development of Algol, *CACM,* 9, 6, 413–431.

[4] Wilkes, M. V. (1964), An experiment with a self-compiling compiler for a simple list processing language, *Annual Review in Automatic Programming,* 4, 1–48.

[5] Brown, P. J. (Ed), (1977), *Software Portability,* Cambridge University Press.

[6] Poole, P. C. (1966), Portable and adaptable compilers, *Lecture Notes in Computer Science,* 21, 427–497, Springer-Verlag.

[7] Lecarme, O., Peyrolle-Thomas, M-C. (1973), Self-compiling compilers: an appraisal of their implementation and portability, *Software, Practice and Experience,* 8, 149–170.

Appendices

APPENDIX A
S-ALGOL SYNTAX

```
< program > ::= < sequence >?

< sequence > ::= < declaration >[;< sequence >]|
                 < clause >[;< sequence >]|
                 < empty >

< clause > ::= if< clause >do< clause >|
               if< clause >then< clause >else< clause >|
               repeat< clause >while< clause >[do< clause >]|
               while< clause >do< clause >|
               for< identifier >=< clause >to< clause >
                  [by< clause >]do< clause >|
               case< clause >of< case.list >default:< clause >|
               < name >:=< clause >|
               < write >|abort|
               < expression >

< expression > ::= < expl >[or< expl >]*

< expl > ::= < exp2 >[and< exp2 >]*

< exp2 > ::= [~]< exp3 >[< relop >< exp3 >]

< exp3 > ::= < exp4 >[< addop >< exp4 >]*

< exp4 > ::= [< addop >]< exp5 >[< multop >< exp5 >]*

< exp5 > ::= < name >|
             < literal >|
             (< clause >)|
             {< sequence >}|
             begin< sequence >end|
             < name >(< clause >< bar > < clause >)|
             @< clause >of< typel >< bra >< clause.list >< ket >|
             vector< bounds >of< clause >

< name > ::= < identifier >|< expression >[(< clause.list >)]*

< clause.list > ::= < clause >[,< clause >]*

< case.list > ::= < clause.list >:< clause >;[< case.list >]

< bounds > ::= < clause >::< clause >[,< bounds >]

< bra > ::= [

< ket > ::= ]

< star > ::= *

< bar > ::= |

< addop > ::= +|-

< multop > ::= < star >|/|div|rem|++

< relop > ::= is|isnt|<|>|<=|>=|~=|=
```

```
< write > ::= write< write.list >|output< clause >,< write.list >|
          out.byte < clause >,< clause >,< clause >

< write.list > ::= < clause >[:< clause >][,< write.list >]

< declaration > ::= < let.decl >|
                    < structure.decl >|
                    < proc.decl >|
                    < forward >|
                    < external >

< let.decl >       ::= let< identifier >< init.op >< clause >

< init.op >        ::= =|:=

< structure.decl > ::= structure< identifier >(< field.list >)

< field.list >     ::= < type1 >< identifier.list >[;< field.list >]

< proc.decl >    ::= procedure< identifier >[< T.spec >];< clause >

< T.spec >       ::= ([< param.list >][< arrow >< type >])

< param.list >   ::= < param.type >[;< param.list >]

< param.type >   ::= < type1 >< identifier.list >|< s.decl >|
                     < proc.type >< identifier.list >

< proc.type >    ::= ([< type2.list >][< arrow >< type >])

< type2.list >   ::= < type1 >[,< type2.list >]|
                     < proc.type >[,< type2.list >]|
                     < s.decl >[,< type2.list >]

< s.decl >       ::= structure< identifier >(< type1 >[,< type1 >]*)

< type1 >        ::= [c]< type >

< arrow >        ::= ->

< external > ::= external< identifier >[< proc.type >]

< forward > ::= forward< identifier >[< proc.type >]

< type > ::= int|real|bool|string|pntr|file|< star >< type1 >

< identifier.list > ::= < identifier >[,< identifier >]*

< identifier > ::= < id >|< standard.id >

< id > ::= < letter >|< id >< letter >|
           < id >< digit >|< id >.

< digit > ::= 0|1|2|3|4|5|6|7|8|9

< letter > ::= a|b|c|d|e|f|g|h|i|j|k|l|m|n|o|p|q|r|s|t|u|v|w|x|y|z|
               A|B|C|D|E|F|G|H|I|J|K|L|M|N|O|P|Q|R|S|T|U|V|W|X|Y|Z

< literal > ::= true|false|
                < u.int >[ .< u.int > ][ e< scale.factor > ]|"[< char >]*"

< char > ::= any ascii character
```

```
< u.int > ::= < digit >[ < digit > ]*

< scale.factor > ::= [ < addop > ]< u.int >

< standard.id > ::= < stand_f >|< stand_s >|< stand_n >

< stand_f > ::= code  | decode | letter | digit | line.number |
                sin | cos | exp | ln | sqrt | atan | truncate | iformat |
                rabs | abs | length | fformat | eformat | fiddle.r |
                options | shift.l | shift.r | b.and | b.or

< stand_s > ::= r.w | i.w | s.w | s.o | s.i |
                maxint | maxreal | epsilon | pi

< stand_n > ::= upb | lwb | float | eof |
                read | readi | readr | readb | peek |
                reads | read.name | read.byte
```

APPENDIX B

TYPE MATCHING RULES

```
< program >< eof > => { void }

< declaration > => { void }
{ void } ; { T } => { T }
< empty > => { void }

if { bool } do { void } => { void }
if { bool } then { T } else { T } => { T }
repeat { void } while { bool } [ do { void } ] => { void }
while { bool } do { void } => { void }
for < identifier > = { int } to { int }
                     [ by { int }] do { void } => { void }
case { T1 } of { T1 },{ T1 }....{ T1 } : { T2 }
              .
              .
              .
              default : { T2 } => { T2 }
{ T } := { T } => { void }
write { T1 },{ T2 },{ T3 }.......... => { void }
output { file },{ T1 },{ T2 }......... => { void }
out.byte { file },{ int },{ int }

{ bool } < or | and > { bool } => { bool }
~ { bool } => { bool }
{ int }< <|>|<=|>= >{ int } => { bool }
{ real }< <|>|<=|>= >{ real } => { bool }
{ string }< <|>|<=|>= >{ string } => { bool }
{ T } < =|~= > { T } => { bool }
{ int } < +|- > { int } => { int }
{ real } < +|- > { real } => { real }
< +|- > { int } => { int }
< +|- > { real } => { real }
{ int } < *|div|rem > { int } => { int }
{ real } < *|/ > { real } => { real }
{ pntr } < is|isnt > (.......)-structure => { bool }
{ string } ++ { string } => { string }
{ string }( { int } | { int } ) => { string }

( { T } ) => { T }
begin { T } end => { T }
< T-literal > => { T }

< T proc >[({ T1 },{ T2 },.......{ Tn })] => { T }

vector { int } :: { int },.......
       { int } :: { int } of { T } => { *......*T }
@{ int }of[c]< type >< bra >{ T },{ T },....{ T }< ket > => { *T }
< structure class >[({ T1 }, .......{ Tn } )] => { pntr }

{ *T }( { int } ) => { T }
{ pntr }( { T-field } ) => { T }
```

APPENDIX C

PROCEDURE NUMBER

```
procedure number
begin
     symb := literal.sy ; literal.type := INT ; let sign := true
     let maxintstr = iformat( maxint )
     let minintstr = { let x = iformat( -maxint - 1 ) ; x( 2|length( x ) - 1 ) }
     let real.literal := float( 0 ) ; let unary.minus := false

     procedure le( cstring s,sl -> bool )
     length( s ) < length( sl ) or length( s ) = length( sl ) and s <= sl

     procedure int.conv( cstring s ; cbool minus -> int )
     begin
          let n := 0
          for i = 1 to length( s ) do
          begin
               let k = decode( s( i|1 ) ) - zero.sy
               n := n * 10 + ( if minus then -k else k )
          end
          n
     end

     procedure integer.string( -> string )
     begin
          let s := ""
          while digit( peek ) do { s := s ++ peek ; let discard = next.ch }
          s
     end

     procedure ex( int scale -> real )
     begin
          let r := float( 1 ) ; let fac := float( 10 )
          while scale ~= 0 do
          begin
               if scale rem 2 = 1 do r := r * fac
               fac := fac * fac
               scale := scale div 2
          end
          r
     end
```

```
procedure real.conv( cstring s ; int scale -> real )
begin
     let n := float( 0 ) ; let no := length( s ) ; let more := true
     while no >= 1 and more do
           if s( no|1 ) = "0" then no := no - 1 else more := false
     for i = 1 to no do n := n * 10 + ( decode( s( i|1 ) ) - zero.sy )
     scale := scale + length( s ) - no
     if scale ~= 0 do n := if scale < 0 then n / ex( -scale )
                                        else n * ex( scale )
     n
end

while peek = "0" do { let discard = next.ch }
let ipart = integer.string
let dpart = if peek = "." then
            begin
                 let discard = next.ch
                 literal.type := REAL
                 integer.string
            end else ""
let epart = if peek = "e" then
            begin
                 let discard = next.ch
                 literal.type := REAL
                 sign := if peek = minus.sy then
                         begin
                              let discard = next.ch
                              true
                         end else
                         begin
                              if peek = plus.sy do { let discard = next.ch }
                              false
                         end
                 integer.string
            end else ""
if literal.type = REAL then
begin
     let scale = int.conv( epart,sign )
     real.literal := real.conv( ipart,scale )
     if dpart ~= "" do
     real.literal := real.literal + real.conv( dpart,scale - length( dpart ) )
     if unary.minus do real.literal := - real.literal
end else
if unary.minus and le( ipart,minintstr ) or
   ~ unary.minus and le( ipart,maxintstr )
then int.literal := if ipart = "" then 0 else int.conv( ipart,unary.minus )
else err.mess1( "Integer literal out of range'n" )
end
```

APPENDIX D

THE ABSTRACT MACHINE CODE

The S-algol abstract machine code, S-code, is designed to fit exactly the needs of the S-algol language. Here the individual instructions are described. They fall naturally into groups.

Jumps

All the jump addresses are relative to the program counter.

fjump(l)	unconditional jump forward to address l
bjump(l)	unconditional jump backwards to address l
jumpf(l)	jump to l if the top stack element is **false**. Remove the top element of the stack
jumptt(l)	jump to l if the top element is **true**. Otherwise remove the top stack element
jumpff(l)	jump to l if the top stack element is **false**. Otherwise remove the top stack element
cjump.ib(l) cjump.r(l) cjump.s(l) cjump.p(l)	the type determines which stack to use. If the top two stack elements are equal, remove both and jump to l. Otherwise remove only the top stack element. Be careful on equality of strings
fortest.op(l)	the control constant, increment and limit are the top three elements of the stack. If the increment is negative and the control constant is less than the limit or the increment is positive and the control constant is greater than the limit then remove them from the stack and jump to l
forstep.op(l)	update the control constant by adding the increment. Then jump to l

Stack Load Instructions

These instructions are used to load any data item which is in scope on to the top of the stack. The data items may be in the local, global or intermediate environments and a separate instruction exists for each form. Different instructions are also used for the separate stacks. The local and global forms of the instruction have a parameter which is the displacement of the item from the stack frame base. The intermediate form of the instruction requires the number of times to chain down the static chain as well as the displacement. Only one form of each type is described.

local(n),global(n),load(r,n)	load on the main stack
plocal(n),pglobal(n),pload(r,n)	load on the pointer stack
localaddr(n),globaladdr(n),loadaddr(r,n)	load address on the main stack
plocaladdr(n),pglobaladdr(n),ploadaddr(r,n)	load the address of the pointer stack item on the main stack
dlocal(n),dglobal(n),dload(r,n)	load double length item main stack

Relational Operations
The relational operations act on the data types int, real and string. The top two elements of the stack are compared and removed. The boolean result **true** or **false** is left on the main stack. Care should again be taken in the equality of strings. Equality is defined on all the data objects in the language. There is a separate form of the instruction for each type. The types are

ib	integer or boolean
r	real
s	string
p	pointer
v	void

ge.i,r,s	greater than or equal to
gt.i,r,s	greater than
le.i,r,s	less than or equal
lt.i,r,s	less than
eq.ib,r,s,p	equal to
neq.ib,r,s,p	not equal to

Arithmetic Operators
These instructions operate on the data types real and integer. The top two elements of the stack are replaced by the result except for negate and float1 which use only the top element and float2 which uses the second top element.

plus,fplus	add
times,ftimes	multiply

minus,fminus	subtract
fdivide	divide real
div	divide int leaving quotient
rem	divide int leaving remainder
neg,fneg	negate
float1	coerce the int to a real on top of the stack
float2	coerce the int to a real second top stack element

Procedure Entry and Exit
The code to execute a procedure begins with the maximum sizes that the main stack and the pointer stack may become in the procedure (this is checked on the call) and ends with a return.

return.ib,r,s,p,v — this is executed on procedure exit. The SF and PSF registers are updated from the MSCW. The SF register is first set to the current dynamic link and then PSF is set to the pointer stack link of the uncovered stack frame. The stack tops must be altered to remove the MSCW and any local items. The new stack tops are the current pointer stack link for the pointer stack and the position of the MSCW for the main stack. If the type of the procedure is not void, the result must be copied to the new stack top

The code sequence to call a procedure is

```
        mst.load
evaluate the parameters
        apply.op
```

The code for the evaluation of the parameters is the same as for any expression. The mark stack and load instruction loads the procedure closure, updates the dynamic link and the pointer stack link and leaves space on the stack for the rest of the MSCW. The apply instruction fills in the MSCW with the line number and the return address. Since procedure names follow the same scope rules as any other names, there are three forms of the instruction. If there are no parameters the mark.stack and apply instructions are combined.

mst.local(n),mst.global(n),mst.load(r,n)
load the procedure closure from the stack, fill in the DL and PSL, and leave space for the rest of the MSCW

apply.op(m,n) fill in the dynamic link and the return address. Update SF and PSF and jump to the address pointed at by SF. Check that there is sufficient stack space to execute the procedure.

local.apply(n),global.apply(n),load.apply(r,n)
load the MSCW and call the procedure.
There are no parameters.

There are two further instructions involved with procedures.

forward.op leave space for the procedure closure on the stack

store.closure(n,m) place the procedure closure on the stack. If the address n is not the top of the stack, it is a forward declared procedure and n is its stack address. m is the code address of the procedure.

Vector and Structure Creation Instructions

These instructions take information off the stack and create heap objects. These objects are then initialised and the pointer to them left on the top of the pointer stack.

make.vector.ib(m,n),r,s,p
m points to the position of the lower bound on the main stack. The difference between PSP and n or SP and m (depending on which stack is in use) gives the number of vector elements. The stack pointers are then reduced to m and n with the pointer to the vector being placed on the pointer stack

iliffe.op.ib(n),r,s,p n pairs of bounds are on the main stack. However, the top of one of the stacks will contain the initial value. The instruction creates an iliffe vector of the shape indicated by the bound pairs and the value of the initial expression is copied into the elements of the last dimension. The expression value and the bound pairs are removed from the stack and the pointer to the vector is placed on the pointer stack

form.structure(n) the expressions which initialise the structure fields have been evaluated on the appropriates stacks. n points to the trademark on the main stack. A structure of the correct size is made up and the fields filled in. To do this the structure table is referred to, to give the number of pointer fields. After removing the fields from the stacks the pointer to the structure is placed on the pointer stack

Vector and Structure Accessing Instructions

These instructions are generated by the compiler to index a vector or a structure. The index of the vector must be checked against the bounds before the indexing is done. Similarly the structure class (trademark) of a structure must be checked.

subv.ib,r,s,p	the vector index is on the top of the main stack and the vector pointer on the pointer stack. These are used to check that the index is legal and then to find the required value. They are removed from the stack and replaced by the value.
subs.ib,r,s,p	the structure pointer is on the top of the pointer stack. The main stack contains the trademark and the field address. The trademark is checked against the structure trademark and if it is the same the field address is added to the pointer to yield the absolute field address. The trademark, field address and structure pointer are replaced on the stack by the result.
subvass.ib,r,s,p	this assigns a value to a vector element. The value is on the top of the stack and the address is calculated as in subv.
subsass.ib,r,s,p	this assigns a value to a structure field. The value is on the top of the stack and the address is calculated as in subs.
lwb	remove the pointer to the vector from the pointer stack and place its lower bound on the main stack
upb	remove the pointer to the vector from the pointer stack and place its upper bound on the main stack
is.op	the trademark is on the main stack and is compared with the trademark of the structure pointed at by the top element of the pointer stack. Remove both and place the boolean result of the comparison on the main stack
isnt.op	this is the same as is.op except it performs the opposite test

Load Literal Instructions

These are used to load the value of a literal onto the stack. The literal usually follows the instruction in the code stream and so the CP register has to be updated accordingly.

ll.nil.string	load the empty string on to the pointer stack.
ll.file	load the nullfile on to the pointer stack
ll.bool(n)	load the boolean value n (**true** or **false**) on to the main stack
ll.sint(n)	load the value of a short integer (–64 to 63) on to the main stack

ll.real(n)	load the real on to the main stack
ll.string(s)	load the string address on to the pointer stack
ll.lint	load a long integer, 16 bits, on to the main stack
ll.char(n)	load the character n as a string of length 1.

String Operations
These are used to perform the string operations in S-algol.

concat.op	remove the two strings from the top of the pointer stack and replace them with a new string which is the concatenation of them
substr.op	a new string is created from the one at the top of the pointer stack and replaces it. It is formed by using the length at the top of the main stack and the starting position at the second top. After checking that these are legal they are removed

Input and Output

read.op(n)	the stream descriptor is on the top of the pointer stack. This is removed and the value read is placed on the appropriate stack. n indicates which read function to use. They are
read	read a character and form it into a string
reads	read a string
readi	read an integer
readr	read a real
readb	read a boolean
read.name	read an S-algol identifier and form it into a string
peek	same as read but do not advance the input stream
read.byte	read an 8 bit byte and return it is an integer
eof	test for end of file on the input stream.
write.op(n)	the field width is on the top of the main stack and the item to be written out either under it or on the pointer stack. The stream descriptor is under all this on the pointer stack. The field width and the item are removed from the stack. In the case of out.byte the file descriptor is also removed from the stack. n indicates which function. They are

write.int	write an integer
write.real	write a real
write.bool	write a boolean
write.string	write a string
out.byte	write an 8 bit byte.

If the field width is not specified then i.w and r.w come into use for int and real. s.w spaces are always written after integers or reals for character streams.

Miscellaneous

rev.ms,rev.ps	swap the top two elements of the stack
erase.ib,r,s,p	remove an element from the stack
finish.op	stop the program's execution
not.op	perform a not on the boolean at the top of the stack
ass.ib,r,s,p	assign the value at the top of the stack to the address on the main stack and remove them
retract.ib(n,m),r,s,p,v	retract the main stack to n and the pointer stack to m. If it is not void move the value at the old stack top to the new stack top

APPENDIX E

S-CODE GENERATED BY THE S-ALGOL COMPILER

A summary of the S-code generated by the S-algol compiler for each syntactic construct is given here. In this description, E in the left hand column represents an expression, and E in the right hand column represents the S-code for that expression. Sometimes the expressions are of type void. A description of the instructions themselves is given in Appendix D.

Source	**S-Code**
~E	E not.op
+E	E
−E	E neg.op
unary.function(E)	E unary.function.op
write E1:E1′, ... En:En′	s.o E1 E1′ write.op. . . . . En En′ write.op erase.op

Write operates for reals, ints, bools and strings.

output E0, E1:E1′. . . . En:En′	E0 E1 E1′ write.op. . . . . En En′ write.op erase.op
out.byte E0,E1,E2	E0 E1 E2 write.op
read	s.i read.op
read(E)	E read.op

similarly for peek, read.name, reads, readi, readb, eof and read.byte.

E1 := E2	E1* E2 ass.op

where E1* is an L-value which may generate a load address.

E1(E2) := E3	E1 E2 E3 subvass or subsass
E1 **or** E2	E1 jumptt(l) E2 1:
E1 **and** E2	E1 jumpff(l) E2 1:
E1 ⟨binary.op⟩ E2	E1 E2 binary.op
(E)	E
E1(E2 | E3)	E1 E2 E3 substr.op
E1(E2)	E1 E2 subs or subv
E(E1, ... En)	mst.load E E1. . . . En apply.op
@E **of** T[E1, ... En]	E E1. . . . . . . En make.vector
E(E1, ... En)	E E1. . . . . . . En form.structure
E ?	E finish.op
abort	finish.op

vector E1::E1′, . . . En::En′ **of** E	E1 E1′. . . En En′ E iliffe.op
if E1 **do** E2	E1 jumpf(l) E2 1:
if E1 **then** E2 **else** E3	E1 jumpf(l) E2 jump(m) 1: E3 m:
repeat E1 **while** E2	1: E1 E2 not.op jumpf(l)
repeat E1 **while** E2 **do** E3	1: E1 E2 jumpf(m) E3 jump(l) m:
while E1 **do** E2	1: E1 jumpf(m) E2 jump(l) m:
for I=E1 **to** E2 **by** E3 **do** E4	E1 E2 E3 1: fortest.op(m) E4 forstep.op(l) m:
begin E **end**	E retract.op
let I = E	E
let I := E	E
procedure I ; E	E return
structure I	ll.int
⟨literal⟩	ll.literal dependent on type
⟨identifier⟩	load.stack

A load.stack instruction may be one of load, local, global, pload, plocal, pglobal, dload, dlocal or dglobal.

The unary functions are upb, lwb, float.

The binary operations are eq.op, neq.op, lt.op, le.op, gt.op, ge.op, plus.op, times.op, minus.op, div.op, rem.op, divide.op, is.op, isnt.op and concat.op.

case E0 **of**	E0
E11,E12, ... E1n : E10	E11 cjump(ll) E12 cjump(ll). . . . . E1n cjump(ll) jump(M1) 11 : E0 jump(xit)
E21,E22, ... E2n : E20	M1:E21 . . . .
.	
.	
.	
.	
.	
default : Ek+1 0	Mk:Ek+1 0
	xit :

Index

A

abstract machine definition, 73, 136 et seq.
abstractions, 70, 136
accessing structures, 134, 184
accessing the symbol table, 126, 130 et seq.
active symbols (*see also* targets, goals), 46
address calculation, 149, 150
address pairs, 139
affix grammars, 37
Aho, A. V., 48, 50, 60, 102, 137
algebra, 24, 27
algol 60, 12, 39, 64, 68
algol 68, 37, 68, 71
algol 68R, 17
algol W, 18, 67, 139, 171
alphabets, 23, 34
ambiguity, 41
Ammann, U., 17, 71, 103
and, 146, 158
annotation of source, 98, 107
ANY, 115
APL, 12
apply.op, 147, 161
arithmetic instructions, 144, 181
assignment, 20, 87, 133, 134
attribute grammars, 37
automatic parser generators, 49
automatically produced programs, 140

B

Backhouse, R., 53, 102
backspaces, 93
backtracking, 46, 50, 52
Backus Naur (Normal) Form, *see* BNF
Backus, J. W., 39
backward jumps, 157
backward references, 151
bad.type, 115
balanced binary trees, 96, 126
base.type, 154
basic symbols (*see also* lexemes, terminals), 13, 76, 88 et seq.
basic units of expressions, 122
BCPL, 17
Berge, C., 26
beta machine, 138
binary chop, 96, 126
binary trees, 73, 96, 126 et seq.
Birkhoff, G., 28
bjump, 151, 157
block counts, 98
block expressions, 21, 83 et seq., 149
blocks, 18, 86, 123, 128, 162
  entry, 138, 144
  exit, 138, 144, 162
BNF (*see also* extended BNF), 34, 39, 78
bool, 18
boolean matrix of a relation, 29
bootstrapping, 164 et seq.
  by pulling, 171
  by pushing, 167
Bornat, R., 50
bottom up parsing, 41, 49
bound checking, 141
Bratman, H., 165
breakfast, 25
Brown, P. J., 173
Burroughs' algol, 12, 17, 71

C

call by value, 20
calling procedures, 133, 140
Cartesian product, 23
case clauses, 20, 151, 157
case expressions, 84
cheating, 63
checking types, *see* type checking
Chomsky, N., 36
civil rights, 141
clauses, 18, 20, 81, 118

closure (*see also* procedure closure), 23, 28
closure calculation, 29, 30
clustering, 127
coalescing storage, 142
code generation, 14, 74, 136 et seq., 149 et seq.
code pointer, 144, 151
collision, 127
comments, 18, 88, 95
compacting store, 142
compatible types, 73
compile and go compiler, 11
compile time, 11
compiler compilation, 165
compiler construction, 67
compiler generators, 50
compiler output, 136 et seq.
compilers, 11, 70 et seq.
composite symbols (*see also* multiple character), 72, 90, 92
concat. op, 145
concatenation, 19, 21, 24
concrete syntax, 72
cons, 128
constant values, 18, 20, 130, 154
context free grammars, 37, 38
context sensitive analysis, parsing, 65, 109 et seq., 125 et seq.
    errors, 73, 115
    grammars, 36
    syntax, 86
cp, 151
cp, 144, 151
creation of structures, 133, 145, 183
cross assembly, 167
cross compilation, 167
cross reference listing, 98

D

dangling else problem, 20
declaration of procedures, 19
declarations, 18, 83, 129 et seq., 153 et seq.
declare, 129, 153
derivations, 41
deterministic parsing, 46, 48, 50, 52
digraphs, 25
Dijkstra, E. W., 50
direct derivations, 41
director sets, 53, 79
displacement from frame, 139
display, 139
distinguished symbol (*see also* start symbol), 34, 38
donor machine, 171
dynamic chain, 138
dynamic link, 138

E

EBCDIC, 74
efficiency, 14, 48, 89, 90, 136
elimination of left recursion, 61
Elliott algol, 17
EMPTY property, 56
empty string (*see also* null string), 35
end of file symbol, 59
enter, 129
environment checking, 73, 125 et seq.
eq, 116
equality of types, 113, 116
equality relation, 28
equivalent grammars, 59
errors, 16, 97 et seq., 125
    diagnosis, 72, 101 et seq.
    messages, 107, 130
    recovery, 72, 101 et seq., 115
    repair, 102
    reporting, 72, 90, 99, 107 et seq., 114
escape character, 93, 94
exp.list, 134
exp1, 120
exp2, 120, 132, 159
exp5, 122, 132, 135, 160
expressions, 21, 83 et seq., 119, 134, 158
extended BNF, 39, 64, 72, 78, 110
external declarations, 19

F

factorisation, 52, 59, 60
field types, 112
fields, 19, 145
file, 18
FINISH, 58
FIRST, 55, 56
first class data objects, 141
fjump, 152
flow of control, 146
Floyd, R. W., 46, 49, 50
FOLLOW, 55, 57
for clauses, 20, 146
form.structure, 145
forstep, 146
fortest, 146
forward declarations, 18
forward references, 151, 156, 157
Foster, J. M., 17, 62, 64

G

garbage collection, 126, 141 et seq., 145
Gaussian elimination, 62
generate.code, 150, 152, 153
generating code, 14, 74, 136 et seq., 149 et seq.
generative parsing, 41
global, 155

global objects, 139, 140, 155
global optimization, 13
goal type, 113, 114
goals (*see also* targets, active symbols), 46, 101, 104
grammars (*see also* syntax), 34
graphical interpretation of relations, 27
graphs, 26
Gries, D., 38, 50
Griffiths, M., 53, 64

H

hand translation, 171, 173
handles, 49
hash functions, 97, 127
hash key, 127
hashing, 73, 96, 126 et seq.
have, 77, 78, 82, 91, 99 et seq.
heap instructions, 145
heaps, 74, 138, 140 et seq.
history, 17
Hoare, C. A. R., 17
horses, 24
hypothetical machine, *see* abstract machine

I

identifiers, 18, 77, 88 et seq.
if clauses, 20, 82, 90, 118, 146, 155, 156
if expressions, 84
Illife, J. K., 146
illife.s, 146
immediate start symbols, 54
implementation language, 165
inclusion, 27
index checking, 141
indirect left recursion, 61
initialising declarations, 18
input and output, 185
input representation, 164
int, 18
intermediate environment, 155
interpreters, 12, 74
Introduction, 11
irrelevant symbols, 103

J

jump if false, 146
jump instructions, 146, 151, 156 et seq., 180
jumpf, 146, 156
jumpff, 146
jumptt, 146

K

keywords, 13, 88, 91, 95 et seq., 125
Kleene star, 24, 40, 79
Knuth, D. E., 17, 50

L

label lists, 156
LALR, parsing, 50
languages, 34
layers, 71, 76, 89, 116, 149
layout, 95
Lecarme, O., 173
left recursion, 48
  elemination, 61
  productions, rules, 43, 47, 55
leftmost derivations, 43, 53
length, 21
left declarations, 129
Lewis, P. M., II, 17
lexemes (*see also* basic symbols, terminals), 36, 38
lexical analysis, 13, 76, 88 et seq.
lexical errors, 97 et seq.
lexicographic levels, 139
line numbers, 98
linear lists, 126
LISP, 12
listing (*see also* printings), 88, 98 et seq., 107
literals, 13, 72, 77, 88 et seq.
LL(l) conditions, 16, 71, 83
LL(l) grammars, 52, 107
LL(k), 17, 53, 71
  grammars, 53
  languages, 53
load, 155, 180
load and go systems, 74
load time, 11
load.int, 162
loading literals to stack, 144, 184
local, 155
local error checking, 106
local objects, 139, 140, 155
lookahead, 53
lookup, 130, 131, 154
loops, 20, 146
lower bound of vector, 145
LR(k) parsing, 50
L values, 131 et seq., 155

M

machine dependent code, 136, 137
machine independence (*see also* system ind.), 98, 101
Mac Lane, S., 28
macro expansion, 14
manipulating grammars, 52
mark stack control word, 138, 140, 143, 160
mark stack instruction, 160
mark.stack, 161
marking phase, 142, 145
match, 114
mathematics, 23

McKeeman, W. M., 165, 173
metalanguages, 34
metasymbols, 40
micro code, 74
microsyntax, 13, 76, 89 et seq.
missing double quote, 98
modelling scope, 128
modularity, 12
Morrison, R., 141
MSCW, 138, 140, 143, 160
mst.load, 147
Multics, 147
multipass compiler, 14
multiple character symbols (*see also* composite), 88
mustbe, 77, 78, 91, 99 et seq., 104 et seq.
mutual left recursion, 47
mutual recursion, 18, 61, 76

N

name.op, 155
names, 84, 125 et seq.
  checking, 125 et seq.
  table, 73, 74, 125 et seq., 153 et seq.
natural machine, 12
Naur, P., 39
nesting, 98
newlines, 88, 93, 95
newpages, 93
next.ch, 92, 98, 107
next.char, 94
next.symbol, 77, 91 et seq.
non-strictness, 146, 158
non-terminal symbols, 34
null string (*see also* empty string), 21, 24
numbers, 94, 178

O

object language, 11, 165
object program, 11, 70
one pass, 14, 16, 67, 71, 89, 137
operator precedence parsing, 50, 87
optimization, 14
or, 146, 158
oracular parsing, 46
ordered sets, 23
outer block globals, 139, 140
overflow, 98

P

P-code, 137
parallelism, 15
parameter types, 133
parameters, 140
parse trees (*see also* syntax trees), 13, 43
parser generators, 49
parsing (*see also* syntax analysis), 13, 41, 76 et seq.
Pascal, 71, 84, 103, 137
Pascal error recovery, 103
pass, 12
peeking, 92
perfect hash function, 96
Peyrolle–Thomas, M-C., 173
phases, 12, 13
phrase structure grammars, 36
pipes, 15
pntr (*see also* pointers), 19, 112
pointer stack, 143 et seq.
  base, 143
  front, 143
  top, 144
pointers, 19, 141 et seq.
Poole, P. C., 173
pop.ms, 150
pop.ps, 150
pop.stack, 157
port, 164 et seq.
portability, 69, 74, 76, 136, 153, 164 et seq.
powers of relations, 28, 30
precedence parsing, 50
Preface, 9
prepass, 14
printing (*see also* listing), 88, 98 et seq.
proc.call, 133, 160
procedures
  apply.op, 161
  bad.type, 115
  bad.types, 114
  base.type, 154
  binary.chop, 97
  bjump, 151, 157
  block, 86, 123, 128, 162
  clause, 81, 118
  compile.bracket, 86
  declare, 129, 153
  display, 114
  enter, 129
  enter.scope, 128
  eq, 113, 116
  exit.scope, 128
  exp.list, 134
  exp1, 85, 120
  exp2, 85, 121, 132, 159
  exp3, 85
  exp4, 85
  exp5, 85, 122, 132, 134, 160
  expression, 85, 119, 158
  fjump, 152
  generate.code, 153
  have, 77, 99
  if.clause, 82, 90, 118, 156
  jumpf, 156

procedures – *continued*
  jumptt, 158
  layout, 95
  let.decl, 83, 129
  load.int, 162
  local, 155
  lookup, 130, 131, 154
  mark.stack, 161
  match, 114
  mustbe, 77, 99, 104, 105
  name.op, 155
  next.ch, 98
  next.char, 94
  next.symbol, 77, 92
  number, 178
  pointer, 154
  pop.ms, 150
  pop.ps, 150
  pop.stack, 157
  proc.call, 133, 160
  program, 80, 116
  push.ms, 150
  push.ps, 150
  push.stack, 161
  read.string, 92, 94
  rel.type, 121
  reserved.word, 96
  retract, 162
  search.table, 131
  search.tree, 131
  sequence, 81, 106, 117
  setlab, 152
  subscript, 134
  substring, 123
  syntax, 104, 105
  try, 92
  try.name, 94, 96
  while.clause, 119, 157
  write.clause, 83
procedures in S–algol, 18
  calls, 133
  closure, 140, 147, 152
  entry and exit, 138, 140, 143, 147, 182
  level addressing, 139, 149
processes, 15
product relations, 27, 30
production rules, productions, 35
program, 80, 116
program text, 88
PSB, 143
PSF, 143
psp, 149
PSP, 144
punctuation, 88, 95
push.ms, 150
push.ps, 150
push.stack, 161

R

Randell, B., 50, 138
read.string, 92, 94, 145
real, 18
recognition, 40
recognition routines, 15
recognitive parsing, 41
recursion, 87
recursive descent, 15, 67 et seq.
reducing, 49
redundancy, 97, 102
refinement (*see also* stepwise refinement), 12
reflexive transitive closure, 24, 29, 32, 54
reflexivity of relations, 27, 32
regular expressions, 88, 89
regular grammars, 37
rel.type, 121
relational operators, 121, 144, 181
relations, relationships, 23, 24
relevant symbols, 103
repeat clauses, 20
representation of types, 111 et seq.
reserved words, 13, 88, 91, 95 et seq., 125
retract, 162
retract.op, 162
retraction, 140, 162
return, 147
reverse polish instruction code, 138
right assignment, 87
right linear grammars, 37
rightmost derivations, 43
Rosencrantz, D. J., 53
run time, 11
Russell, L. J., 50, 138
R values, 131 et seq., 155

S

S–algol, 18, 67
  abstract machine, 138 et seq., 149, 180 et seq.
  error recovery, 104 et seq.
  syntax, 174
  type matching rules, 177
S–code generation, 149 et seq., 187
S–code interpreter, 171
SASL, 103, 104
SB, 140
scalar data types, 111, 112
scanning, 88 et seq.
scope, 18, 125 et seq., 138
scope checking, 73, 125 et seq.
screening, 88, 95 et seq.
search.table, 131
search.tree, 131
segment, 140, 151 et seq.
semantic actions, 64
semantics, 11, 45

semi-Thue grammar, 36
sentences, 34
  generation, 40
  recognition, 40
sentential forms, 41
sequence, 81, 106, 117
setlab, 152
sets, 25
SF, 140
shift-reduce principle, 49
shifting, 49
shunting algorithm, 50
SID, 17, 64
simple precedence parsers, 50
simulated evaluation of code, 74, 136, 149 et seq., 157
single character symbols, 90
source language, 11, 165
source program, 11, 70, 98
sp, 149
SP, 144
spaces, 88, 95
special purposes registers, 144
stacks, 74, 138 et seq.
  base, 140
  frame, 138
  front, 140
  instructions, 144
  load instructions, 180
  retraction, 140, 144, 162
  top, 144
START, 54
start set, 54
start symbols (*see also* distinguished symbol), 34, 80
static analysis, 136
static chain, 138
static link, 138
Stearns, R. E., 17
stepwise refinement (*see also* refinement), 16, 69 et seq., 76, 89, 109, 116, 132, 155
storage layout, 74
string operations, 145, 185
string quotes, 24, 98
strings, 18, 21, 23, 86, 141
strong LL(k), 53
structure class declarations, 19
structures
  cons, 113
  const, 130
  field, 113
  link, 129, 153
  proc, 112
  scalar, 112
  STRUCTURE, 113
  var, 130
  VECTOR, 112
structures in S-algol, 19, 112, 133, 134, 141
  class checking, 141
  classes, 19
subject languages, 34
subscript, 134
substitution, 59, 60
substr.op, 145
substrings, 21, 86, 123
sum relations, 28, 30
symbol, 77
symbol table, 73, 74, 125 et seq., 153 et seq.
syntax (*see also* grammar, 34
syntax analyser, 80 et seq., 132
syntax analysis (*see also* parsing), 13, 71 et seq., 76 et seq.
syntax errors, *see* errors
Syntax Improving Device, 17, 64
syntax trees (*see also* parse trees), 16, 42, 43
system independence (*see also* machine ind.), 98

T

T-diagrams, 165 et seq.
table driven compilers, 49
tabs, 88, 93, 95
tagged architecture, 143
tail recursion, 89
target machines, 74, 136
targets (*see also* goals, active symbols), 46
terminal symbols (*see also* basic symbols), 34, 72, 76, 88
testing for LL(l) conditions, 52
testing the parser, 88
top down parsing, 41, 45
trademarks, 141, 145
transformational grammars, 40
transforming grammars, 59
transition state diagrams, 89
transitive closure, 24, 28, 32, 61
transitivity, 27
transporting compilers, *see* portability
transpose, 27
traversal, 45
try, 92
try.name, 94, 96
Turner, D., 70, 103, 104
two-level grammars, 37
type 0 grammar, 36
type 1 grammar, 36
type 2 grammars, 37
type 3 grammars and expressions, 37, 88
types, 18
  ANY, 115
  checking, 72, 116 et seq.
  equality, 113
  errors, 114
  matching rules, 78, 109 et seq., 117

types, 18 – *continued*
of a procedure, 111
of a structure, 112
rules (*see also* type matching), 37, 110 et seq.
void, 110, 112

U

Ullman, J. H., 48, 50, 60, 102, 137
unary operators, 120
unconditional jumps, 146
underlining reserved words, 98
UNIX, 15, 98

V

value, call by, 20
van Wijngaarden, A., 37
variability of a name, 130, 134, 154
variables
cp, 151
env.list, 128
identifier, 89
lex.level, 153
psp, 149
variables – *continued*
recovering, 105
sp, 149
symbol, 77, 91
the.name, 91
vector and structure accessing, 184
vector and structure creation, 183
vectors, 20, 112, 134, 141, 145
Von Neumann machines, 70

W

Warshall, S., 32
Weber, H., 50
Whetstone algol, 67
while clauses, 20, 119, 157
Wichmann, B., 139
Wilkes, M. V., 172
Wilson, R. J., 26
Wirth, N., 50, 95
write clause, 82

Y

YACC, 50